MW00835552

Technological Innovation, Modernity, and Electric Goods in Late State Socialist Poland

Technological Innovation, Modernity, and Electric Goods in Late State Socialist Poland

Patryk Wasiak

LEXINGTON BOOKS
Lanham • Boulder • New York • London

Published by Lexington Books
An imprint of The Rowman & Littlefield Publishing Group, Inc.
4501 Forbes Boulevard, Suite 200, Lanham, Maryland 20706
www.rowman.com

86-90 Paul Street, London EC2A 4NE

Copyright © 2024 by The Rowman & Littlefield Publishing Group, Inc.

All rights reserved. No part of this book may be reproduced in any form or by any electronic or mechanical means, including information storage and retrieval systems, without
written permission from the publisher, except by a reviewer who may quote passages
in a review.

British Library Cataloguing in Publication Information Available

Library of Congress Cataloging-in-Publication Data

Names: Wasiak, Patryk, author.
Title: Technological innovation, modernity, and electric goods in late state socialist
    Poland / Patryk Wasiak.
Description: Lanham: Lexington Books, [2024] | Includes bibliographical references and
    index. | Summary: "This book deconstructs the public performance of technological
    innovation and imagined modernity in relation to the home technologies market in late
    state socialist Poland. Patryk Wasiak goes on to discuss how these technologies would
    have an impact on the creation of a desirable future social order and economy"—
    Provided by publisher.
Identifiers: LCCN 2023034526 | ISBN 9781666924084 (cloth) |
    ISBN 9781666924091 (ebook)
Subjects: LCSH: Socialism—Poland. | Poland—History—1945–1980. | Poland—
    Economic conditions—1945–1981. | Household electronics Industry—Poland—
    History—20th century. | Technology and State—Poland—History—20th century.
Classification: LCC HX315.7.A6 W37 2023 | DDC 335.009438—dc23/eng/20230830
    LC record available at https://lccn.loc.gov/2023034526

∞™ The paper used in this publication meets the minimum requirements of American
National Standard for Information Sciences—Permanence of Paper for Printed Library
Materials, ANSI/NISO Z39.48-1992.

Contents

Acknowledgments

Research for this book was supported with the National Science Centre, Poland, grant 2016/23/D/HS3/03199. I would like to express my gratitude to two persons from Lexington Books. Jasper Mislak provided me with a lot of support at different stages of editing my book and later Caitlin Palmer substantially helped my with her editorial work. I also would like to thank two anonymous reviewers for their comments, which helped me to revise and improve my book. Finally, I would like to thank Peter Charles Gee for proofreading the first version of my manuscript, and providing me with a lot of insightful questions and comments.

List of Abbreviations

CAF	Centralna Agencja Fotograficzna, Central Photographic Agency
COBRESPU	Centralny Ośrodek Badawczo Rozwojowy Elektronicznego Sprzętu Powszechnego Użytku, Central Institute for the Research and Development of Consumer Electronics
COO	Country of origin
FK	Federacja Konsumentów, Federation of Consumers
FMCG	Fast Moving Consumer Goods
FYP	Five Year Plan
IRWiK	Instytut Rynku Wewnętrznego i Konsumpcji, Institute for Domestic Market and Consumption
IWP	Instytut Wzornictwa Przemysłowego, Institute for the Industrial Design
KGD	Komitet Gospodarstwa Domowego, Home Economics Committee
KNiM	Komitet Normalizacji i Miar, Committee for Normalization and Measures
MITI	Ministry of International Trade and Industry (Japan)
MNE	Multinational enterprise
NIK	Najwyższa Izba Kontroli, the Highest Council for Control
NPSG	Narodowy Plan Społeczno Gospodarczy, National Social and Economic Plan
NOT	Naczelna Organizacja Techniczna, Main Technical Organization
OBR	Ośrodek Badawczo Rozwojowy, Center for Research and Development

OEM	Original Equipment Manufacturer
PHW	Przedsiębiorstwo Handlu Wewnętrznego, Enterprise for Domestic Retail Trade
R&D	Research and Development
SEP	Stowarzyszenie Elektryków Polskich, Association of Polish Electricians
STR	Scientific and Technological Revolution
VCR	Video Cassette Recorder
WOG	Wielkie Organizacje Gospodarcze, Large Economic Organizations
WZT	Warszawskie Zakłady Telewizyjne, Warsaw Television Works
ZOJT	Zakłady Odbioru Jakościowego Towarów
ZRK	Zakłady Radiowe im. Kasprzaka Kasprzak Radio Works

Introduction

THE AIM OF THIS BOOK

In this book, I aim to deconstruct the public performance of technological innovation and imagined modernity in the home technologies market in late state socialist Poland. While doing so, I will shed light on the politics that accompanied the representations of the new innovative consumer technologies in the public sphere and the agenda of actors who performed such representations. I hope that this investigation will improve our understanding of how the social actors who took part in the politics of material culture in state socialism embraced the narratives of innovation, progress, and modernization as key slogans in their public performances and the expression of their identities and objectives.

I argue that the central form of the mediation of home technologies was the projection of specific "sociotechnical imaginaries" that included visions of how these technologies would impact the creation of a desirable future social order and economy. Later, such imaginaries were renegotiated and challenged as infeasible or undesirable. Although the manufacturers of electric goods will regularly appear in my book, I primarily pay attention to other actors such as the electric engineering community, the home-efficiency movement, the consumer protection movement, circles of economic technocrats, technological research and development centers, trade organizations, and milieus of researchers and experts from the fields of consumer research and commodity economics.

A host of these social actors, who were interwoven into state power, extensively used slogans related to the imagined modernity in public communications about the policies of governmental institutions and state-owned manufacturers. Several interest groups collaborated in the co-construction of the public images of an industry identified as being at the forefront of the technological modernity of the 1970s and 1980s. Moreover, these key interest groups presented the mass production and abundance of electric goods as crucial factors in the process of economic and social modernization. The category of electric goods discussed in my book includes two subcategories.

1

The first is popularly referred to as "brown goods," that is, technologies used for home entertainment such as televisions, radio receivers, stereos, and video-cassette recorders. The second subcategory is "white goods," which include products used for housework like washing machines, electric ovens, food processors, and dishwashers.

These same interest groups attempted to convince others that their agenda corresponded with the objective of constructing a new society through technological innovation, and I investigate how such groups were capable of exercising power through the production and sharing of knowledge related to "technological promises." I also highlight how such knowledge was used to enroll other actors into some form of collaborative action. Such a discussion sheds light on how those interest groups were able to express their expectations to other actors and how those who were expected to take action responded to or ignored such requests.

Understanding such mediations can help us to grasp different views of the possible course of modernization and the corresponding social imaginaries of a bright future under state socialism. Such an instance of "technological promise" occurred in the late 1970s, at the peak of the prosperity of Edward Gierek's decade-long rule and at a time of actual successes in introducing technical innovation. Poland's electronic engineering lobby claimed that the huge investments in electronics had helped to begin the process of transforming Poland from an agricultural country into the "Hong Kong of the Eastern Bloc."[1] Hong Kong at that time was one of the developing Far East countries, or "Far East tigers," that had secured their global position due to investing in high technology industries, particularly those concerned in the production of consumer electronics. The Polish engineering lobby was dissatisfied with the end of the investment program and requested that it should be continued to finish the transition. With its claims that Poland could become another Hong Kong, the electronic engineering lobby had a clear agenda of building public awareness of electronics as a technology that offered a possibility of economic growth. Such an awareness also sought to have a tangible impact on other social actors who could help to secure further governmental investments in this sector.

I use historical accounts of several key technological innovations such as new models of radio receivers, television sets, and automatic washing machines to discuss the politics of the intermediary actors who co-constructed such technologies by creating, sharing, or eventually challenging the public knowledge that accompanied such innovations. I intentionally move away from discussing in detail the technological and organizational issues related to the production of technological products to instead pay attention to the process of "mediating technology" and the public sharing of knowledge related to the design, manufacturing, retail, and consumption of such technologies.

Aside from exploring how interest groups publicly performed technological innovation and modernity, I seek to highlight the tensions between the actors who took part in such performances and offer insight into the circumstances in which such tensions emerged and the possibilities of articulating them. I do this by highlighting the scale of tensions between governmental institutions, state enterprises, and nongovernmental organizations under state socialism.

One of the key elements of the public imagery of capitalism in the state socialist mass media was the notion of the inevitable social and economic conflicts that emerge as a result of ruthless profit-seeking. Economists and social critics explained the politics of greedy American corporations as the contemporary equivalent of the nineteenth-century robber barons. They reminded readers that such "economic pathologies" were the expressions of the internal contradictions and conflicts within capitalism, a key theme of Marxist political economy. The public image of the social life and economy of state socialism was the opposite, with the state media regularly reminding citizens that the state-party structure and centrally controlled economy resulted in a tensionless background for the pursuit of economic, social, and technological progress. Understandably therefore, the issues of internal tensions and conflicts in the economy and society under state socialism were, to a large extent, subjected to censorship. My study sheds light on the public articulation of such contradictions.

My book focuses on the 1970s and 1980s, the period generally referred to in the scholarship as late state socialism, and I will use this term accordingly. My study covers two distinct periods. The first includes the years 1970–1980, the era of the rule of the First Secretary of PZPR, Polska Zjednoczona Partia Robotnicza, or the Polish United Workers' Party, Edward Gierek, who imposed the policy of building so-called "consumer socialism." This was a key element of a broader policy of securing steady economic, technological, and social progress, which was related to a policy of strengthening bonds with the West and the Third World. The second period is from 1981 to 1989, a time of social upheaval after the establishment of the Solidarity movement and the imposition of martial law in 1981. During this decade, the deepening economic crisis resulted in a decrease in the standard of living of many people, which led to a questioning of the feasibility of achieving the ambitious social goals formulated in the 1970s.[2]

How did "telling stories" through textual and visual narratives allow these social actors to perform the social imaginaries of modernity in Poland in the period I discuss? And how did these actors use this imagery to express their identities and pursue their agenda? Such stories about technology-based modernity were based upon two key themes. First, in the 1970s, the central theme was to communicate to Polish consumers that they were experiencing the ongoing benefits of a centrally planned and efficient process of modernization through the steady introduction of novelties and an increase in the production quotas of home technologies. Later, in the 1980s, an era of economic and social crises, these propaganda-laden narratives were accompanied by critical counter-narratives that challenged the official imagery of steady progress and abundance. Such criticism was strongly influenced by the emerging consumer movement that openly challenged the claims of success in modernization with the bleak imagery of stagnation, the lack of innovation, poor quality, and the obsolescence of domestically made consumer technologies.

A recently published volume on the imaginary "good life" and consumer culture in the Eastern Bloc, edited by Cristofer Scarboro, Zsuzsa Gille, and Diana Mincyte, provokes several questions.[3] For instance, to what extent did the collective consumption programs in the Eastern Bloc succeed or fail in delivering the promised "good life?" And how did a host of historical actors define and negotiate the notion of the "good life?" I avoid writing a Whig history in which the past is the inexorable march of progress toward modernity or is eventually interpreted to explain the failure of a political or economic system in the future. For that reason, I do not offer any clear answer to the question of whether late state socialist Poland became a "modern" country or rather if instead the socialist project was a failure that left Poland a backwater country in a dire financial condition. Rather, I investigate the rules of public representations of achievements, failures, and inefficiencies that accompanied the policy of modernization as they were perceived by contemporaries.

The Chernobyl nuclear accident was a definitive technological failure with tremendous environmental, social, and economic costs.[4] But should we view the massively produced East German Trabant, one of the icons of the contemporary German "Ostalgie," an affordable car with an outdated two-stroke engine and chassis made of fiberglass, as a success or a failure?[5] There is no clear answer to this question, and we can argue that the Trabi, as it was diminutively called by Germans, was both a modern and obsolete car.

Instead of giving straightforward answers to the questions I've raised, I seek to emphasize the problem of defining how social actors establish what constitutes success and failure in technological innovation, and more broadly, modernization projects, under late state socialism?[6] I focus on the social actors' power of defining what exactly constitutes modernity and obsolescence and their use of such definitions to enroll other actors to take part in collaborative actions.

Many of the recent works on late state socialism show a myriad of problems with the manufacturing, retail, and use of consumer goods such as unreliable electric goods, unfashionable clothes, tasteless foodstuffs, and ugly toys. Instead of primarily covering the failures of state socialism, however, my book examines its inefficiencies, particularly related to production, complaints about the qualities and shortages of consumer products, and the inefficient actions of those who tried to introduce reforms to improve the quality of such products.

My book covers the issue of technological innovation, but it also addresses the much broader issue of the lack of theoretically informed works on how interest groups created social imaginaries in state socialism. I investigate how within the political, economic, and social context of state socialism several interest groups that operated both within the power relations of the state apparatus or on its margins used such imaginaries to achieve their objectives. I demonstrate how expert groups, the industry lobby, research institutes, and nongovernmental organizations attempted to secure their role as intermediary actors in order to have a tangible impact on not only the production of a range of commodities but also, more importantly, on the definition of which commodity or product feature is modern and innovative and which is obsolete.

The notion of "social and economic progress" (orig. postęp społeczny i ekonomiczny) was an overarching theme of the public narrative performed by the PZPR in the 1970s and 1980s. According to this narrative, which was extensively communicated in the mass media, technological development was supposed to play a vital role in such processes. I investigate the specific features of public debates on innovation in consumer technologies, which refer to several key terms used to describe the technological, economic, and social orders. I have equally considered both desired (such as modernity and progress) and undesired (irrationality, backwardness, wastefulness of resources, obsolescence) elements of these range of orders.

The industrial production of home technologies, and particularly the constant innovation of this production under state socialism, was supposed to produce well-being. Scarboro has emphasized the importance of such imagery in the introduction to *The Good Life*, to which I will regularly refer to in further chapters. As he notes:

> The historical task of relating consumption to ideology haunted late socialist Eastern Europe. This should not surprise us. From the beginning, communist readings of political economy were tied to the promise that industrial production would produce plenty, generating new and improved social relationships.[7]

This notion of "social progress" was an example of the generation of new social relationships. In Hungary, the reforms during the long János Kádár era (1956–1989) for better provisions were popularly referred to as "Goulash Socialism." Instead of goulash, a traditional Hungarian dish, Scarboro proposes a more broadly applicable term of "refrigerator socialism," which highlights the central role of the production of home technologies in shaping the material world of consumption under state socialism:

Was refrigerator socialism a proper goal for the socialist good society? If so, what exactly was *socialist* about it? The absence, or poor quality, of these very goods—refrigerator capitalism made better refrigerators after all—seemed to point to the inadequate fulfillment of the socialist social contract.[8]

In the mid-century era, the refrigerator was one of the most important elements of both capitalist and state socialist imaginaries of technological and social progress in terms of improving the standard of living.[9] I will address Scarboro's questions and indeed, refrigerators will regularly appear in my book. However, I also discuss other technologies that were defined as symbols of the modernity of the 1970s and 1980s: automatic washing machines, microwave ovens, stereophonic and high-fidelity audio-cassette players and radio receivers, stacking systems, and color television sets with remotes. These were the global symbols of modernity in consumer technologies of the 1970s and 1980s. I investigate the controversy over the question if the Polish electric goods industry was capable of providing consumers with such products.[10] With regard to Scarboro's comments, key actors did define the provision of "modern" goods as an element of the socialist social contract, while later interest groups who challenged public claims about the successes of modernization articulated the inefficiencies in delivering such products as a possible breach of such a contract.

THE INTENDED AUDIENCE

My book combines selected investigative toolsets from recent works on the cultural history of the Eastern Bloc, science and technology studies (STS), design studies, and consumer culture studies. I draw from selected concepts from STS as the most relevant tool for delivering a multifaceted investigation of the cultural, social, political, and economic aspects of technological innovation in state socialism. This toolset is supplemented by concepts from other fields, which I use to highlight some concurrent trends. Such a convergence has enabled me to deliver a theoretically informed, scholarly investigation that can shed more light on public debates on the cultural significance of technological innovation in the historical setting of late state socialism.

Most recent works on the cultural history of the Eastern Bloc have been primarily grounded in the cultural, economic, and social history of this region and were addressed to scholars both interested and familiar with the history of the region. My approach is different: I have intentionally grounded my research in a composite toolset to demonstrate how a case study about technological innovation in an Eastern Bloc country can have a broader impact on academia. I strongly believe that such an approach can make this case relevant to a broad audience of scholars interested in the politics of modernization in the Cold War era, not only historians of Eastern Europe. While working on this book, my primary concern was to make it accessible, relevant, and interesting to scholars from all academic fields.

Writing a book that aims to reach scholars with different backgrounds and interests is a challenging process. To make it accessible for those unfamiliar with the history of the Eastern Bloc, state socialist Poland, and the cultural logic of the centrally planned economy, I have included relevant accessible explanations of the basic features of state socialism and historical facts from Polish history in the 1970s and 1980s. At the same time, this book is also aimed at historians of Eastern Europe, so when I introduce any concepts from other scholarly fields, I provide a brief and accessible introduction to such concepts and make references to the relevant literature.

KEY CONCEPTS

Aside from delivering a theoretically informed investigation of the how technological innovation was imagined under state socialism, I also intend to make this an exploratory study by seeking to demonstrate the usefulness of a set of key concepts from different scholarly fields. Here, I provide a brief overview of the key concepts used in my book. Such concepts will be further discussed in detail in subsequent chapters and supplemented with other concepts relevant to specific chapters.

My book refers to a number of key interpretative frameworks useful in studying how social actors publicly perform the imagery of technological innovation. The most significant framework is the concept of "sociotechnical imaginary," proposed by Sheila Jasanoff and Sang-Hyun Kim.[11] Such imaginaries are visions of desirable futures driven by technological development. In Jasanoff and Kim's approach, such desirable futures are primarily structured on specific new social orders and positive social change. I will address how the imagined modernity of late state socialist Poland included representations of home technologies and relevant desirable economic and social order.

The concept of sociotechnical imaginaries is grounded in philosopher Charles Taylor's concept of social imagery which is widely used in contemporary social research.[12] The sociotechnical imaginaries toolset has been extensively used in STS scholarship, represented by this overview of the usefulness of his concept in studying the interconnections and power relations between a host of social actors.

Implicit in the notion of sociotechnical imaginaries is the assumption that some
actors and institutions have more power than others to project their imaginations
and to get others to buy into them, whether voluntarily, as through consumer
behavior, or through discipline and governmentality, as in the work of states and
state-like actors. Studies at the intersection of science and technology studies
and political science investigate how such powerful imaginaries are constructed
and how they gain and retain power.[13]

My primary point of interest is how social actors performed their roles and
used their power to allocate other actors and objects with projected roles in
the imagined process of modernization. While referring to this concept, I
am particularly interested in using it to shed more light on, as Jasanoff and
colleagues note, "the relationship between national political cultures and the
production of *sociotechnical imaginaries.*"[14]

Social actors shape worlds not only through the production of material
artifacts but also by "telling stories" about artifacts produced by them or
some other actors. Historian of technology John Law provided a seminal
study of "telling stories" in his book on "the project" of the British Aircraft
Corporation's canceled strike and reconnaissance aircraft TSR-2 from the
1960s.[15] Law applies the strategy of the decentralization of the material
object, the aircraft itself, and focuses on how this object is discursively constructed, or "performed," with drawings, diagrams, technical specifications,
and claims about its possible use on a battlefield in what he called the "projectness," a key element of modernity. As he elaborates:

> This is the idea (which is also a performance) that many technologies and
> other social arrangements are properly narrated and organized as "projects,"
> "programs," "operations" or other closely related terms such as "organization,"
> "system," "network," . . . Think of the TSR2 project. Or the Manhattan Project.
> Or the mission statements of organizations. Or indeed "the modern project." . . .
> This kind of telling and performing is a standard narrative trope in late moder-
> nity. And it is, of course, performative of that modernity, tending as it is told and
> enacted to order social relations in an image of projectness. It is one of the aims
> of this book to interfere with this trope, to erode the assumptions performed in
> projectness, or at least to explore what is involved in their enactment.[16]

For Law, the TSR-2 is a set of images, norms, and projected applications in
real life. As I will demonstrate, the governmental policy of building socialist modernity was performed by several institutional actors through similar
"projects," "systems," and "networks."

A similar reflection on the role of the performance of social actors in the
creation of public imagery of specific technologies can be found in an influential essay by cultural studies scholar Dick Hebdige on the Italian Vespa

scooter.[17] For Hebdige, the scooter is not a material object but rather an enactment of promotional images and texts. Hebdige's work has been substantially inspired by Roland Barthes' work on the cultural significance of the Citroen car and how it performed within the framework of French postwar consumer culture.[18] Similarly, consumer culture studies scholar Don Slater, in his work on how the images of modernity are embedded in contemporary consumer culture, notes: "Consumer culture is notoriously awash with signs, images, publicity. Most obviously, it involves an aestheticization of commodities and their environment: advertising, packaging, shop display, point of sale material, product design etc."[19] Later, we will see several signs and images of domestically made Polish electric goods, and I will demonstrate how the public performance of modernity and innovation has been accompanied by the aestheticization of such commodities.

I do not consider the world of state socialism as a predefined political, economic, and social structure. I rather view it as a constantly shifting assemblage of humans, institutions, artifacts, ideologies, procedures, norms, and bodies of knowledge. The possibilities of interaction within such a network were to a large extent structured by the power relations dictated by the cultural logic of the political system. As sociologist Michel Callon notes, scientific discovery and technological innovation can be abstracted as "the simultaneous production of knowledge and construction of a network of relationships in which social and natural entities mutually control who they are and what they want."[20]

Another inspiration for this work comes from cultural anthropologist Arjun Appadurai's classic study on the social life of commodities in which the central point of investigation is how human actors "encode things with significance."[21] Appadurai notes that the creation of value is a "politically mediated process."[22] Later in this book, we will see how the creation of the values of technologically innovative electric goods in late state socialist Poland was also an example of a politically mediated process.

Appadurai also discusses the role of such knowledge in the cultural biography of things. He notes what constitutes the knowledge related to the commodities: "Culturally constructed stories and ideologies about commodity flows."[23] This remark emphasizes the performative aspect of the sharing of knowledge and corresponds with the previously quoted works by Law, Hebdige, and Slater. Appadurai notes different types of relevant knowledge:

Commodities represent very complex social forms and distributions of knowledge. In the first place, and crudely, such knowledge can be of two sorts: the knowledge (technical, social, aesthetic, and so forth) that goes into the production of the commodity; and the knowledge that goes into appropriately consuming the commodity. . . . Knowledge at both poles has technical, mythological, and evaluative components, and the two poles are susceptible to mutual and dialectical interaction.[24]

When it comes to technical knowledge, which is particularly relevant for this book, Appudarai also offers a useful insight: "with all commodities, . . . technical knowledge is always deeply interpenetrated with cosmological, sociological, and ritual assumptions that are likely to be shared."[25]

When Appadurai discusses a "politically mediated process," he refers to the process of mediation as a value-neutral description of the specificity of interactions between social actors. His remark corresponds with the emerging popularity of mediation as a stage between production and consumption, an area of scholarly interest in the history of technology and design studies. In my book, I particularly refer to the concept of "technology mediation junction" proposed by historian of technology Ruth Schwartz Cowan and later expanded by historians of consumer technologies such as Ruth Oldenziel, Adri Albert de la Bruhèze, and Onno de Wit. They describe this junction as "an area of expertise situated between production and consumption."[26] Historians of material culture and design Elizabeth Shove and Martin Hand provide an instance of what constitutes such expertise in the case of home technologies in their study of the British housekeeping periodicals: "competences, and technologies assumed and represented in each cohort of advertisements, features, and editorial comment."[27] Design historian Kjetil Fallan, in his work on the history of aluminum as a material for durable goods, notes how such an approach connects studying production and consumption: "Studying how aluminum products have been visualized and envisioned in the space between the factory floor and the kitchen counter also challenges another, equally stubborn dichotomy: the division of the world of goods into separate spheres of production and consumption."[28]

To better grasp the role of the agendas of several actors that took part in such a junction I will refer to the concept of "technological promises" and "technological expectations," proposed by historians of technology Harro van Lente and Arie Rip, to shed more light on the repertoire of social actors, who take part in this "technology mediation junction" and how they attempt to influence other actors. As they note:

> Once technical promises are shared, they demand action, and it appears necessary for technologists to develop them, and for others to support them. At the same time, the options which are considered feasible and promising are translated into requirements, guidelines and specifications.[29]

[. . .]

Because expectation statements contain a script of the future world, they position the relevant actors, explicitly or implicitly, exactly as characters in a story are positioned. Since the expectations are public or semipublic statements that can be drawn upon by others, expectation statements require some response from the actors being positioned. An actor who rejects the role allocated by the script must react, either by protesting against the role, or by contesting the nature of the expectations.[30]

The notion of "technological promises" and "technological expectations" will be useful for investigating the politics of the intermediary actors that attempt to facilitate the several stages of the social life of the technological products, from their design, manufacturing, testing, and retail trade, to the consumption, and evaluation.

THE STRUCTURE OF THE BOOK

My book is divided into four chapters that discuss different aspects of sociotechnical imaginaries of technical innovation in the electric goods industry. However, all the chapters are connected, and when I discuss a specific issue, I inform the reader that I will cover a similar topic in other chapters from a different angle or offer a more detailed analysis of a specific issue. Each chapter also includes an introduction that outlines the theoretical frameworks to which I refer to in that chapter.

In chapter 1, I introduce the most significant intermediary actors and present their identities, agendas, and repertoire that they used in the public communication of knowledge. This chapter provides an extensive introduction to the subsequent chapters by presenting the most relevant features of a centrally planned economy, their significance for technological innovation, and the power relations between the manufacturers, intermediary actors, and consumers. I first outline the cultural logic of state socialism, particularly the system of economic plans and the process of the communication of technological novelties in the state media and then present the agenda and repertoire of the most important interest groups: the electronic engineering community, the home efficiency movement, and the consumer protection lobby. While discussing all these topics, I highlight how they help to understand how technological innovation was embedded in the power relations between the key interest groups.

Chapter 2 is dedicated to the investigation of how specific actors took part in performing modernity by claiming how the introduction of specific technologies could bring a desirable future, or "modernity," with particular positively valued economic and social changes. In this chapter, I discuss selected aspects of the performance of modernity such as the practices of using the "Scientific Technological Revolution" phrase; the intersection of debates on technological innovation and the "social goals" of the governmental policy; the use of measurable indicators of modernity; and the narratives about how Poland was capable of joining the globalizing world of electronic goods. Finally, I discuss the narratives about the constant improvement of the production profile and the dedication to the regular release of "novelty" products.

In chapter 3, I investigate a range of controversies related to the quality of electric goods. In most of the recent studies on consumer culture in the Eastern Bloc, many authors discuss the experience of consumers, which was that the state offered them not only a limited quantity of products but also products of poor quality. I also deconstruct the experience of the "poor quality" of electric goods.

First, I explore how manufacturers and a range of governmental institutions co-constructed the system for quality control and how they performed in public their attention to improving electric goods through elaborate systems of quality tests and discursive practices related to the awarding of certificates of "high quality." Later, I outline how the inability to successfully collaborate between manufacturers and contractors became identified as a key reason for the poor quality of consumer goods. Finally, I consider how the consumer protection movement problematized the unreliability of electric goods and their poor design by articulating this issue as a breach of the social contract between the state and consumers.

Chapter 4 consists of five case studies that supplement the analysis that I present in the first three chapters with a more detailed investigation of selected products and practices. This chapter includes a study of practices of narratives about the workplaces and workers in electric goods manufacturers, a study of the application of industrial design systems to the production of electric goods, and a study of the most significant and publicly visible technological innovation from the era, that of the color television set. The final case study is dedicated to the construction of cultural memory and nostalgia for the world of "modern" domestic manufacturers that release high-quality and modern products. As I will show, such memory refers to the construct of unfulfilled alternative modernity.

NOTE ON SOURCES

I do not consider the mediation of design in terms of shaping the actual industrial design of specific commodities but rather "telling stories" and taking part in debates on specific design trends. My research base corresponds with my research agenda. I am primarily interested not in technological objects themselves but rather in their images and the narratives about them as well as narratives on practices relevant to design and manufacturing. As source material, I use primarily published materials to analyze both written content such as public statements of officials and representatives of manufacturers. I mostly refer to the press sources, which include, to quote Appadurai, "culturally constructed stories and ideologies about commodity production and flows."[31] Such stories were told by specific authors that represented the interests of specific groups with their agenda.

Both in popular press and trade journals, I have found a unique combination of technical and economic expert discourse and normalized propaganda-laden phrases. My sources offer the same content as sources employed by Serguei Oushakine in his paper on Soviet consumer culture. He summarizes the cultural logic of "stories" in his sources:

> Scholars of late Soviet consumption for the most part have been ignoring numerous books, pamphlets, and trade magazines published by academic and professional organizations during the last three decades of Soviet history. And for good reason: often written in a highly technical prose, these texts are saturated with political clichés, ritualistic incantations, and citational ornamentation, making it next to impossible to determine when a scholarly argument morphs into a piece of propaganda, and vice versa.[32]

The main research for this book is a content analysis of five press titles that were the main sites for the mediation of technological innovation in the electric goods industry. I argue that these were sites where different actors expressed their voices and attempted to enroll other actors in their projects This analysis includes *Przegląd Techniczny* (issues from 1970 to 1989), a leading weekly periodical of the engineering community; *Życie Gospodarcze* (issues from 1970 to 1989), a weekly periodical of the economic experts' community; *Veto* (1982–1989), an unofficial press organ of the Federacja Konsumentów, FK, or the Consumers' Federation; *Atut* (1988–1989), a short-lived official organ of this organization; and, finally, *Gospodarstwo Domowe* (1970–1989), a monthly periodical published by Komitet Gospodarstwa Domowego, KGD, or the Home Economics Committee. These titles represented the agenda of three different relevant milieus that attempted to build their position as experts through the production and communication of knowledge.

These sources are supplemented by content analysis of other relevant periodicals: *Ekran, Audio Hi-Fi Video, Radioamator, Magazyn Rodzinny, Razem, Polityka, Handel Wewnętrzny, Polityka Społeczna,* and a collection of unpublished press photographs from the Narodowe Archiwum Cyforwe, which owns a collection of press photographs from Centralna Agencja

Fotograficzna, the main photo press agency in state socialist Poland. When relevant, I also refer to selected archival documents from the archival collections of Ministerstwo Przemysłu i Handlu, or the Ministry of Industry and Trade, and UNITRA and PREDOM industrial associations. All these archival collections are available in Archiwum Akt Nowych in Warsaw.

While quoting sources, when relevant, I use the original Polish phrases because they were part of the normal vocabulary used in public communications in the state media. Such vocabulary includes phrases such as, for instance: "modernizacja produkcji" (the modernization of production), "poprawa jakości wyrobów" (the improvement of the quality of products), and "walka o jakość produkcji" (the struggle for the quality of production). Such phrases are worth closer examination since they tell us much about how social actors used discursive practices and how they ground their repertoire in broader cultural frameworks driven by the dominant political ideology. I also use Polish abbreviations, for instance, PZPR rather than PUWP. For the sake of clarity, I have provided a list of all abbreviations.

NOTES

1. *Przegląd Techniczny*, July 4, 1982, 23.

2. For a general history of postwar Poland, see: Andrzej Paczkowski, *The Spring Will Be Ours. Poland and the Poles from Occupation to Freedom* (University Park: Pennsylvania State University Press, 2003 [1995]); Brian Porter-Szűcs, *Poland in the Modern World: Beyond Martyrdom* (Chichester: Wiley Blackwell, 2014). For an overview of economic history of both eras, see: Kazimierz Z. Poznanski, *Poland's Protracted Transition. Institutional Change and Economic Growth 1970–1994* (Cambridge: Cambridge University Press, 1996).

3. Zsuzsa Gille, Cristofer Scarboro, and Diana Mincytė, "The Pleasures of Backwardness," in *The Socialist Good Life. Desire, Development, and Standards of Living in Eastern Europe*, ed. Cristofer Scarboro, Diana Mincytė, and Zsuzsa Gille (Bloomington: Indiana University Press, 2020), epub.

4. Sonja D. Schmid, *Producing Power: The Pre-Chernobyl History of the Soviet Nuclear Industry* (Cambridge and London: MIT Press, 2015).

5. Eli Rubin, "The Trabant: Consumption, Eigen-Sinn, and Movement," History Workshop Journal 68, no. 1 (Autumn 2009): 27–44.

6. Graeme Gooday, "Re-writing the 'book of blots': Critical reflections on histories of technological 'failure,'" *History and Technology* 14, no. 4 (1998): 265–91, here 268–71.

7. Gille et al., "The Pleasures," epub.

8. Cristofer Scarboro, "The Late Socialist Good Life and Its Discontents: *Bit, Kultura*, and the Social Life of Goods," in *The Socialist Good Life. Desire, Development,*

and Standards of Living in Eastern Europe, ed. Cristofer Scarboro, Diana Mincytė, and Zsuzsa Gille (Bloomington: Indiana University Press, 2020), epub.

9. Cf., for instance, Sandy Isenstadt, "Visions of Plenty: Refrigerators in America around 1950," *Journal of Design History* 11, no. 4 (1998): 311–21.

10. For a discussion on the global trends in electric goods during the 1970s and 1980s, see: Alfred D. Chandler, *Inventing the Electronic Century. The Epic Story of the Consumer Electronics and Computer Industries*, (Cambridge, MA: Harvard University Press, 2005).

11. Sheila Jasanoff and Sang-Hyun Kim, "Containing the Atom: Sociotechnical Imaginaries and Nuclear Power in the United States and South Korea," *Minerva* 47 (2009): 119–46, here 121; Cf. also Sheila Jasanoff and Sang-Hyun Kim, eds., *Dreamscapes of Modernity. Sociotechnical Imaginaries and The Fabrication of Power* (Chicago and London: University of Chicago Press, 2015).

12. Charles Taylor, *Modern Social Imaginaries* (Durham and London: Duke University Press, 2004).

13. Taylor, "Modernity's Powerful Imaginations."

14. Sheila Jasanoff, Sang-Hyun Kim, and Stefan Sperling, "Sociotechnical Imaginaries and Science and Technology Policy: A Cross-National Comparison," https://sts.hks.harvard.edu/research/platforms/imaginaries/iii.proj/nsf-summary-and-proposal/.

15. John Law, *Aircraft Stories. Decentering the Object in Technoscience* (Durham and London: Duke University Press, 2002).

16. Law, *Aircraft Stories*, 7–8.

17. Dick Hebdige, "Object as Image: The Italian Scooter Cycle," in Dick Hebdige, *Hiding in the Light. On Images and Things* (London and New York: Routledge 2002 [1988]): 77–115.

18. Roland Barthes, "The New Citröen," in Roland Barthes, *Mythologies* (New York: The Noonday Press, 1972 (1957), 88–90.

19. Don Slater, *Consumer Culture and Modernity* (Cambridge: Polity Press, 1997), 31.

20. Michel Callon, "Some elements of a sociology of translation: domestication of the scallops and the fishermen of St Brieuc Bay," in Mario Biagioloi, ed., *The Science Studies Reader* (London and New York: Routledge, 1999): 67–83, here 68. First published in John Law, ed., *Power, Action and Belief: A New Sociology of Knowledge?* (London: Routledge, 1986): 196–223.

21. Arjun Appadurai, "Introduction: Commodities and the Politics of Value," in *The Social Life of Things. Commodities in Cultural Perspective*, ed. Arjun Appadurai (Cambridge: Cambridge University Press, 1986), 3–63, here 5.

22. Appadurai, "Introduction," 6.

23. Appadurai, "Introduction," 48.

24. Appadurai, "Introduction," 41.

25. Appadurai, "Introduction," 42.

26. Ruth Oldenziel, Adri Albert de la Bruhèze, and Onno de Wit, "Europe's Mediation Junction: Technology and Consumer Society in the 20th Century," *History and Technology* 21, no. 1 (March 2005): 107–39, here 111. For the most important studies that elaborate on the concept of mediation" in design studies, see: Grace Lees-Maffei,

"The Production-Consumption-Mediation Paradigm," *Journal of Design History* 22 no. 4 (December 2009): 351–76; Section 11: "Mediation," in *The Design History Reader*, ed. Grace Lees-Maffei and Rebecca Houze (Oxford and New York: BERG, 2010), 427–66.

27. Martin Hand and Elizabeth Shove, "Orchestrating Concepts: Kitchen Dynamics and Regime Change in Good Housekeeping And Ideal Home, 1922–2002," *Home Cultures: The Journal of Architecture, Design and Domestic Space* 1, no. 3. (2004): 235–56, here 240.

28. Kjetil Fallan, "Culture by Design: Co-Constructing Material and Meaning," in Kjerstin Aukrust, ed., Assigning Cultural Values (Frankfurt: Peter Lang Publishing, 2013): 135–63, here 141.

29. Harro van Lente and Arie Rip, "Expectations in Technological Developments: An Example of Prospective Structures to be Filled in by Agency," in *Getting New Technologies Together Studies in Making Sociotechnical Order*, ed. Cornelis Disco and Barend van der Meulen (Berlin and New York: Waiter de Gruyter: 1998), 203–29, here 218–19.

30. van Lente and Rip, "Expectations," 216.

31. Appadurai, "Introduction," 48.

32. Serguei Oushakine, "'Against the Cult of Things': On Soviet Productivism, Storage Economy, and Commodities with No Destination," *Russian Review* 73 (April 2014): 198–236, here 206.

Chapter 1

The Cultural Logic of State Socialism, Intermediary Actors, and Technological Innovation

INTRODUCTION

This chapter first identifies the most significant structural features of the state socialist economy and the consumer culture relevant to technological innovation in home technologies. Secondly, it introduces a host of relevant social actors that co-constructed the public imagery of such technologies. It also provides an introduction for readers not versed in the economy, politics, and culture of late state socialism. For this reason, I aim to offer an accessible explanation of the peculiarities of the Second World's economic planning, designing, manufacturing, retailing, and advertising of consumer technologies. I also discuss the identities and agenda of the main social actors that will regularly appear in later chapters and highlight the main features that governed power relations between these actors. An understanding of the structures that governed the relationships between social actors, their identities, and repertoires of producing knowledge, coalition building, and the tensions between them, is essential for further discussions on their role in mediating technological innovation.

The most obvious key actors in the cultural biography of consumer products from the electric goods sector were state enterprises that designed and manufactured such products, but I intentionally shift the focus from production to the space of mediation. Such an approach decentralizes the manufacturers and moves the attention to a host of intermediary actors that influenced the cultural biographies of consumer technologies. As I will further discuss, they did it primarily by producing and circulating knowledge through public channels of communication such as popular press titles, television broadcasts, specialist publications, research reports, and quality certificates. Such actors extensively collaborated with manufacturers by, for instance, helping them to communicate the release of recent novelties and to facilitate the public performance of labor that took place on the factory floor, including the efforts of engineers who designed the new products and the work crews that assembled them.

This chapter helps readers to understand how several interest groups were capable of exercising their agency by projecting the imagery of a possible, desirable future and an equally alternative undesirable future in relation to technology, the economy, and the social order. I subsequently focus on the strategies they employed to shape and perform their identities in public, and how they cooperated, shared, and communicated knowledge on design, manufacturing, retail, and the use of technological novelties in the household environment.

Such actors were embedded in a network of power relations that in some cases enabled opportunities for interactions between them. In other situations, such a network hindered such interactions and caused tensions that were driven by conflict of interests. For this reason, I equally consider both collaborative actions driven by similar goals as well as conflicts between interest groups. Moreover, paying attention to such conflicts enables me to investigate to what extent it was possible to publicly articulate not only a generalized discontent on the state of the electric goods industry but also openly reveal in detail some structural sources for conflicts and inefficiencies that existed in the state socialist economy and consumer culture.

While discussing such interactions, I make a novel contribution to the research by outlining not only the conflicts and tensions themselves but also discussing the possibilities of articulating such conflicts in the public sphere in state socialism. This is because according to propaganda narratives, state socialism was supposed to offer a frictionless alternative to a capitalist system that was burdened by conflicts of interest caused by the ruthless desire to maximize profits. In this chapter, however, we will see several internal conflicts under state socialism such as rivalries within the state apparatus, the struggle between different industries and state enterprises for centrally distributed resources, and acute conflicts between producers, retailers, and consumers.

I also introduce several microscale case studies to illustrate the broader forms of interactions and mediations between intermediary actors, and these cases will be discussed more extensively in the later chapters. When such a case study is mentioned, I will inform the reader about where it will be subsequently discussed in detail. I do not address in detail, however, the policies of the departments of the Central Committee of the PZPR and central governmental agencies, such as the ministries, that shaped the economic and social planning that indirectly governed the electric goods industry.

Rather than a top-down perspective of hierarchical relations within the state apparatus itself, my approach is to pay attention to the boundaries of the state apparatus, a space where intermediary actors were capable of formulating and pursuing their objectives. Moreover, several studies on the consumer culture of the Eastern Bloc have extensively discussed the political economy of the central institutions that dictated the rules for the production of consumer products in state socialism.[1] I also do not include a detailed discussion about governmental policy toward consumption in late state socialist Poland, since such a topic has been discussed by Brian Porter-Szűcs, Małgorzata Mazurek, and Matthew Hilton.[2] Mila Oiva also offers insights into the emergence of consumerism in Poland in the 1960s, and Joanna Zalewska's article on the experience of consumption of home technologies in Poland in years 1945–1980 is highly relevant to my investigation.[3]

A historian of consumption, Frank Trentmann, outlines in his study of the production of knowledge relevant to the practices of consumption in various historical settings the need to pay attention to the agenda of those who produced such knowledge: "What groups and agencies have spoken as consumers or on their behalf, for what reasons and with what implications?"[4] While answering this question in this chapter, I investigate how such groups, which I consider to be intermediary actors, were situated within the network of power relations between manufacturers and consumers and what their sources of authority were. To better grasp the interconnections and power relations between historical actors, I first refer to the concept of "consumer mediation junction" that highlights "mediation" or "negotiation" as a key form of interaction between social actors that took part in the politics of consumption. The authors of the seminal paper on the "mediation junction" framework outline the significance of intermediary actors in shaping European consumer cultures: "In this ongoing process of negotiation, a host of intermediary groups—from women's associations and transatlantic expert groups to Soviet black marketers—were crucial in shaping Europe's particular patterns of consumption. These intermediaries included consumer lobby groups, labor unions, business associations, and government agencies."[5]

They note further the focal point of inequalities of power that govern interactions between various actors in mediation junctions: "We examine the dynamics of three arenas—the state, the market, and civil society—to understand why the negotiating space expanded or contracted and why some stakeholders had more power than others did in these negotiations."[6]

Similarly, a historian of technology, Per Lundin, emphasizes in his introduction to an edited volume on the history of consumption in Europe the proactive role of intermediaries and their agendas in influencing the process

of negotiation: "In the negotiation processes that took place, rarely did intermediary actors function as neutral partners: rather, they were proactive advo-
cates of particular interests, ideals, and norms."[7]

I follow these remarks with an investigation into what rules governed the
"negotiating space" in state socialism, how such rules changed over time,
and how actors could pursue their agenda while operating in such space.
Working at the intersection of STS and economic history, Harro van Lente
and Arie Rip explain how social actors initiate their engagement with technological innovation by sharing an interest in future possibilities opened by
new technology:

> Actors start to take mutual account of each other because of the opportunities
> they perceive in the future technology. Initially, the participating actors belong
> to different organizations and different sectors, but by commonly anticipating
> a future technology, they become interconnected. These interconnections are
> not like producer-client relationships or hierarchical relations: actors do not
> exchange products, but ideas about technology and technical opportunities.[8]

While the authors use the term "future technology," it is equally suitable
to refer here to Jasanoff and Kim's "sociotechnical imaginary," since most
actors join such coalitions because of the projected imagery of possible social
opportunities and economic profits that can be induced by technological innovation.[9] Later, I will highlight several situations when a host of social actors
formed a coalition, which lobbied for specific technology and products.

I support this framework with sociologist Michel Callon's concept of
"translation." As Callon notes, an emergence of a structured relationship
between a nexus of human and nonhuman actors can be referred to as "translation," "during which the identity of actors, the possibility of interaction, and
the margins of maneuver are negotiated and delimited."[10] Further, he highlights the advantages of using such a concept as an interpretative framework:

The repertoire of translation is not only designed to give a symmetrical and
tolerant description of a complex process which constantly mixes together a
variety of social and natural entities. It also permits an explanation of how
a few obtain the right to express and represent the many silent actors of the
social and natural worlds they have mobilized.[11]

In Callon's original study, the silent actors of the natural world were scallops, sea creatures similar to oysters, who were represented by "the social
entities," that is, French fishermen and scientists interested in scallops'
reproduction. My study instead focuses on the social world, and I primarily
pay attention to how a host of "social entities," that is, intermediary actors,
manufacturers, and retailers, used their authority to speak about and represent
consumers who can be considered as "silent actors."[12]

Although the manufacturers of the electric goods themselves are not the main protagonists of my book, I have included here a table that lists the main manufacturers and their production profiles to provide some background information. I hope this will help the reader when I later refer to specific enterprises.

This chapter is structured as follows. First, I outline the intersection between the governmental policy of consumption and the home technologies production industry in state socialist Poland. I then discuss how the goals of the governmental policy toward consumption stimulated the design and manufacture of specific electric goods. While doing so, I outline the basics of the organization of production of such goods. Next, I discuss how technological innovations were communicated in the public sphere. The final section introduces key intermediary actors: the electric engineering community, the home efficiency and consumer protection movements, economic experts, and the emerging market research and commodity knowledge experts. I discuss their identities, agendas, and how it was possible for them to exercise power through the production of knowledge and the collaboration and tensions between them and other interest groups.

POLISH CONSUMER CULTURE AND TECHNOLOGICAL INNOVATION

During the post-Stalinist era, the Polish government, like most other state socialist countries, took significant measures to shift the allocation of resources from extensive industrial production to improving living conditions through mass housing projects and the manufacturing of consumer goods.[13] In 1956, the newly appointed First Secretary of the PZPR, Władysław Gomułka (1956–1970), began the era of the so-called "mała stabilizacja" ("small stabilization").[14] This term refers to both a decrease in the level of forceful industrialization driven by ideological principles and an increased focus on citizens' welfare through a housing program and well-provisioned retail stores.[15] The post-Stalinist period was also the era of increased economic contacts within the rest of the Eastern Bloc and a steady flow of consumer products exported by the USSR.[16] Zalewska discusses how Polish consumers embedded the availability of new home technologies in that era in the experience of progress and positive change in their lives and their households.[17] She argues that the government beginning to pay attention to the issues of consumption in the post-Stalinist era can be interpreted as a "consumer revolution," and that this was similar to shifts in the West that had been discussed by historians of consumption.

Table 1.1. Main Polish Manufacturers of Electric Appliances

Name	Location	Main Products	Years of Activity
Zakłady Zmechanizowanego Sprzętu Domowego -Polar	Wrocław	Refrigerators, automatic washing machines	1951 to present. In 2002, acquired by Whirpool Polska, http://www.polar.sm.pl/
Zakłady Sprzętu Grzejnego Predom-Wrozamet	Wrocław	Gas ovens, electric ovens, microwave ovens	1946–2013 (liquidated) From 1993, products sold under Mastercook brand
ZELMER Rzeszowskie Zakłady Elektromechaniczne im. Augustyna Micała	Rzeszów	Vacuum cleaners, coffee grinders, food processors	1937 to present. Privatized in 2001, http://www.zelmer.pl/
Warszawskie Zakłady Telewizyjne, In 1993 renamed as Elemis	Warsaw	Television sets	1955–2003 (liquidated)
Zakłady Radiowe Diora	Dzierżoniów (near Wrocław)	Record players, audio cassette players, stack systems, VCRs	1945–2001 (liquidated)
Zakłady Radiowe im. Kasprzaka	Warszawa	Radios, audio cassette players, stack systems, VCRs	1949–1999 (liquidated)
Gdańskie Zakłady Elektroniczne "Unimor"	Gdańsk	Black and white television sets, color television sets	1957–1997 (liquidated)
Zakłady Radiowe Radmor	Gdynia	Audio cassette players, radios, amplifiers	1947 to present. Since 1989. Radmor manufactures only specialized communications equipment, http://www.radmor.com.pl/.
Zakłady Wytwórcze Magnetofonów Unitra-Lubartów.	Lubartów (near Lublin)	Audio cassette players	1971–1996 (liquidated)
Łódzkie Zakłady Radiowe Fonica	Łódź	Record players, Amplifiers	1945–2002 (liquidated)
Zakłady Kineskopowe "Unitra-Polkolor"	Piaseczno (near Warsaw)	Color kinescopes	1976–Since 1991, joint venture with Thomson Consumer Electronics. Production ceased in 2009.

Beginning in the late 1950s, the USSR became a juggernaut in the production of durable goods that were distributed domestically and exported to other Eastern Bloc states.[18] In Polish households, the most visible durable goods from the USSR were imported refrigerators and black and white television sets. At the same time, domestic electric goods manufacturing industry also underwent significant development and expansion. The most prominent state enterprises in that industry were Warszawskie Zakłady Telewizyjne, hereafter WZT (Warsaw Television Works, production profile: television sets), Zakłady Radiowe im. Kasprzaka in Warsaw, hereafter ZRK (Kasprzak Radio Works: radios, reel-to-reel audio recorders, audio-cassette recorders), Zakłady Radiowe Diora (in the small city of Dzierżoniów in the region of Lower Silesia: radio receivers, stacking systems), Polar in Wroclaw (refrigerators, washing machines), and Zelmer in Rzeszów (vacuum cleaners, small appliances).[19] We will regularly see such manufacturers and their products in later chapters, where I will also introduce some other smaller manufacturers not listed previously.

Aside from the television sets and refrigerators from the USSR and small shipments of products from other Eastern Bloc states, most of the electric goods available from the retail trade in the 1960s were designed and manufactured domestically. In the early phase of the development of black-and-white television broadcasting in the 1950s, Poland received technological support from the USSR with the know-how, blueprints, and prototype models of television sets.[20] I will not discuss the history of this technology, as it was recently discussed from the perspective of media studies in a volume by Piotr Sitarski, Maria Garda and Krzysztof Jajko.[21]

The distribution of black and white television sets to a substantial percentage of Polish households in the 1960s was the result of the successful development of the mass-scale production of television kinescopes by ZELOS, a dedicated manufacturer of kinescopes in Piaseczno, near Warsaw. This enterprise closely collaborated with WZT, which manufactured television sets. It is also important to note that ZELOS became the foundation for Polkolor, the sole domestic manufacturer of color kinescopes (cf. chapter 4). Some enterprises from the consumer electronics sector established contacts with companies in Western Europe and signed licensing agreements. Such practices took place only on a small scale, and these efforts were initiated by the enterprises themselves, without any central plan or support from the government.

The rule of Gomułka ended in December 1970 after mass protests in the port cities of Gdańsk and Szczecin were brutally suppressed by the military. These protests were sparked by the introduction of steep price increases for meat and other staples. In response to this discontent, the new government under First Secretary of the PZPR Edward Gierek (1970–1980) undertook an extensive policy to improve the standard of living, reform the central and intermediate levels of economic management, and to greatly increase technological development through the purchase of Western licenses.[22] The two overarching aims of the licensing policy were to stimulate the domestic manufacturing of high-value-added technological products that could be successfully exported to First and Third World countries and, in the case of electric goods, to greatly increase the ownership of such products by Polish households.[23]

In the 1970s, the government also established an orchestrated system of propaganda. This media campaign of showing people that they live in a modern and highly prospering country was referred to as "propaganda sukcesu" or "the propaganda of success."[24] According to Lente and van Rip, the propaganda-laden public coverage of technological developments can be interpreted as a body of publicly shared "technological promises" made by the government to citizens.[25] In later chapters, I will discuss the construction of the sociotechnical imaginary included in such promises and the articulation of controversies related to the feasibility of fulfilling such promises.

Many home technologies were appropriated by such propaganda texts as indicators of the modernization of the industry, and of a steep improvement in the levels of comfort enjoyed in Polish households. These technologies included an automatic washing machine introduced by Polar in 1972, several models of audio-cassette tape recorders introduced by ZRK under the license by West German Grundig, and the building of a manufacturing plant for color kinescopes by the newly established Polkolor (1976), the most spectacular project. The capacity to domestically mass produce color kinescopes had two objectives. First, it sought to facilitate the production of the first model of a domestically manufactured color television set. Secondly, the government envisioned color kinescopes as a flagship electronic export product that would enable Polkolor to become a reliable original equipment manufacturer, or OEM, and one of the world's top-ranked players in the consumer electronics industry.

According to the plan of the economic policy-makers, the costs of purchasing technologies manufactured under Western licenses were to be paid from shipments of licensed products on an OEM basis. These hopes for the successful export of home technologies regularly appear in my book. In the 1960s, Poland was able to some extent to achieve technological autarky in the production of electric goods since most components and materials could be delivered by domestic subcontractors. One of the side effects of the introduction of new more complex technologies in the 1970s was the need for components and materials with much higher quality standards than before. These could not be manufactured domestically and had to be imported from the West. For this reason, dollars and West German marks became an important non-human component of an assemblage of "home technologies."

The first cracks in the image of the Polish prosperity of the 1970s appeared in 1976 when, after a price hike for staple food products, organized protests took place in factories in Warsaw and Radom.[26] Such protests were easily suppressed, but the deepening economic crisis of the second half of the 1970s led to the next wave of mass protests that began in Gdańsk in 1980, which resulted in the establishment of the legal Solidarity movement in the same year, followed by a government crackdown with the imposition of martial law in December 1981. Poland returned to more or less normal when martial law was finally abolished in late 1982.[27] However, the emergence of the severe economic crisis that accompanied the social upheaval of 1980–1981, and which lasted until 1989, had a significant impact on the possibility for the further modernization of the production of home technologies.

One of the persistent trends of the 1980s was that electric goods became increasingly unaffordable for many people, the result of high inflation, regular price hikes, and stagnation in technological innovation. Moreover, martial law disrupted the production of electric goods due to the impossibility of importing the necessary materials and components and the loss of income due to missed export shipments.

The main topic of public debates on technological innovation in the 1980s was the need to limit "technological expectations" in the sector of high-end consumer technologies. Such cutbacks from the early 1980s were officially referred to creatively as "racjonalizacja struktury produkcji' (the rationalization of the production structure.) As a columnist in *Przegląd Techniczny* in 1983 noted, the economic planners ordered the electric goods industry to "verify its production program and to eliminate a range of products that, when considered from a technological and functional point of view, does not fit in a current situation of crisis."[28] The policy-makers ordered the industry to discontinue the production of a range of products that were considered novelties as they were too expensive to produce and too expensive for consumers to purchase. For example, in the late 1970s, the industry planned to start manufacturing a dishwasher which was considered both a significant innovation and an expensive luxury product. This plan was abandoned after 1981. I will discuss the cutbacks in the project of domestic production of high-end audio technologies and the failure of the project to manufacture color televisions in chapter 4.

The second element of the public experience of the crisis was the number of public voices that warned about the deepening technological gap between Poland and the world's electronics powers: the United States, Japan, and other Far East countries. Such warnings were expressed by economists and technology experts and were illustrated by elaborate presentations of this gap through tables and graphs (see chapter 2). To cope with this problem, in 1985, the government established the Office for Technological Progress

(Urząd Postępu Technicznego), affiliated with the Council of Ministers, that was to fund technological innovation through governmental orders.[29] To some extent, this office was supposed to play a role similar to the famous Japanese Ministry of International Trade and Industry (1949–2001), better known as the MITI, which was frequently discussed in public as an example that the Polish authorities and economic planners should follow.[30] However, the Polish institution had a limited budget and could do little to help the industry. Indeed, two highly publicized projects of technological innovation funded through this system, the Polish educational computer Elwro 800 Junior and two competing video-cassette recorders, were considered failures that were later, after 1989, identified as costly blunders which contributed to the rapid demise of their manufacturers (Elwro, ZRK, and Diora).[31]

THE SYSTEM OF PRODUCTION AND THE PLAN

State socialist governments that imposed the system of central economic planning used "Five Year Plans," hereafter FYPs, for the long-term planning of economic development. Such plans not only included declarations of the specific quotas for both industrial and consumer goods production but also in some cases defined plans for technological innovation.[32] The translation of the guidelines drafted by the congresses of the ruling communist parties into such FYPs for the production of consumer goods has been extensively discussed by several authors who specialize in the consumer culture in the Eastern Bloc, such as Krisztina Fehérváry, Natalya Chernyshova, and Patrick Hyder Patterson.[33] The system of economic planning in state socialist Poland was analyzed in-depth by Jean Woodall and Kazimierz Poznański.[34] In particular, Woodall's work has been important for my research as she extensively discusses the process of the translation of FYPs into factory floor-level production management practices. Moreover, she discusses several inefficiencies, tensions, and conflicts of interest that were the side effects of the policy of micromanaging the economy in the 1970s by a circle of economic experts, popularly referred to as "technocrats."[35]

The system of state socialist FYPs is an excellent real-life example of John Law's focus on the central role of "projectness" in shaping modernity. This concept, which I will discuss in great depth in chapter 2, refers to the pursuit of large-scale collaborative actions by several institutions and economic entities that together expect to achieve a projected future.[36] The production system in state socialism was based on a procedure that involved turning specific ideologically driven principles and guidelines into a nationwide "plan." The instructions included in such a plan determined the course of action for governmental agencies and production quotas for the production sector. The future in FYPs was projected through the vocabulary of steady "improvement" (poprawa, or polepszenie) or "increase" (wzrost) of some tangible indicators of modernity, prosperity, and efficiency. Such indicators included, for example, the number of durable goods per one hundred households or access to services such as one kindergarten or hospital for a specific number of citizens.

I quote the original terms used in both documents and the mass media since such phrases became elements of normalized political communications related to the imaginary future-oriented communist project. In a study of the youth culture of the late USSR, Alexei Yurchak discusses, as he calls it, "normalized" language with well-defined phrasing and visual language that referred to the body of central principles of communism and the trio of Marx, Engels, and Lenin, supplemented with the image of the current First Secretary of the Communist Party of the Soviet Union.[37] Stories presented in the mass media that were used to perform state socialist "projectness" include several similar "normalized" phrasing as well as distinctive visual conventions of associating the processes of production with workers on the factory floor (see chapter 4).

Central planning and the tensions that arose during the carrying out of such a plan significantly determined the roles and identities of the social actors embedded in the structure that were tasked with carrying out the plan. Beginning with the classic work by Fredrick Jameson, there is a continuous field of research on the cultural logic of late capitalism.[38] Similarly, the aforementioned works on consumer cultures in state socialism address the issue of the cultural logic of this political, economic, and social system. Here, I would like to refer to a particular feature of this system by quoting the seminal work by Sergei Oushakine on the commodity culture of the USSR. He argues that the Soviet production system should be viewed not merely as a system that produces a specific quota of material objects determined by the current FYP but rather as a more complex massive "commodity-transmitting network" that includes "multiple institutional associations, nomenclatures of things, protocols of interactions and codes of behavior, which were supposed to manage the Soviet things system on rational grounds."[39]

Later, I will illustrate how the system of technological innovation is an instance of such a network that was established to control the social life of technological products on rational grounds. Such a system was used to determine how a new product was designed, manufactured; tested under a quality control regime, possibly marked with a quality certificate; presented during trade shows, where it could be nominated for a category of "best new product" or with one of the myriad other awards; announced through public communications channels and quas-advertisements; delivered to the consumer through retail trade and rationally used by consumers; and eventually properly serviced under warranty if it should be faulty.

The state socialist economic system was accompanied by the promise that it is capable of efficiently governing the introduction of new technologies, while at the same time fulfilling "social needs" specific to state socialist society. If we refer to Lente and van Rip's framework of the "expectation/ promise" repertoire of social actors, declarations toward the production quotas and technological innovation in the electric goods industry constitute a set of technological expectations. As they note: "Expectations about possible developments, especially as these are put forward and taken up in statements, brief stories or scenarios. These lead to action, not because there is a structure behind the backs of the actors, but because now actors are creating one before them."[40]

In later chapters, I will introduce several instances of public debates that included such a repertoire. I will investigate how the intermediary actors expressed their expectations of the industry, as they claimed to speak on the behalf of consumers or the more abstract "common good," and the promises made by representatives of the industry. While confronting expectations and promises, I will discuss several cases when intermediary actors used a failure to deliver a promise by the industry as an opportunity to problematize the flaws in consumer goods production, inefficiency in the introduction of technological innovation, and the lack of dedication to the fulfillment of social goals that such innovation was supposed to achieve.

FYPs dictated a specific set of goals for all institutions and industries within the state apparatus. In state socialism, the government-party system was supposed to rationally allocate the roles for all relevant social actors for the tensionless process of the introduction of new technologies. Oldenziel and colleagues provide a useful remark on the specificity of a socialist-style consumption junction:

> After Stalin's death, the socialist states dealt with the intersection between consumption and production in a different fashion than was common in the West. They sought to subsume individual consumption under the regime of collective consumption. Although Cowan's consumption junction in technological development had liberal market arrangements in mind, there was also a specifically socialist-style consumption junction, in which the state tried to directly manage the gap between production and consumption. Instead of working through civil society, the government incorporated the mediations within the state apparatus.[41]

Later in this chapter, I will identify the specific institutions that were supposed to take part in managing the gap between production and consumption. This discussion will provide the background for a better understanding of how the central planning policy governed the relationship between manufacturers, intermediary groups, and consumers. I will also address the questions of how the processes of mediation relevant to specific technological innovations were incorporated into the state apparatus, how some actors joined these mediations, and the reasons behind the emergence of tensions between them.

In Poland, as in the whole Eastern Bloc, the Central Committee of the PZPR regularly held major party congresses during which high-ranking party members discussed what had been achieved in recent years, publicized previous successes, or, if the specific congress was held after a regime change (e.g., 1956, 1970), they would conduct a ritual which condemned the shortcomings and mistakes of the previous ruling circle. Further, the congresses presented new ideas for upcoming reforms that enable state socialist Poland to go further in the pursuit of both economic and social development. Later, such congresses issued a collection of documents with guidelines concerning the goals of the governmental body Komisja Planowania, the Planning Commission, which used such guidelines to formulate the draft of the upcoming Narodowy Plan Społeczno-Gospodarczy, or the National Social and Economic Plan (hereafter NPSG), a Polish term for FYP. Every NPSG included several quantitative goals for the production of consumer goods, but it also set targets for the statistical indicators of household consumption. For the sake of this study, the most relevant indicator was the percentage of households that owned specific electric appliances.

The authors of the NPSG drafts extensively consulted with economic experts to garner their opinions. The debates on these plans took place during meetings of several party and governmental bodies that were accompanied by public coverage in central news outlets. The formulation of every NPSG was extensively covered in several issues of *Życie Gospodarcze*. To some extent, such publicly held debates were presented as "public consultations'" but were in fact political rituals. However, such debates also revealed the power struggles between competing industries since the FYP dictated the resource allocation between different production sectors.[42]

After the acknowledgment and publication of the final version of NPSG, *zjednoczenia*, or product-based industrial associations, were responsible for achieving specific goals concerning the production of industrial products and consumer goods as well as the development of new infrastructure: housing, hospitals, and schools. The system of *zjednoczenia*, which had its counterparts in East Germany (Vereinigung) and in the USSR (Объединение предприятий), was first introduced in Poland in the 1960s.[43] Later, in the 1970s, this system was substantially expanded under the policy of creating Wielkie Organizacje Gospodarcze (WOG), or the Large Economic Organizations, and was another instance of socialist "projectness."[44] With such organizations, the policy-makers sought to expand the possibility to directly manage the centrally planned economy. *Zjednoczenia* were compulsory organizations that governed all major state enterprises from a specific economic sector, and their function was to coordinate the production of specific products and to achieve specific quotas declared in NPSG. Two relevant *zjednoczenia* for my study were the association of enterprises from the consumer electronics industry UNITRA (1961–1980) and the home appliance industry PREDOM (1974–1989). Representatives of *zjednoczenia* rarely appeared in the media when it came to public communications about new home technologies. In fact, the majority of the press materials that were relevant to my research were interviews with the directors, managers, and chief engineers of specific enterprises.

Each *zjednoczenie* was responsible for the management of production quotas, ensured that all enterprises within its structure fulfilled their required quotas, and oversaw the cooperation between these enterprises. In addition to instructing specific enterprises on the quantities of products they should manufacture, each *zjednoczenie* could exercise its power through the quality control protocols. Another way of exercising control over specific enterprises was ordering them to manufacture specific innovative technologies designed in Ośrodek Badawczo Rozwojowy, the Center for Research and Development (hereafter OBR), which were affiliated directly with the specific *zjednoczenie* instead of technologies designed in the research centers affiliated with specific enterprises. This issue will be discussed in subsequent chapters.

In a centrally planned economy, at least in the home technologies industry, there was very little vertical integration. Moreover, the specificity of this industry was that production of materials and components was particularly dependent on subcontractors, some of whom had a monopoly on the supply of components. This was exacerbated by the fact that specific state enterprises were obliged to manufacture specific products with specific designs given to them by their *zjednoczenia*. This issue was a major problem for this industry. In chapter 3, which discusses the quality of electric goods, I will investigate the narrative of problems with "dostawcy" (subcontractors) as the weakest link in the production process that also significantly hindered technological innovation.

The system of *zjednoczenia* was supposed to solve the issue of capitalist-style competition between enterprises with similar production profiles. The reality was rather different. Brian Porter-Szűcs provides an insightful comment on the cultural logic of the competition in the Polish economy:

> There was also a great deal more micromanagement in Polish planning, and more rigidity when plans turned out to be poorly designed. On the other hand, the PRL didn't really have *one* planned economy: rather, many different economic ministries functioned on parallel tracks and competed with each other

for resources. Anyone who thinks planning in communist Poland eliminated competition should have seen the battles for allocations or raw materials and financial resources that the managers of every firm had to constantly fight. This wasn't *capitalist* competition, but it was competition nonetheless.[45]

Moreover, drawing exclusively from publicly available sources, Woodall discusses several examples of the rivalry between different ministries, industries, and enterprises gathered in a single *zjednoczenie,* different divisions in an enterprise, and finally conflicts between management and workforce.[46]

In addition to the logic of system being a significant flaw, the Hungarian economist János Kornai in his influential work discusses the logic of "soft budget constraints" and their impact on the inefficiency of the centrally planned economy.[47] And here, I would like to discuss another, rather overlooked feature of this system. To offer a glimpse of the tensions in the socialist economy, I have included an excerpt from a speech by Zdzisław Grudzień, the First Secretary of the Katowice Voivodeship Committee of the PZPR, a close associate of Gierek and one of the most prominent political figures in Poland of the 1970s. In a public speech during the VIII PZPR Congress in 1980, Grudzień openly acknowledged that enterprises and *zjednoczenia* notoriously neglected the objectives of the FYP and instead pursued their own agenda by fulfilling only the elements of the plan that make them eligible for governmental bonuses: "In too many cases state enterprises and even zjednoczenia, to benefit by receiving bonuses, have learned how to manipulate the plan, . . . [the] Plan has to be a compulsory directive for all enterprises and economic organizations. We need to fiercely work against the inappropriate understanding of the openness of the plan."[48]

Grudzień's public speech revealed the feature of a centrally planned economy that we may call "soft plan constraints," which enabled enterprises and *zjednoczenia* to manipulate the data used as indicators of fulfilling the production quota or simply neglect it altogether if there was no bonus for fulfilling it. While studying such practices is an issue for economic historians, I raise this issue to illustrate how severe tensions in the planned economy were openly articulated. In chapter 2, I will discuss the public controversies over a similar practice of declaring technological innovation with public exhibits of prototypes of appliances that the manufacturer did not intend to produce in the near future. Such exhibitions of technological innovation were used by enterprises to receive some economic benefits for enterprises that fill the criteria of technological innovativeness. In all three subsequent chapters, I will address several other tensions and conflicts that had an impact on the innovativeness and qualities of electric goods.

SOCIALIST-STYLE ADVERTISEMENT
AND PUBLIC COMMUNICATIONS

In an introduction to a comparative study of European systems of the production of domestic technologies, technology historian Cynthia Cockburn
compares capitalism and state socialism in terms of orchestrated systems for
introducing innovations:

> In a profit-governed society there is no socially-responsible agent of techno-
> logical planning. The latest model from the drawing board of a manufacturer is
> designed only to compete with that of his rivals for space in the actually-existing
> household. However, our collective European project showed that, even in the
> formerly centrally-planned economies, there was no systematic approach to the
> development of household technologies.[49]

Although this remark, in general, is relevant for the state socialist management of the production of home technologies, there were some attempts to
introduce such a coordinated system. Karin Zachmann, in her chapter in the
book *Cold War Kitchen*, discusses a short-lasting East German ministry-level
advisory committee that in the late 1950s attempted to introduce a centrally
coordinated plan for the development of home appliances.[50] However, there
was no such thing as a "systematic approach" to the development of home
appliances in Poland. This lack of a coherent system for introducing technological innovation and for building an efficient "commodity-transmitting
network" was articulated in public debates as a problem for the centrally
planned economy. A report on the problems with the introduction of novelties
in audio electronics from 1983 noted this flaw: "There is a lack of a comprehensive policy for introducing new products to the market, setting up prices,
and communicating novelties to consumers. Both the industry and retail trade
organizations are to be blamed for such a situation."[51]

Although there was no coordinated system for the implementation of technological innovation, I outline here an orchestrated system of announcing the
release of new products to consumers. This system, which was a pivotal element of the mediation junction, was facilitated by several actors that used it
to pursue their own agenda. In market economies, manufacturers of consumer
technologies communicate the release of new products with advertising campaigns that emphasize technological innovativeness, ergonomics, and design.
These seek to show how the product fits into or improves an individual's
lifestyle. In state socialism, there were very few directly organized advertising campaigns comparable with the market economy. Yet, such a form of
communication was used, and I will briefly outline the practice of advertising
electric goods.[52]

Such communication was based on the production and circulation of textual and visual representations of consumer products. While studying such representations, I note Hebdige's remark on the role of the product image in advertising: "The narrative is ordered according to the dictates of an economic principle: the circulation of the Image precedes the selling of the Thing. Before looking at what the scooter came to mean in use, it is necessary to consider how it was made to appear before the market."[53] Later, Hebdige uses the appropriate term "support structure" to describe a range of practices that accompany the design of a new product: "All these support structures can be regarded as extensions of the original design project: to produce a new category of machines, a new type of consumer."[54]

In his remarks about the role of the Yugoslav mass media in shaping consumer culture, Patterson notes that the orchestrated system of providing consumer goods was accompanied by a system of presenting narratives and images that can be interpreted as a socialist-style equivalent of the despised culture industry in the West. As he argues, such a system of public communications ultimately harmed society due to the arousal of expectations that could not be fulfilled through the actual delivery of consumer goods.

> Structural flaws in the functioning of the socialist economies hampered the effort from the start, but even when there were early and genuinely impressive successes in raising living standards, these proved insufficient. The problem was exacerbated by the governments' efforts to celebrate those successes and promote a culture of consumption in the media, in advertising, and in other sectors of what became, in remarkably short order, a socialist "culture industry" with real similarities to the media machines so derided.[55]

Here, I outline key features of the aforementioned "support structures," or a local equivalent of the "culture industry," in late state socialist Poland. This issue will also be explored, where relevant, in later chapters.

Public communications about the release of new home technologies included propaganda-laden texts on recent developments and the steady progress in the manufacturing of consumer goods and the achievements of governmental policy in improving the standard of living. This was an orchestrated effort by the state media, which closely collaborated with the manufacturers, trade organizations, and several intermediary actors that contributed to these campaigns. Such public announcements were a pivotal element of the "commodity transmitting network" in state socialism. The texts and visual images related to technological innovation were ascribed with the imaginary of technological modernization that would have a positive impact on society.

A new major product introduced by a state enterprise was usually released in the following manner. First, the manufacturer brought a new product to its exhibition during Targi Krajowe (Domestic Fair), the main event for the domestic trade, which was held twice a year as Targi Wiosenne (Spring Fair) and Targi Jesienne (Autumn Fair) in the city of Poznań. These fairs were primarily for representatives of trade organizations, who then evaluated the new selection of products and made preliminary agreements with the manufacturers to deliver a specific quota of the exhibited products to their stores. Some high-profile, newly released products considered as possible export successes were also exhibited during the international fair Międzynarodowe Targi Poznańskie (Poznań International Fair) to get the attention of potential foreign buyers.

Such fairs were widely covered by the mass media. In the 1970s, public communications about new products released during the fairs were extensively embedded in the propaganda that was designed to convince citizens that the policy-makers were actively pursuing a policy of technological and social modernization. Such media coverage particularly emphasized the innovativeness of the electric goods industry, which, it was claimed, carried out extensive R&D programs and regularly introduced novelties with new features that corresponded to global trends. After the crisis of 1980, there was a significant change in the content of such coverage. Reports from the fairs in the 1980s were frequently used to problematize the stagnation and the crisis in the industry. The repertoire of these texts usually included a contrast between the promises that had been made about the technology with the disappointing reality, for example, tthat there was a limited number of novelties, or that most of the production quota of an attractive novelty would be exported and Polish consumers would not see such products in retail stores anytime soon.

There were also large one-off dedicated exhibitions that contributed to the public communication of recently released electric goods. For instance, in 1980 IRWiK, IWP, and KGD organized a major exhibition titled "Dom i rodzina" ("Household and Family") that was first presented in the Palace of Science and Culture in Warsaw and later displayed in several large cities.[56] Here, I give an excerpt from a report on this event:

> The exhibition presents the rational equipment of a standard M4 [three bedrooms and a kitchen] apartment with home appliances, that includes the newest propositions from PREDOM . . . One can also see a set of consumer electronics from UNITRA DOM . . . The exhibition is highly popular among visitors. Among them are families, representatives of manufacturers and trade organizations, and schoolchildren . . . It is worth emphasizing that virtually all exhibits came from the current production and are available from the retail trade.[57]

Such a narrative in the report provides an instance of the performance of modernity with claims of what exactly constitutes a "modern" apartment, that such modernity is within the reach of consumers since new products are available in the stores, and that consumers can embrace the modernization project by frequenting such an exhibition.

Aside from this major event, there were other much smaller, locally held exhibitions of novelties from the electric goods industry. Such small-scale local exhibitions were usually coorganized by one of several retail trade organizations, such as those belonging to the main structure of PHW, Przedsiębiorstwo Handlu Wewnętrznego, or the Enterprise for Domestic Retail Trade, or, in rural areas, of Samopomoc Chłopska (Peasant Self-Help), a rural cooperative. The organizing of these exhibitions usually received support from the KGD, and they included some educational elements with posters and demonstrations on the efficient use of home appliances that could relieve women from the burden of housework.

In state socialism, the personnel of retail stores were burdened with the responsibility of helping the consumer to make an informed and rational decision about their purchase. In the 1970s, one of the major goals of "polityka konsumpcji" was not only to improve the quality of consumer goods but also the quality of the relevant services such as the education of such personnel.[58] *Handel Wewnętrzny (Domestic Trade)*, a trade journal of the community of commodity knowledge experts, regularly published postulates on how to assist store workers to provide consumers with expert knowledge. Such duties included informing consumers about the new products that had arrived from the electric goods industry and the ability to demonstrate their technical features. One of the experts outlined this policy as a "collaboration of manufacturers and retail trade organizations in the creation of 'image' (a term originally used in English) of products and the conditions in which they are offered to consumers."[59] She noted the "correct exposition of products in a retail store, professional service by store clerks and delivering information about a product" as key elements of this strategy. These instructions show us the attention paid to how to locally organize the performance of a "modern" product in the space of a retail store.

The public creation of an image of a product in state socialism also involved advertisements, published mostly in female magazines, that communicated the release of new designs of home appliances from PREDOM. Other popular magazines occasionally published advertisements for consumer electronics from the UNITRA enterprises. The advertisements of PREDOM products were usually full-page color illustrations of products, refrigerators, automatic washing machines, and vacuum cleaners, but they were published on behalf of the PHW, or occasionally Samopomoc Chłopska, not the manufacturers. This practice of advertising shows how retail trade organizations, not manufacturers, were tasked with communicating the availability of new products. The single most popular format was an advertisement for refrigerators that usually included an open refrigerator full of attractive products and a young female leaning in to reach one of the products. If we were to obscure the names PREDOM, Polar, Zelmer, and PHW, as well as the bottles of Polish vodka in refrigerators, the visual content of such adverts could be mistaken for an advert from a market economy from that era.[60]

Another channel of public communications about new products the state media. Information about the release of new products was used for the public performance of sociotechnical imaginaries related to the modernization project. Such communications consisted of short articles in newspapers and weeklies, customarily titled "nowości z . . . " (novelties from . . . [manufacturer's name]), with a list of the recently released novelties and their basic features. Such short notes, and sometimes full-page articles, were regularly accompanied by photos with propaganda-laden captions from CAF (Centralna Agencja Fotograficzna), or the Central Photographic Agency.[61] A similar format was employed by announcements on the television news and newsreels. In later chapters, I discuss some specific discursive practices used in such communications.

Every major periodical included in my source base, including *Przegląd Techniczny*, *Życie Gospodarcze*, *Veto*, and *Gospodarstwo Domowe*, regularly published articles about the electric goods industry. These could be short "novelties from . . . " communiqués, reports about specific manufacturers, or a more general article on the state of the industry as a whole. The longer publications usually gave a voice to one of the enterprise managers or a chief engineer, who explained what the enterprise would be releasing in the upcoming months or responded to a recent critique.

In the 1970s, critical voices in such communications were rather scarce and referred to general problems with inadequate production quotas and indirect complaints concerning the quality of products. Such complaints were written in the passive voice and used normalized phrasing that carefully avoided putting the blame on any institution or enterprise. Only in the 1980s did magazine editors regularly problematize such issues and openly discuss conflicts, economic problems, and question the feasibility of the further modernization of the industry. However, even in this decade of deepening economic and social crisis, we can regularly find narratives written with normalized phrasing that communicate a story of the harmonious cooperation between actors that took part in the production and mediation of home technologies and of steady technological progress.

THE ELECTRONIC ENGINEERING LOBBY

One of the most influential intermediary actors that shaped the sociotechnical imaginary related to home technologies was a loose coalition that represented the electric engineering community.[62] This community was a nexus that included engineers working for electric goods manufacturers, researchers at polytechnic universities and state research centers, and journalists from a range of technical and popular science press titles. From the early 1970s onward, this group extensively promoted electronics as the technology of the future that would play a pivotal role in the economic and social development of the decades to follow (cf. chapter 2).

Although there was also a powerful lobby that represented home appliances manufacturers and PREDOM, this lobby did not publicly share a similar coherent sociotechnical imaginary related to home appliances such as washing machines and refrigerators as technologies of the future. Managers from PREDOM enterprises mostly publicly expressed claims about the role of such goods in improving the standard of living and the imagery of the "modern household." However, they did not offer a coherent imagery of a technology-based future. For this reason, I focus here on the identity and repertoire of the electronic engineering community, which played a significant role in terms of shaping public knowledge and "telling stories" that accompany the production and consumption of home technologies.

This lobby had an organizational background with Stowarzyszenie Elektryków Polskich, or the Association of Polish Electricians (SEP), a professional association of electric engineers. The SEP in the 1970s was dominated by the electronic engineers, and their voices were primarily expressed on the pages of *Przegląd Techniczny* (*Technical Review*), the oldest (est. in 1866) and most influential Polish periodical dedicated to technological development that represented the interests and the worldview of the technical intelligentsia. To illustrate the agenda of *Przegląd Techniczny*, I refer to a study on the role of the technological press by technology historian Jeffrey Herf. In his study of the engineering community in the Third Reich, and its repertoire of public voices, Herf provides an insightful and broadly applicable remark on the role of the popular technology press: "The contributors to the journals of the engineering associations and the lecturers at the technical universities fashioned a tradition, a shared set of texts, basic terms, and common metaphors with which they hoped to lift technology from the alien world of Zivilisation to the familiar world of Kultur."[63]

Przegląd Techniczy played exactly such a role. In the postwar period, the editors and invited experts from different branches of technology-based industries used the pages of the magazine to bring accessible communication on the recent developments in the ongoing "Scientific Technological Revolution" (cf. chapter 2) and to show how new technologies provide positive social, cultural, and economic change. *Przegląd Techniczny* was also a key media platform in the communications about the release of new home technologies. Novelties from this market were primarily communicated by CAF photographs accompanied by normalized, propaganda-laden captions published in a section with a selection of press photographs that illustrated the recent technological developments from Poland and abroad.

Aside from regularly expressing their voices on the pages of *Przegląd Techniczny*, electronic engineers also had their own periodical, *Radioamator*, which in 1979 was renamed *Radioelektronik*. This monthly was primarily a niche periodical for electronics and ham radio hobbyists that published electronic blueprints and other content that required expert knowledge about electronics. However, its editors regularly published "novelties from. . . . " materials about UNITRA products, extensive product tests (cf. chapter 4), information about recent SEP activities such as conferences and publications, and other materials relevant to technological innovation in electronics.

In 1978, at the peak of the period of the "consumer socialism" policy, UNITRA established a large (about three hundred employees) research institute named Centralny Ośrodek Badawczo-Rozwojowy Elektronicznego Sprzętu Powszechnego Użytku, or the Central Institute for the Research and Development of Consumer Electronics (hereafter COBRESPU). Officially, this institute had two goals. The first one was to carry out R&D and provide UNITRA enterprises with the know-how for technical innovation. The second goal was to provide external quality control of electronic products made by these enterprises to address complaints about the poor manufacturing and the regular failures of consumer electronics. The unofficial objective of this institute was to enhance the control by UNITRA over electronics manufacturers (cf. chapter 3). The COBRESPU also played a significant role in the promotion of the technical culture related to electronic technologies, particularly in the promotion of the audiophile culture, which I have discussed elsewhere.[64] In 1984, a circle of electronics engineers linked to the COBRESPU started publishing *Hi-Fi Audio Video* monthly. The magazine had a subtitle, "progress in consumer electronics," and aside from publishing Do-It-Yourself blueprints, it regularly informed readers about the global trends in audio and video electronics and recent products from domestic manufacturers.

The electronic engineering community will regularly appear in subsequent chapters as the most significant intermediary actors that took part in the mediation of technological innovation in home technologies. Here, I would like to make a brief comparison between this lobby and another interest group, the economic expert lobby, to highlight the source of tensions between different expert groups. The key cause of this tension was the justification and profitability of very costly governmental investment in the R&D of electronic technologies. To explain the social context of the tensions between both communities, it is necessary to point out a significant factory-floor trend. Woodall notes the dominance of engineers at senior positions in the management of state enterprises: "Polish industrial managers tended to be trained in engineering, ignorant of formal economics and business training."[65]

For economic experts, the central platform for expressing their voices was *Życie Gospodarcze*, a leading economic weekly that represented the interests of this community, including ministry-level experts, university researchers, and managers from state enterprises. In Polish, they were referred to as "ekonomista," or "economist," since the term "manager" appeared in Polish economic culture only in the 1980s. Factory managers had to compete for participation in the decision-making process with engineers. As Woodall noted, the managers were often sidelined since the latter group was favored when it came to promotion to senior positions. Usually, the director of an enterprise had a degree in engineering and previously held a position of "główny technolog," or chief technologist.

Woodall offers several instances of how in the 1960s and 1970s influential economic experts used *Życie Gospodarcze* to publish opeds and give interviews to enroll others in their vision of specific economic policies. For economists, in public discussions on technological innovation, the key issue was the profitability of investing a substantial amount of financial and material resources in the pursuit of innovation.[66] A range of voices on this matter expressed by the technical engineering and economic expert's communities can be put in two main binary categories. The first was an argument that the pursuit of technical innovation, despite the lack of short-term profits and a heavy burden on the budget, would make a profit in the long run. The second argument was that Poland had already lost the "technological race" (cf. chapter 2), and therefore, such investments would not bring any measurable benefits to the economy or society.

State enterprises operated under the centrally planned economy under the conditions of "the soft-budget constraints," yet state enterprises that manufactured consumer products also had to sell them and make a profit. *Życie Gospodarcze* covered extensively the need for hard currency investments referred to in Polish as "wkład dewizowy," which were necessary for innovation in home technologies. While state enterprises were mostly dependent on other enterprises for most resources, materials, and components (cf. chapter 3), the central government rarely shared another key resource, the convertible currency (dollars or West German marks), which was necessary to import some materials and components unavailable in Poland, or those which were manufactured in Poland but were of insufficient quality. For this reason, state enterprises from the electric goods industry had to pay attention to the development of a strategy of exporting their products to obtain hard currency on their own and to favor foreign markets with the supply of their products. As we will see in subsequent chapters, these complex economic transactions were regularly discussed in public during debates on technological innovation.

KOMITET GOSPODARSTWA DOMOWEGO
(HOME ECONOMICS COMMITTEE)

Historians of consumer culture discuss the home efficiency movement, also referred to as the home economics movement, that emerged in Western Europe and the United States during the early twentieth century as a nongovernmental organization that played a substantial role as an intermediary actor that helped shape consumer culture by carving its niche between producers, consumers, and governmental institutions.[67] Here, I address the question of how exactly such a nongovernmental organization named Komitet Kospodarstwa Domowego (the Home Economics Committee) was able to operate in state socialism on the margins of the state apparatus. The KGD became an influential expert group that built its position through the production of knowledge about the practices of housework and home appliances and by collaborating with other actors from the mediation junction. I wish to highlight how this organization actively worked together with institutions, trade organizations, and home appliance manufacturers in campaigns organized under the slogans of "modernization" and the "mechanization of households." The authors of the intellectual agenda document of the Tensions of Europe research project noted the role of the home efficiency movement in Western Europe as a key actor in the emerging civil society of consumers. As they argue, such organizations "helped organize women and workers into social activists, responsible citizens, and critical consumers of new technologies."[68] I will now outline the agenda and repertoire of the KGD to note similarities and differences with the role of the previously mentioned movements in Western Europe.[69]

The KGD was established in 1957 as a nongovernmental organization referred to in Polish as "organizacja społeczna" (societal organization), formed under the umbrella of Liga Kobiet (the League of Women) due to the presumed need for an expert group that would address both the social and economic problems faced by women responsible for households. The KGD formed its identity as an expert group that drew from the scientific expertise of its members, including experts in industrial design, commodity knowledge, consumer research, and nutritional science. The organization built its identity on its academic credentials since most experts were employed as researchers at either universities or state research centers. For instance, a longtime activist and chairperson of the KGD, Alicja Zdybel (1968–1989), who was a prolific writer of articles and regularly represented the KGD in the media as an interviewee, was at the same time employed as a research coordinator at the Instytut Wzornictwa Przemysłowego (IWP), the Institute of Industrial Design.

The most appropriate term to describe the position of the KGD in the power structure of state socialism would be to call it "a quasi-NGO." In Polish jargon, organizations such as these are referred to pejoratively as "transmission belts" that helped the authorities to carry out their social and economic policies without their agency. The "transmission belt" term was originally used by Lenin to discuss the role of trade unions in helping the Communist Party in building the communist project.[70] The KGD itself was not under the direct control of the state apparatus, but in a nondemocratic country, the state allowed only organizations whose activities were perceived as desirable from the point of view of the interests of the state to operate.

The KGD's agenda was to support the modernization of households and help them to more efficiently fill their roles in society. Such a goal was consistent with state policy since the steady increase in efficiency was one of the key objectives of the communist project.[71] The term "efficiently" was primarily used to describe economic performance, and in state socialist Poland, one of the most frequently used public slogans was "wzrost wydajności produkcji" (an increase in the efficiency of production) at state enterprises. However, Porter-Szűcs notes an important trend related to the notion of efficiency. In the 1960s, "the object of efficiency maximization shifted from the firm to 'society.'"[72] Thus, the term "an increase of the efficiency of production" became accompanied by "wzrost wydajności pracy" (an increase in the efficiency of work), which referred to the efficiency of a single worker on the factory floor. Such efficient workers also needed to live in efficiently run households operated by housewifes. For this reason, the KGD's agenda of maximizing the efficiency of households was consistent with the government's social policy. It was not only allowed to operate but was also enabled to extensively collaborate with governmental institutions in performing educational activities.

There were several key KGD strategies relevant to this book. First, the organization carried out extensive educational campaigns by organizing courses that were conducted by local female instructors and usually held in rural areas. In addition, the KGD provided materials for other institutions with educational activities. For instance, the KGD published ready-to-use scripts for courses and other educational materials. KGD experts also communicated their knowledge through publishing books, publications in its periodical *Gospodarstwo Domowe* (the *Household*), and also in a more accessible form in women's magazines and brochures on rational housework.

The KGD played a pivotal role in the establishment of the regular large-scale testing of durable goods outside of state enterprises and OBRs from the industry (cf. chapter 4). The testing was coorganized with Instytut Towaroznawstwa, the Institute for Commodity Knowledge, and its communications were also published in *Gospodarstwo Domowe* and women's magazines. KGD activists also conducted research on households and consumers in collaboration with Instytut Rynku Wewnętrznego i Konsumpcji, IRWiK (Institute for Domestic Market and Consumption) to carry out surveys on time use and household spending.

The KGD was also capable of enrolling other social actors into its educational campaigns, such as local branches of governmental agencies, other NGOs, manufacturers, retailers, and trade organizations. To illustrate the mundane aspects of the organization's role as an intermediary actor, I have included a report from a course on using electric ovens from the early 1970s that offers a glimpse of how the KGD performed modernity in a rural area. Such a course represents one of the most basic and frequent activities of the KGD and was organized with the collaboration of the local "Nowoczesna Gospodyni," or "Modern Housewife" center, one of the hundreds of local educational centers run by Samopomoc Chłopska.[73] The goal of such a course was to familiarize young rural females with electric ovens as an appliance for cooking as a modern alternative to coal stoves. The course was run by a local KGD female instructor, and the KGD also provided all the necessary appliances demonstrated during this event.

In her study, Karin Zachmann discusses an intermediary actor that for a short time had a significant impact on the planning of the production of home appliances.[74] Did the KGD play a similar role? The organization regularly informed consumers about technological innovations with articles in *Gospodarstwo Domowe* and by organizing exhibitions on novelties with retail trade organizations. The KGD activists in their publications and interviews suggested that they directly collaborated with the industry through informal channels and urged state enterprises to increase their production quotas of home appliances and improve quality control. But it is doubtful that the organization was somehow capable of influencing the actual design of specific products. In 1989, Alicja Zdybel in an interview in *Atut*, the official monthly of the FK, outlined the KGD's activities and pointed out that the organization was only capable of successfully halting the end of the production of impractical appliances such as "spulchniacz do kotletów," a device to make cutlets, a Polish traditional dish, and portable coffee machines.[75] It is worth noting that the production of portable coffee machines is something of a mystery since as far as I am aware, no enterprise was manufacturing ordinary coffee machines in any significant quantities. Besides, Poles did not need such a device, as they simply put a spoon or two of coffee into a cup and poured boiling water into it. Therefore, claiming influence over such peculiar products as examples of the KGD's agency to influence the design and production of new home appliances, suggests that the organization had little impact in that regard.

Nevertheless, the KGD played a vital role in the shaping of public knowledge about the role that a well-equipped modern household could play in challenging irrational backwardness and encouraging female empowerment. Furthermore, when such issues became addressed in official governmental documents and party propaganda, the KGD used such materials to enhance its position as an expert group by showing how its activities corresponded with the social policy of the government. In the early 1970s, an article in *Gospodarstwo Domowe* used extracts from a speech by Gierek to support the organization's claim for authority: "We have to remove the remains of backwardness in the economy, culture, and lifestyle as soon as possible . . . We also want every household to be equipped with modern home appliances that ease the work of our sisters, mothers, and wives."[76]

The KGD claimed to represent consumers by constantly appealing to manufacturers and state institutions for more production quotas, better quality products, and more affordable consumer goods that were necessary for running a household, but it did not represent actual consumers, as we will see in the case of the FK discussed later, but rather used "consumer" as a figure of speech. The KGD did not develop any system of receiving feedback from actual consumers but only considered them as subjects for research that needed to undergo the process of education. The KGD strongly promoted a normative "consumption regime" based on the dichotomy of rational (positive) and backward (negative) forms of consumption.[77]

The KGD's agenda of sharing a normative discourse on both the material culture of the household and the relevant social role of a housewife is an instance of the politics of expert groups discussed by historian of technology Boel Berner. As she notes in her paper on Swedish educational "housewives' films," "The experts wanted to serve the housewife, but also to remake her."[78] Moreover, she refers to Zygmunt Bauman's notes on the role of contemporary expert cultures: "The user is reduced to a rhetorical figure in the experts' game. His or her own definition of the problems rarely reach the experts. Instead, they are represented by the experts (or other proxies) and addressed, at a distance, as a social construction in experts' discourse."[79] This remark corresponds with the aforementioned work by Frank Trentmann on the role of expert groups in "the making of the consumer."

Materials produced by the KGD reminded readers-consumers that they were obliged to behave rationally, obtain know-how, and enhance their cultural capital to be more effective while undertaking their role in the system of production both as efficient workers and as efficient housewives who support male workers by carrying out domestic chores.[80] The normative model of the modern household projected by the KGD was a detailed sociotechnical imaginary at a microscale level that was connected with the macroscale level imaginary of the progress of state socialist Poland. Later, we will examine the activities of the KGD in the discussions on performing modernity (chapter 2) and the emergence of electric goods testing (chapter 3).

The KGD was an organization whose objectives of building "modern" and "rational" households corresponded with the official ideology and the policy of the state apparatus. In the next section, we will discuss an organization that similarly built its identity as an expert group, but its structure and agenda were different when it came to the allocation of the role of the consumer.

FEDERACJA KONSUMENTÓW (THE FEDERATION OF CONSUMERS) AND *VETO* MAGAZINE

The Federacja Konsumentów (Federation of Consumers), hereafter the FK, was a consumer protection organization established in 1981 and led by its energetic chairperson, Małgorzata Niepokulczycka, who worked as an economics researcher at the University of Gdańsk. There had been several previous initiatives intended to represent the consumer lobby in the state apparatus, for instance, Biuro Współpracy z Konsumentem (Office for Collaboration with Consumer), where an unsatisfied consumer could submit a complaint about a manufacturer or a retailer. However, the FK as a mass-scale societal organization with an agenda based on Western consumer protection movement ideology was something entirely different. Mazurek and Hilton in their seminal paper offer an in-depth discussion of the formation and repertoire of the FK as a civic expression of discontent by consumers.[81]

Despite the breadth of recent works on consumer culture in the Eastern Bloc, the study by Mazurek and Hilton seems to be the only study of a consumer protection organization in state socialism. Mazurek and Hilton argue that the FK was an instance of civil society that actively represented the interests of consumers, as it openly questioned several elements of state policy toward consumption. Moreover, in contrast to the KGD that I discussed earlier, the FK openly articulated the existence of conflict between producers, retailers, and consumers.[82]

However, the FK did not attempt to openly challenge state socialism itself and only appealed for substantial reforms that would secure the rights of consumers. After a series of workers' strikes in Poland in 1980 and the establishment of the Solidarity movement that offered the possibility of expressing social discontent as workers, the authorities brutally suppressed the possibility of expressing discontent as workers. In such a context, the FK carved out a niche as an organization that offered the possibility of expressing discontent as consumers. Beginning in 1982, FK activists expressed their opinions through *Veto* weekly (1982–1995), the informal press organ of the organization. In 1988 and 1989, the FK also published its short-lasting official monthly, *Atut*. In later chapters, I discuss how both magazines played an important role as sites for the mediation of technological innovation in home technologies.

Here, I highlight the central difference between the KGD and the FK as two different forms of public expression of the consumption lobby. Mazurek and Hilton make a clear distinction between other forms of the consumer lobby and the FK:

> As in East Germany, although the consumer figured little in party-state planning, during periods of economic liberalization following moments of socio-political upheaval (especially 1956 and 1970–1), greater attention was paid to the needs of the consumer and a consumer lobby can be detected in the party-state apparatus. However, only with the events of the early 1980s—those associated with Solidarity—did a more independent form of consumer activism emerge: one which could lay claim to being something of a social movement.[83]

There was also a significant difference between both organizations in the roles they allocated for the consumer. To understand the difference in their respective approaches to consumers by the KGD and the FK, I refer to the notion of "implicated actors" formulated by technology historians Nelly Oudshoorn and Trevor Pinch and science historian Adele Clarke, where both users and particularly nonusers, are "implicated actors." As Clarke and colleagues note:

> *Implicated actors* are actors silenced or only discursively present in situations. In discourse data, they are usually constructed by others for others' purposes. There are at least two kinds. The first, while physically present, are silenced, ignored, or made invisible by those having greater power in the situation. Second are those *not* physically present but *solely* discursively constructed by others, usually disadvantageously. *Neither* kind of implicated actor is actively involved in self-representation.[84]

For KGD activists, consumers were primarily "implicated actors." They mostly imagined consumers as the passive recipients of educational campaigns, and their behavior was evaluated through a normative binary opposition rational-irrational, modern-backward. In contrast, the FK gave voice to consumers and offered them a platform to express their opinions and complaints. Mazurek and Hilton note that:

> In the West, these were the individuals who would be associated with non-governmental organizations, new social movements and what has been loosely termed "civil society." Such a phenomenon did not exist under state socialism, yet nevertheless equivalent experts formed the backbone of FK. Their concerns and interests were no longer focused solely on improving consumer supply under a command economy, but were adapted also from an emerging global discourse of consumer rights and protection to which they, as educated professionals, had access.[85]

In the 1980s, the growing consumer movement used the strategy of problematization to openly articulate complaints that the plans and governmental policy to some extent had failed to deliver specific promises. Thus, the magazine *Veto* openly deconstructed the normalized phrasing of "wzrost ilości," or the increase of the quantity, and "poprawa jakości," or the improvement of quality of consumer products as empty slogans (cf. chapter 3). However, it is important to note that FK activists carefully used vocabulary that was to a large extent compatible with the normalized vocabulary of state media discourse. The FK activists, the editors of *Veto,* and *Atut* were all careful to articulate social conflicts in a way that neither undermined the legitimization of the whole political system nor proposed any political change.

The KGD built a coalition with the FK, and both organizations regularly collaborated. Usually, the KGD provided some form of expertise used in *Veto*, for instance, consumer tests on electric appliances or research on their pricing. The FK, however, was primarily a social movement that strongly emphasized that the whole organization was built by consumers themselves. Thus, the editors not only published complaints about some aspects of the consumer culture but also figuratively presented themselves as consumers by sharing a specific anecdote from a retail store or by using the "mystery client" participant-observer style of ad hoc research to demonstrate the experience of searching for some specific product in a store or describing the experience of using a product. The editorial board of *Veto* was flooded with letters with all sorts of complaints that were used to support their arguments with "czytelnicy piszą nam, że . . .," "the readers wrote us that . . . " statements, and sometimes they published such letters. The genre of letters from frustrated consumers published in *Veto* is referred to by Appadurai: "Mythologies produced by consumers (or potential consumers) alienated from the production and distribution of key commodities."[86]

Veto's editors, although highly critical of manufacturers, tried to deconstruct some mythologies, for instance, with a campaign of providing detailed information on the complex process of fixing the price for electric goods based on honest information from manufacturers that explain the peculiarities of establishing a price for a complex technological product. This was one of the forms of collaboration between *Veto*'s editors and manufacturers. To further explain the tensions and collaboration between consumers, *Veto* editors, and manufacturers, I will once again refer to Hess's examination of instances of technology and product movements that operate in the market economy and facilitate interactions of such movements with the private sector. Hess calls this a "private-sector symbiosis with SMs" that generates collaborations and conflicts between manufacturers, intermediary actors, and consumers.[87] It is still important, however, to note that *Veto* actively collaborated with the electric goods industry and included the "novelties from . . . " genre, only usually with a more critical approach.

The FK was formed by a group of experts from a range of institutions and academic centers that legitimized the project. It is necessary to emphasize that while this organization represented consumers, it had a core of insiders, and they were welcomed by other actors that instantly helped to legitimize the movement and allocated its role as an important and purposeful element of the mediation junction. Lente and van Rip note: "At first, actors not involved in the new technology need not consider themselves excluded, or as being outsiders—but insiders will nevertheless define them as such. Such labeling by insiders, and associated behaviors, can in fact create coherent groups of commentators/critics which were not there before."[88]

The central form of the repertoire of *Veto*'s editors and other authors invited to express their opinion on *Veto*'s pages was to articulate controversies over design, shortages, reliability, or the pricing of electric goods. Virtually all the articles in *Veto* presented a severe critique and instead of addressing indirect problems presented detailed articulations of some flaws in the production system with vocabulary that emphasized the point of view of the consumer. *Veto* was a platform that played a pivotal role in raising such controversies, but as we will see in the section on testing new television sets (chapter 4), *Veto* also built its position as an actor that could ease tensions between manufacturers and users and enroll them into a common initiative.

SUMMARY

This chapter has outlined the main features of production, the sharing of knowledge, and the "support structures" that accompanied the production of electric goods in state socialism. In addition, it introduced the main actors that will regularly appear in the subsequent chapters. I have discussed the most important interest groups, their agendas, and highlighted possible forms of interaction, collaboration, and the tensions between them.

I also noted how the process of mediation of technological innovation took place both within and at the boundaries of the state apparatus. This chapter illustrates how actors that operated within the state apparatus or at its margins engaged in a process of enrollment for common action. Most of the repertoires of the relevant interest groups can be interpreted in terms of "technological expectations" and "technological promises." Later, we will see several instances of how these repertoires were related to the notions of modernity and the quality of electric goods, two central elements of the sociotechnical imaginary of consumer technologies from that era.

Aside from the aforementioned main intermediary actors, there were several other actors that to some extent mediated the production and consumption of home technologies. In later chapters, we will briefly examine the role of the Polish standardization committee, Polski Komitet Norm i Jakości, or the Polish Committee for Norms and Quality, and institutions such as the research center ZETOM, which was tasked with the compulsory testing of the safety of all durable goods, and the IRWiK, an economic research institute that carried out extensive research on practices of consumption. The authors of "Tensions of Europe Intellectual Agenda" discussed instances of where the standardization committees "sought to mediate fierce business competition, government safety concerns, and consumer pressures for labor standards, fair pricing and user-friendly designs of products."[89] Such institutions and organizations produced knowledge about products and consumers, but their primary agenda was to use such knowledge in a professional setting rather than communicate it publicly. For this reason, they will only appear briefly when I discuss their collaborations with other actors within the mediation junction.

NOTES

1. The most significant recent works that address the history of consumption in the Eastern Bloc are: Paulina Bren and Mary Neuburger, eds., *Communism Unwrapped: Consumption in Cold War Eastern Europe* (Oxford: Oxford University Press, 2012); Scarboro et al., *The Socialist Good Life*.

2. Porter-Szűcs, *Poland*, 258–84; Brian Porter-Szűcs, "Conceptualizing Consumption in the Polish People's Republic," in *The Socialist Good Life*; Malgorzata Mazurek and Matthew Hilton, "Consumerism, Solidarity and Communism: Consumer Protection and the Consumer Movement in Poland," *Journal of Contemporary History* 42, no. 2 (April 2007): 315–43.

3. Mila Oiva, "Something New In The Eastern Market. Polish Perceptions of the Developing Soviet Consumerism, 1961–1972," in *Fashion, Consumption and Everyday Culture in the Soviet Union between 1945 and 1985,* ed. Eva Hausbacher, Elena Huber, Julia Hargaßner (München, Berlin, and Washington, D.C.: Verlag Otto Sagner, 2014), 99–113; Joanna Zalewska, "Consumer revolution in People's Poland: Technologies in everyday life and the negotiation between custom and fashion (1945–1980)," *Journal of Consumer Culture* 17, no. 2 (2017) 321–39.

4. Frank Trentmann, "Knowing consumers—histories, identities, practices: an introduction," in *The making of the consumer: knowledge, power and identity in the modern world,* ed. Frank Trentmann (Oxford: Berg Publishers: 2005), 1–27, here 2.

5. Oldenziel et al., "Europe's Mediation," 110.

6. Oldenziel et al., "Europe's Mediation," 111.

7. Per Lundin, "Introduction," in *The Making of European Consumption: Facing the American Challenge,* ed. Per Lundin and Thomas Kaiserfeld (Houndmills: Palgrave Macmillan, 2015), 1–16, here 3.

8. van Lente and Rip, "Expectations," 207.

9. In STS, such a process of coalition-building is also referred to as the formation of "technology- and product-oriented movements." Cf. David J. Hess, "Technology- and Product-Oriented Movements: Approximating Social Movement Studies and Science and Technology Studies," *Science, Technology, & Human Values* 30, no. 4 (Autumn 2005): 515–35.

10. Callon, "Some elements," 68.

11. Callon, "Some elements," 82.

12. Cf. also: Trentmann, "Knowing consumers."

13. For an overview of the history of state socialist Poland, see: Paczkowski, *The Spring*; Porter-Szűcs, *Poland.*

14. Paczkowski, *The Spring,* 279–350.

15. For a discussion on the shift in the Polish consumer culture in that period, see: Porter-Szűcs, "Conceptualizing Consumption."

16. For a discussion on economic and cultural trends related to the processes of globalization in the Eastern Bloc, see: Anne E. Gorsuch and Diane P. Koenker, eds., *The Socialist Sixties, Crossing Borders in the Second World* (Bloomington: Indiana University Press, 2013); Oscar Sanchez-Sibony, *Red Globalization: The Political Economy of the Soviet Cold War from Stalin to Khrushchev* (Cambridge and New York: Cambridge University Press, 2014); André Steiner, "The globalisation process and the Eastern Bloc countries in the 1970s and 1980s," European Review of History 21, no. 2 (June 2014): 165–81.

17. Zalewska, "Consumer revolution."

18. For an outline of the production of home appliance in the USSR at that time, see: Susan E. Reid, "The Khrushchev Kitchen: Domesticating the Scientific-Technological Revolution," *Journal of Contemporary History* 40, no. 2 (April 2005): 289–316. Mila Oiva, in both her doctoral thesis and an article, discusses the emergence of Polish-Soviet trade: Mila Oiva, "Creation of a Market Space. The Polish Clothing Industry, Soviet Union, and the Rise of Marketing, 1949–1961," PhD thesis, Cultural History, University of Turku, 2017; Mila Oiva, "Selling fashion to Soviets.

Competitive practices in Polish clothes export in the early 1960s," in *Competition in Socialist Society*, ed. Katalin Miklóssy and Melanie Illic (London and New York: Routledge, 2015), 71–88.

19. For an overview of the development of the consumer electronics industry in Poland, see: Mieczysław Hutnik and Tadeusz Pachniewicz, *Zarys historii polskiego przemysłu elektronicznego do 1985 r.* (Warszawa: Stowarzyszenie Elektryków Polskich, 1994); Zeszyt Historyczny SEP 1994 no. 2.

20. For a detailed history of Polish television broadcasting, see: Jerzy Myśliński, *Kalendarium polskiej prasy, radia i telewizji* (Warszawa: Bel Studio, 2012). The history of the television system in the USSR has been discussed in: Kristin Roth-Ey, *Moscow Prime Time, How the Soviet Union Built the Media Empire that Lost the Cultural Cold War* (Ithaca and New York: Cornell University Press, 2014).

21. Piotr Sitarski, Maria B. Garda, and Krzysztof Jajko, *New Media Behind the Iron Curtain: Cultural History of Video, Microcomputers and Satellite Television in Communist Poland* (Kraków: Jagiellonian University Press, 2021).

22. Paczkowski, *The Spring,* 351–410.

23. Polish economic historian Kazimierz Poznanski offers a comprehensive discussion on the so-called "import-led growth policy" of the 1970s: Poznanski, *Poland's Protracted Transition*, 1–80. See also: Paczkowski, *The Spring*, 353–60.

24. Paczkowski, *The Spring*, 360–69.

25. van Lente and Rip, "Expectations."

26. Paczkowski, *The Spring*, 369–410.

27. Paczkowski, *The Spring*, 411–506.

28. Janusz Dąbrowski, "Strategia 'oszczędnego dobrobytu,'" *Przegląd Techniczny*, January 9, 1983, 10–11, here 11.

29. "Ustawa z dnia 3 grudnia 1984 r. o utworzeniu Komitetu do Spraw Nauki i Postępu Technicznego przy Radzie Ministrów oraz Urzędu Postępu Naukowo-Technicznego i Wdrożeń," *Dziennik Ustaw* 1984 nr 55 poz. 280; "Rozporządzenie Rady Ministrów z dnia 25 marca 1985 r. w sprawie szczegółowego zakresu działania Urzędu Postępu Naukowo-Technicznego i Wdrożeń," *Dziennik Ustaw* 1985, nr 21 poz. 93.

30. Chalmers A. Johnson, *MITI and the Japanese Miracle: The Growth of Industrial Policy, 1925–1975* (Stanford, CA: Stanford University Press, 1982). Simon Partner discusses the role of the MITI in the international success of the Japanese consumer electronics: Simon Partner, *Assembled in Japan. Electrical Goods and the Making of the Japanese Consumer* (Berkeley, Los Angeles and London: University of California Press, 1999).

31. Patryk Wasiak and Jaroslav Švelch, "Designing educational and home computers in state socialism. Polish and Czechoslovak experience," *Journal of Design History*, forthcoming; Patryk Wasiak, "VCRs, Modernity, and Consumer Culture in Late State Socialist Poland," in Cristofer Scarboro, Diana Mincyte, and Zsuzsa Gille, eds., *The Socialist Good Life: Desire, Development, and Standards of Living in Eastern Europe* (Bloomington: Indiana University Press, 2020), epub.

32. Paul Josephson and Raymond Stokes discuss the role of planning system for technical innovation in the USSR and GDR: Paul R. Josephson, *Would Trotsky Wear a Bluetooth? Technological Utopianism under Socialism 1917–1989* (Baltimore:

Johns Hopkins University Press, 2009); Raymond G. Stokes, *Constructing Socialism: Technology and Change in East Germany 1945–1990* (Baltimore et al.: Johns Hopkins University Press, 2000).

33. Krisztina Fehérváry, "Goods and States: The Political Logic of State-Socialist Material Culture," *Comparative Studies in Society and History* 51, no 2 (April 2009): 426–59; Natalya Chernyshova, *Soviet Consumer Culture in the Brezhnev Era* (London and New York: Routledge, 2013); Patrick Hyder Patterson, *Bought and Sold: Living and Losing the Good Life in Socialist Yugoslavia* (New York: Cornell University Press, 2011). The impact of the FYP system for consumer cultures is also extensively discussed in: Bren and Neuburger, *Communism Unwrapped.*

34. Poznanski, *Poland's Protracted Transition*; Jean Woodall, *The Socialist Corporation and Technocratic Power: The Polish United Workers' Party, Industrial Organisation and Workforce Control 1958–1980* (Cambridge et al.: Cambridge University Press, 1982).

35. Woodall, *The Socialist Corporation*, 80–117.

36. Law, *Aircraft Stories,* 8–9.

37. Alexei Yurchak, *Everything Was Forever, Until It Was No More: The Last Soviet Generation* (Princeton and Oxford: Princeton University Press, 2005).

38. Fredric Jameson, *Postmodernism, or, The Cultural Logic of Late Capitalism* (Durham, NC: Duke University Press, 1991).

39. Oushakine, "Against the Cult," 204.

40. van Lente and Rip, "Expectations," 205.

41. Oldenziel et al., "Europe's Mediation," 122.

42. Woodall, *The Socialist Corporation*, 80–117.

43. Cf.: Robert Lewis, "Hierarchy and Technological Innovation in Soviet Industry: The Science-Production Associations," *Minerva* 22, no. 2 (June 1984): 129–59.

44. Michał Budziński, "Utworzenie Wielkich Organizacji Gospodarczych—założenia reformy przemysłu PRL lat 70," *Kwartalnik Kolegium Ekonomiczno-Społecznego. Studia i Prace*, no. 3 (2018): 163–77; Janusz G. Zielinski, "New Polish reform proposals," *Soviet Studies* 32, no. 1 (1980): 5–27; Ben Slay, *The Polish Economy: Crisis, Reform, and Transformation* (Princeton, NJ: Princeton University Press, 1994), 38; Poznanski, *Poland's Protracted Transition,* 12–14.

45. Porter-Szűcs, *Poland*, 264. Cf. also Katalin Miklóssy and Melanie Ilic, eds., *Competition in Socialist Society* (London and New York: Routledge, 2014).

46. Woodall, *The Socialist Corporation*, 80–117.

47. János Kornai, "The Soft Budget Constraint," *Kyklos* 39, no. 1 (February 1986): 3–30.

48. *Przegląd Techniczny*, March 9, 1980, 8.

49. Cynthia Cockburn, "Domestic Technologies: Cinderella and The Engineers," *Women's Studies International Forum* 20, no. 3 (May-June 1997): 361–71, here 365–66.

50. Karin Zachmann, "Managing Choice: Constructing the Socialist Consumption Junction in the German Democratic Republic," in *Cold War Kitchen: Americanization, Technology, and European Users,* ed. Ruth Oldenziel and Karin Zachmann (Cambridge and London: MIT Press, 2010), 259–84.

51. Mateusz Jędrzejczak, "Problemy dystrybucji nowości w branży elektroakustycznej," *Handel Wewnętrzny,* Issue 5, 1980, 50–53, here 51.

52. It is worth noting that there was even a slogan, "state socialist advertisement," "socjalistyczna reklama," coined in the 1970s by the emerging community of economic experts interested in the introduction of elements of marketing in local economic systems; see: Klemens Białecki, Zygmunt Kossut, Andrzej Szanjder, "System socjalistycznej reklamy," *Życie Gospodarcze*, September 16, 1973, 11.

53. Hebdige, "Object as Image," 95.

54. Hebdige, "Object as Image," 96–97.

55. Patrick Hyder Patterson, "Just Rewards: The Social Contract and Communism's Hard Bargain with the Citizen-Consumer," in Scarboro et al., *The Socialist Good Life*, epub.

56. "Z działalności edukacyjnej Instytutu Handlu Wewnętrznego i Usług," *Handel Wewnętrzny*, Issue 4, 1980, 62–63.

57. "Z działalności edukacyjnej," 63.

58. For an outline of the goals of "polityka konsumpcji" of the 1970s, see: Jan Duraj, *Socjalistyczny model konsumpcji* (Warszawa: Książka i Wiedza, 1973); Edward Wiszniewski, *Polityka konsumpcji w Polsce* (Warszawa: Państwowe Wydawnictwo Ekonomiczne, 1979).

59. Elżbieta Ostrowska, "Handel—zapora czy autostrada między produkcją i konsumpcją," in unpublished collection of conference papers from the IRWiK seminar "Konsumpcja-Rynek-Wzrost Gospodarczy" 1988, IRWiK, archive, file 203, p. 5, Archiwum Akt Nowych.

60. For instance, see: Isenstadt, "Visions of Plenty."

61. Polish historian Paweł Miedziński extensively discusses such "normalized" visual conventions used in CAF photographs: Paweł Miedziński, *Centralna Agencja Fotograficzna 1951–1991* (Szczecin and Warszawa, Instytut Pamięci Narodowej, 2021).

62. For a study of engineering community under state socialism, see: Dolores L. Augustine, *Red Prometheus: Engineering and Dictatorship in East Germany, 1945–1990* (Cambridge and London: MIT Press, 2007).

63. Jeffrey Herf, *Reactionary modernism: Technology, culture, and politics in Weimar and the Third Reich* (Cambridge and New York, Cambridge University Press, 1984), 173.

64. Patryk Wasiak, "The production of High Fidelity audio electronics, and the politics of technological and social modernization in late state socialist Poland," *Journal of Sonic Studies*, forthcoming.

65. Woodall, *The Socialist Corporation*, 141–42.

66. For instance, cf. an interview with Jan Kaczmarek, the chairman of the Committee for Science and Technology: "Opłacalność postępu technicznego," *Życie Gospodarcze*, January 18, 1970, 1–2.

67. See: Janice Williams Rutherford, *Selling Mrs. Consumer: Christine Frederick and The Rise of Household Efficiency* (Athens and London: University of Georgia Press, 2003); Sarah Stage and Virginia B. Vincenti, eds., *Rethinking Home Economics: Women and the History of a Profession* (Ithaca, NY: Cornell University Press,

1997); Megan J. Elias, *Stir it Up: Home Economics in American Culture* (Philadelphia: University of Pennsylvania Press, 2010); Danielle Dreilinger, *The Secret History of Home Economics: How Trailblazing Women Harnessed the Power of Home and Changed the Way We Live* (New York: W.W. Norton & Company, 2021).

68. "Tensions of Europe Intellectual Agenda," 2005, 16, https://www.histech.nl/projects/SHT/www/nl/files/get/Intellectual_Agenda.pdf.

69. Elsewhere, I have discussed the role of the KGD as an organization that shaped the gender role of "nowoczesna gospodyni," or a rural housewife, and facilitated access to knowledge on using home appliances in rural areas: Patryk Wasiak, and Katarzyna Stańczak Wiślicz, "Deconstructing 'nowoczesna gospodyni.' The home efficiency movement, gender roles, and material culture in late state socialist Poland," *Slavic Review*, forthcoming.

70. Vladimir Ilyich Lenin, "The role and functions of trade unions under the New Economic Policy," in *Lenin's Collected Works*, 2nd English ed. (Moscow: Progress Publishers, [1922] 1965), vol. 33, 188–96.

71. For the cultural history of the notion of efficiency, see: Jennifer Karn Alexander, *The Mantra of Efficiency: From Waterwheel to Social Control* (Baltimore: Johns Hopkins University Press, 2008).

72. Porter-Szűcs, "Conceptualizing Consumption." Originally in Polish public discourse, this shift and the emphasis on the "efficiency of society" in fulfilling its role in a socialist state was referred to as "efektywność społeczna," literarily "social efficiency." See cf.: Władysław Dudziński, "Efektywność społeczna," *Życie Gospodarcze*, January 18, 1970, 1, 4.

73. Anna Marcinakówna, "Kto pomoże Nowoczesnej Gospodyni," *Miesięcznik ZMW*, March 1972, 14–15.

74. Zachmann, "Managing Choice."

75. "Daleko nam do luksusu," *Atut*, Issue 10–12, 1989, 22.

76. *Gospodarstwo Domowe*, Special Issue, 1971, 1.

77. Frank Trentmann, "Beyond Consumerism: New Historical Perspectives on Consumption," *Journal of Contemporary History* 39, no. 3 (July 2004): 373–401, here 374.

78. Boel Berner, "'Housewives' films' and the modern housewife. Experts, users and household modernization: Sweden in the 1950s and 1960s," *History and Technology* 18, no. 3 (January 2002): 155–79, here 163.

79. Berner, "Housewives' films," 159. Quotation after: Zygmunt Bauman, "Life-world and expertise: Social production of dependency," in Nico Stehr and Richard V. Ericson, eds., *The culture and power of knowledge: Inquiries into contemporary societies* (Berlin: Walter de Gruyter, 1992), 81–106, here 90.

80. Ryszard Kurzyk, "Edukacja konsumenta jako działalność informacyjna," *Gospodarstwo Domowe*, January–February, 1971, 6–8.

81. Mazurek and Hilton, "Consumerism."

82. Mazurek and Hilton, "Consumerism," 316–17.

83. Mazurek and Hilton, "Consumerism," 317.

84. Adele. E. Clarke, Carrie Friese, and Rachel Washburn, eds., *Situational Analysis in Practice: Mapping Research with Grounded Theory* (Walnut Creek, CA: Left

Coast Press, 2015). Cf. Nelly Oudshoorn and Trevor Pinch, "Introduction: How Users and Non-Users Matter," in *How Users Matter: The Co-Construction of Users and Technology,* ed. Nelly Oudshoorn and Trevor Pinch (Cambridge and London: MIT Press, 2003), 1–25, here 6.

85. Mazurek and Hilton, "Consumerism," 318.

86. Appadurai, "Introduction," 48.

87. Hess, "Technology," 521.

88. Arie Rip and Siebe Talma, "Antagonistic Patterns and New Technologies, in *Getting New Technologies Together Studies in Making Sociotechnical Order*, ed. Cornelis Disco and Barend van der Meulen (Berlin and New York: Walter de Gruyter, 1998), 299–322, here 301.

89. "Tensions of Europe Intellectual Agenda," 16–17.

Chapter 2

The Performance of Modernity

INTRODUCTION

This chapter investigates how, and for what reason, the relevant social actors formulated their own stories on what constituted the desired state of "being modern" and juxtaposed this with stories about obsolescence and backwardness. I discuss how manufacturers together with intermediary actors "performed modernity" through their repertoires of public communications. With publicly shared narratives, they ascribed the term "modernity" with the projections of desirable technological, economic, and social developments that corresponded with their agenda. While doing so, they discursively allocated themselves prescribed roles in the shaping of technological modernization or identified other actors, those who are obliged to contribute to the modernization, and those social actors who may hinder this process or at least do not perform their roles with enough diligence.

The theme of modernity, accompanied by the narratives of backwardness and obsolescence, was a central element of the imagery used in public expressions of technological innovation in the Polish home technologies industry of the 1970s and 1980s.[1] Virtually all the media narratives from the 1970s about the production of home technologies by state enterprises included claims about the ongoing process of "unowocześnianie produkcji" ("modernization of production process") and assurances that the industry not only already produces "nowoczesne wyroby" ("modern products") but also invests in the design of further novelties that follow global trends in home technologies. In the 1980s, such claims became more and more extensively accompanied by critical voices that questioned the feasibility of technical modernization.

I refer to such debates as a performance of modernity. I contend that such a performance was a key element in social actors' expressions of technological expectations and promises related to the process of technological

55

modernization of the industry as well as the desired economic and social modernization.[2] I borrow the term "performing modernity" from cultural anthropologist Louisa Schein who emphasizes that, aside from studying what constitutes specific imagery of "being modern," it is equally important to research how modernity is constituted as a discursive regime through the performances carried out by social actors.[3]

In chapter 1, while outlining the identities of a host of intermediary actors, I discussed what kind of authority enabled them to successfully carry out such performances and have an impact on other actors. Here, I investigate the repertoire of discursive practices that they used in these performances. Historians of design and technology share similar research agendas when it comes to studying how actors perform modernity while presenting new designs and technological innovations. Kjetil Fallan in his paper on the aluminum industry in Norway uses the term "producing progress" not only to discuss the production of material objects made of aluminum, one of the icons of twentieth-century modernity, but also to establish a discursive regime in which aluminum was the material that brought economic and social progress.[4] Similarly, John Law uses the term "performing progress" to discuss how intermediary actors, while presenting the vision of a new military aircraft, were publicly telling stories about which technologies are modern and which technologies have become obsolete.[5]

For this chapter, I have selected the key strategies that were regularly used in the public narratives on the role of home technologies in the modernization of the Polish economy and society. My investigation of these subsequent key strategies is not only inspired by the aforementioned discussions on technological modernity but is also driven by historian of consumption Don Slater's work on the notion of modernity as being a feature of "modern consumer culture."[6] Here I follow his question of how certain modern experiences and dilemmas have been formulated.[7] Slater notes the centrality of the issue of modernity as a constitutive element of the "modern" consumer culture that began in the late nineteenth century:

> consumer culture is bound up with the *idea* of modernity, of modern experience and of modern social subjects. In so far as "the modern" constitutes itself around a sense of the world experienced by a social actor who is deemed individually free and rational, within a world no longer governed by tradition but rather by flux, and a world produced through rational organization and scientific know-how, then the figure of the consumer and the experience of consumerism is both exemplary of the new world and integral to its making.[8]

Here, I would like to emphasize the importance of paying attention to the issue of which social actors formulated such experiences and dilemmas and what was their agenda. Historian of technology Per Lundin, in his work on the identity of urban planners who designed car-friendly "modern" European cities, coined the term "mediators of modernity."[9] I find this term suitable for my study and will later evaluate how specific actors performed their roles as such "mediators of modernity." As I will show, they primarily built their authority through their expert knowledge of how to efficiently plan and carry out the modernization process.

The notion of modernization as a social process and its connection to the development of consumer cultures in the Eastern Bloc has been addressed recently in a range of works on the history of consumption of the region.[10] For the sake of brevity, here, I only note that Mary Neuburger offers the most extensive investigation on this subject with her study on the interconnections between the experience of modernity and the evolving culture of using tobacco in twentieth-century Bulgaria. She also provides an extensive review of the relevant literature.[11] Surprisingly, there are few studies that investigate technological modernity in the Eastern Bloc. In his seminal work on large-scale technological projects in the USSR, technology historian Paul Josephson makes a remark that is still relevant to this day: "In spite of the centrality of modern technology to the economic successes and political legitimacy of the socialist experiment, and in the views of socialist leaders, we remain at an early stage of appreciation of its place in that history."[12]

In addition to Josephson's work on the USSR, there are a number of relatively recent works that examine the connections between specific technological projects and the experience of technological modernity in the Eastern Bloc.[13] The most relevant work to which I will refer to in several places is Raymond Stokes' study of technological development and the legitimization of the political system in the GDR.[14] And Joanna Zalewska notes how the personal testimonies of her interviewees include narratives on progress both in terms of changing society and lifestyles and also progress in terms of changing available home technologies.[15]

Besides the key concept of sociotechnical imaginary by Jasanoff and Kim, this chapter is also inspired by *Technology and Modernity*, an edited volume on the pivotal role of the imaginary of modernity in technological projects. The most relevant work here is Philip Brey's essay on bridging the gap between modernization studies and the STS. As he notes:

> In modernity theory, technology is often treated as a "black box" that is discussed, if at all, in abstract and often essentialist and technological determinist terms. In technology studies, the black box of technology is opemned, and technologies and their development are studied in great empirical detail, yet technology studies generate their own black box, which is society. The larger sociocultural and economic context in which actors operate is either treated as

a background phenomenon to which some hand-waving references are made, or it is not treated at all—a black box returned to sender, address unknown.[16]

I address this issue by discussing how technological modernization was embedded in both the sociocultural and economic currents of the 1970s and 1980s, particularly the emerging processes of globalization. Brey also notes another significant gap between works on modernity theory and STS, namely the difference of scale that is put under scrutiny:

> A key conclusion is that the major obstacle to a future synthesis of modernity theory and technology studies is that technology studies mostly operate at the micro (and meso) level, whereas modernity theory operates at the macrolevel, and it is difficult to link the two. I analyze the micro-macro problem and ways in which it may be overcome in technology studies and modernity theory.[17]

Investigation of the mediation process helps to narrow this gap by highlighting how meso-level processes of the introduction of new technological designs, specific governmental policies, and public debates on technological modernization are connected with the macroscale imaginaries of the desirable future of state socialism. Josephson explains his agenda of focusing on the grandiose projects pursued under state socialism and how such projects were embedded in technological utopias:

> I explore the place of technology under socialism as a symbol, an engine of progress, and an all-too-real force of political, economic, and cultural change. I highlight the utopian aspects of the quest for modern technology to solve economic and social challenges that faced such nations as the Soviet Union, the People's Republic of North Korea, and the newly socialist countries of East Central Europe in the postwar world.[18]

My book focuses on the less utopian and more pragmatic dimensions of modernity and progress in the postindustrial era. In the 1970s, instead of the utopian visions of using technology to reshape nature, we can rather see discussions on joining emerging global supply chains established by MNEs. Moreover, at that time, one of the most significant indicators of "being modern" was the capability of earning a hard currency from the high-value-added international commodity trade.

This chapter is structured as follows. Firstly, I will discuss the notion of the ongoing "Scientific and Technological Revolution," as this is a theme extensively used in performances of modernity as an unprecedented global-scale process that has tremendous consequences for economies and societies. Secondly, I discuss how the process of technological modernization was embedded into the pursuit of social goals related to "social progress."[19] The next section focuses on the specific criteria that was used to evaluate whether state socialist Poland was a modern or still-backward country, and how social actors used them. The subsequent section investigates how the notion of technological progress was interconnected with the policies of establishing connections with foreign trade partners. Finally, I discuss how the steady pursuit of innovation in design and manufacturing was a central element of the imagery of technological modernity.

THE SCIENTIFIC AND TECHNOLOGICAL REVOLUTION: THE TECHNOLOGICAL RACE, AND GOVERNMENTAL POLICY

One of the key elements of the imaginary of postwar technological development was the ongoing "Scientific and Technological Revolution," hereafter STR, and how this would have a tremendous impact on societies and economies. The cultural logic of the postwar STR is extensively discussed by several authors, who also investigate the notion of "technological revolutions" in history.[20] In the current popular history of the postwar era, this term is usually used as a synonym for the twentieth-century "information revolution" that took place roughly in the period 1945–1970 through the development of the semiconductor industry that resulted in the mass dissemination of electronic technologies. However, the term STR was originally used more broadly and referred to developments in chemistry, engineering, and materials science that led to several achievements such as new medicines, fertilizers, and pesticides that enhanced agricultural production; plastic polymers, which had a substantial impact on everyday life; information and communication technologies; and transportation, particularly aviation.[21]

One of the most important features of the imagery of the STR was the conviction that this was not a one-time structural change based on the introduction of a single new technology but rather a new, long-lasting era that would see the steady introduction of more and more advanced technologies. The cultural logic of the STR can be illustrated with one of its most important symbols, Moore's Law, which refers to a steady and unending progress through the miniaturization of electronics. The imagery of the STR also included the constant need to compete with others in order to stay in the vanguard of technological progress to avoid running the risk of being left behind in a state of backwardness. This feature can be illustrated by the concept of the "technological race." Two of the most spectacular Cold War–era races were the nuclear arms race and the space race, but more relevant here are two other races. First is the American and European race to compete with the emerging "Far East tigers," primarily Japan. The second is the Eastern Bloc's race to "catch up and overtake the West" in terms of technological innovation and industrial production beyond that of military and space technologies.[22] Later, I will discuss several instances of public debates on the need and feasibility for Polish participation in such technological races.

The STR term became a popular buzzword in the USSR in the 1960s. It was used broadly as the justification for the policies that applied recent scientific and technological developments to economic and social planning. Unfortunately, aside from a book on cybernetics, there is little scholarship on the politics of using the STR term in the bloc.[23] For my purposes, the most relevant paper is Susan Reid's study of the application of the STR in kitchen design.[24] As she notes, "'STR' was a central term in official pronouncements of the Khrushchev era, which made it a defining characteristic of socialist modernity."[25] Moreover, Reid argues that this term was used rather vaguely by political factions and industry lobbies as the slogan to justify the application of scientific inventions and developments in designing new, and presumably more modern, material culture such as for housing, home interiors, or electric goods.[26]

Woodall examines how the technocratic circles in the ruling elite of the PZPR in the 1960s entrenched their power through the use of the imaginary of the ongoing STR to formulate new guidelines for economic policy. The essential part of their proposed reforms was a shift from the policy of extensive growth to a more focused development of a few selected industries identified as the forefront of the STR:

> The Resolution of the Fifth Congress and the statement at the ensuing II Plenum of the PZPR Central Committee in 1969 proposed a new strategy of "intensive selective development" which would take advantage of the "scientific-technological revolution" by accelerating investment and output in the chemical and engineering industries and would encourage more exports of these goods.[27]

The policy-makers subsequently increased the amount of resources invested in the engineering industry from the early 1970s. At that time, the government strongly promoted the growth of this industry through the purchases of foreign licenses and encouraged *zjednoczenia* and state enterprises to invest in the modernization of production processes. The notion of the ongoing STR was still present in the public discourse in the 1980s and was used to formulate policies for technological innovation. The most notable case of this was the establishment of the Urząd Postępu Technicznego, or the Office for Technological Progress, affiliated with the Council of Ministers. This institution, which was established in 1986, coordinated governmental orders for the development of technologies identified as key projects for securing technological progress. An example of its operation was the very costly project for a Polish video-cassette recorder, which I have discussed elsewhere.[28]

The policy of investments in the 1970s is discussed by Polish economist Joanna Kotowicz-Jawor, who outlines the economic context for the extensive purchases of foreign technological licenses that peaked in the mid-1970s.[29] As she notes, the policy-makers declared that this large-scale, highly expensive program was of "strategic importance for the state economy to the year 1990."[30] As a result, in 1972, the Komisja Planowania, or the Planning Commission, the governmental body responsible for the central control of the economy, prepared the detailed guidelines for the NPSG 1976–1980.[31] Such a plan is an instance of "projectness" as the key feature of modernity. It included several "programs," among them the "program for modernization and development of market production," which was focused on the modernization of the production of consumer goods, and the "program for electronization of the state economy," to increase the production of both industrial and consumer electronics.[32]

The purchases of licenses and other incentives from the government for *zjednoczenia* from technology-based industries ready to embrace the STR were referred to in the official vocabulary with the frequently used phrase "narzędzia tworzenia inwestycji modernizacyjnych," or "the means for the creation of modernization investments."[33] The term "modernization investment" itself was one of the buzzwords of the economic reforms of Gierek's era. The "modernity" term in the 1970s was also appropriated by the circles of economists interested in the broader implementation of the "modern" management culture inspired by the developments in management science in the West. This process was generally referred to as the "modernization of the organizational structure of the economy."[34]

In the 1970s, the government offered substantial financial resources to support this program and to help to purchase licenses. However, this support led to the growth of the belief that this should not be merely a one-time investment and that the state should offer further resources to help the electronic industry to keep pace in the technological race. Kotowicz –Jawor notes the emergence of such expectations: "demands for 'the right to grow' contributed to the emergence of the forces that fought for more sustained investment. These forces existed at the level of specific regions, industries, and in the central government."[35]

Indeed, for the whole decade of the 1980s, despite the continuation of the program for the support of the development of the electronic industry, this program was perceived as insufficient by the electronic engineering community. The representatives of the industry and prominent figures in the community regularly expressed "technological expectations" for an increase in the level of the investment in electronics. The community also expressed resentment toward economic experts, who argued that investment in the electronic industry should be limited since it did not bring any measurable profits. These economists claimed that Poland was unable to compete with the MNEs that led the race for technological development in electronics and information and communication technologies, so there was no point in allocating resources to take part in a race which Poland had already lost.

Karol Mieczykowski, a prominent *Przegląd Techniczny* columnist with expertise in electronics, defended the costly investment in the color kinescopes manufacturing plant Polkolor (cf. also chapter 4). As he noted, those who criticize investments in the domestic electronic industry "do not comprehend the realities of the contemporary world that takes part in the technological race and suggest that we can afford to ignore the world's development in electronics. They suggest that the result of such an approach will be negligible. However, the times when one can somehow live without electronics are gone."[36]

This quote illustrates the central tension between these interest groups. The economic experts evaluated investments in the production of consumer electronics in terms of short-term measurable profits. The electronic engineering community attempted to exercise their "right to grow" with an argument that despite the lack of such short-term profits, participation in the technological race, even with the lack of prospects for being in the vanguard, was necessary to have any chance for long-term economic development because of the rapid increase in the role of electronic technologies in the economy.

Thus, the imagery of the ongoing technological race was employed in the repertoire of social actors expressing "technological expectations." Van Lente and Rip note how the use of arguments about "unstoppable trains" and the need to compete with Japan were used in the claims of social actors who expressed some form of "technological expectations."[37] The electronic engineering community used these terms in public to fight for an increase in government investment in this industry.

Aside from the aforementioned investments, policy-makers attempted to foster the production of modern electric goods through the development of the structures of *zjednoczenia*. This was a key element of the policy of the formation of WOGs, discussed in chapter 1. In the years 1961–1978, all producers of both industrial and consumer electronics were grouped together under UNITRA. In 1978, these two branches were separated, and from that time on, UNITRA DOM, literally UNITRA HOME, was the grouping of all manufacturers of consumer electronics, while the manufacturers of home appliances were grouped as PREDOM, established in 1974. However, it is necessary to note that this system of extensive oversight of the electric goods industry lasted for a short period, because after the regime change in 1980, new economic policy-makers quickly discontinued the policy of WOGs. In

1982, UNITRA and PREDOM, as well as other compulsory *zjednoczenia*, were disbanded and replaced by voluntary *zrzeszenia* (associations) of producers with the same names. After this reform, *zrzeszenia* had significantly diminished capabilities of exercising power over state enterprises.

One of the main objectives of *zjednoczenia* was to foster technological innovativeness in the production of industrial and consumer products. This policy was a direct result of the implementation of the aforementioned "program for the modernization and development of market production." The founding document of PREDOM outlines its objectives and is an example of the "projectness" in the electric goods industry. The overarching objective of the PREDOM was "to create favorable conditions for the further development of consumer goods for the domestic market and export."[38] This document further elaborated that:

> The Ministry for Machine Industry, while fulfilling social and economic goals formulated by the VI PZPR Congress [1971], undertook several technological and organizational initiatives to accelerate the production quota for market goods and to increase their quality standard.[39]

These objectives were followed by declarations on the means of achieving them: Zjednoczenie organizes, coordinates, and oversees:

1. Research and development
2. The design of new products
3. Work related to the expansion and modernization of state enterprises
4. Production and preparation of the shipments [of new products]
5. Selling products in domestic retail trade and for export
6. Servicing users of appliances /technical and warranty services/
7. Providing spare parts and repairs
8. Market research and management of a network of exemplary department stores with services [this network was never established].[40]

To paraphrase the title of the work of Appadurai, this list illustrated how a single nationwide organization was supposed to efficiently organize all the stages of the social life of electric goods in state socialism.[41] Woodall notes the issue of "projectness" related to the formation of *zjednoczenia*: "the assumption was made that large production units and enterprise integration would encourage greater technological innovation."[42] This was an attempt to shape modernity with a single organizational structure that coordinated and supervised R&D, distributed the products, and provided services. Later, in this and in the following chapters, we will examine in more detail the

extent to which UNITRA, PREDOM, and selected enterprises carried out
these tasks.

TECHNOLOGY AND SOCIAL GOALS

The title of this section comes from the title of an article by the chief ideolo-
gist of the PZPR, Andrzej Werblan, and a sociologist named Zbigniew Sufin
that was published in *Przegląd Techniczny* in a series of articles that covered
the Eighth PZPR Congress in February 1980.[43] In this paper, the authors
argue that state socialism can shape the conditions under which technological
progress could be harnessed by policy-makers and state-owned industries to
achieve projected "cele społeczne" ("social goals"). In contrast, they claimed
that any technological progress made by the market economies is used by
interest groups to maximize their profits.

Here I outline how the adjective "social" was used in public communications related to technical innovation in the electric goods industry. The publicly shared imagery of the ongoing advancements of the STR was embedded
within the broader narratives of the pursuit of macroscale goals for the
society by the party and the government. In this section, I discuss how home
technologies became embedded in the articulation of social goals related to
a positively valued vision of a future society and economy. While doing so,
I demonstrate how modernity was performed not only by "telling stories"
about new technologies but also about a future society and the methods for
achieving this new desired sociotechnical order. This section also highlights
the existing knowledge gap about the complex epistemology of the adjective
"social" in state socialism.

Socio-technical imaginaries are built upon complex narratives that allocate
specific technologies as harbingers of a new desirable social order. Those who
project such imaginaries use a repertoire of explanations to show how a new
technology will provide a positive social change or address an acute social
problem. Some technologies, such as the internet, were widely presented in
the public sphere as "revolutionary technologies" that could contribute to the
removal of some preexisting conditions that limit social and economic development.[44] A good example of the revolutionary, or to use Silicon Valley jargon, "disruptive," character of some of the internet-related technologies can
be illustrated with the infamous "move fast and break things" slogan used by
Mark Zuckerberg. Similarly, an annual San Francisco information technology
gathering called TechCrunch Disrupt is intended as an event for the "founders
and investors shaping the future of disruptive technology."[45]

However, such imaginaries can also include narratives on how technology
can offer a desirable social and economic change without challenging the

preexisting political, legal, or economic framework. Sheila Jasanoff notes how such an imaginary can be used in a reactionary way: "The identities, institutions, languages, and representations created by science and technology can be *politically* sustaining, by helping societies to accommodate new knowledges and technological capabilities without tearing apart (indeed, often by reaffirming) the legitimacy of existing social arrangements."[46]

This remark illustrates how policy-makers can formulate policies toward technological innovation to be not only politically sustaining but even to enhance the legitimization of a political regime or prevailing social and economic models. For example, the political regime of Gierek paid close attention to publicly communicating how it embraces technological innovation to strengthen the legitimization of the ruling elite. Zsuzsa Gille and colleagues in their introduction to the *Good Life* offer a brief remark that insightfully explains the core objective of the social policies of the political regimes of state socialism: "to cultivate and promote an ideologically sound and profoundly meaningful——perhaps even pleasurablegood life in socialist Eastern Europe."[47]

These state socialist governments tried to impose a social policy that would engage societies in the communist project through the visions of a future "good life." Such policies were broadly imposed in the 1960s and 1970s and replaced the ideological motivation of the Stalinist era. Probably the most famous slogan related to the socialist "good life" is the Hungarian "Goulash Communism" during the long János Kádár era (1956–1988). In Poland, such a trend began in the 1960s with the regularly used slogan "materialne bodźce zaangażowania," or material stimuli for engagement. This term referred to the policy of offering citizens tangible incentives, such as a good salary, an apartment, or a private car, to motivate them to perform their work duties diligently.

Most of the media texts related to the introduction of new home technologies, an increase of the production quotas, and the development of retail trade, were accompanied by claims of how a specific improvement would contribute to society. Such texts regularly included the adjective "social," with phrasing such as "social planning," "social policy," "social goals," "social interests," or "social progress." An example of the role played by words such as "social" and "society" in the phrasing of public discourse in state socialism comes from a paragraph from the Polish Constitution from 1976, which emphasizes the "progress of socialist society" as an overarching objective of the state apparatus: "The primary objective of the state in the People's Republic of Poland is the all-embracing (orig. wszechstronny) development of socialist society, the development of the creative forces of the nation (orig. rozwój twórczych sił narodu) and every individual, and the better and better fulfillment of the needs of the citizens."[48]

The narratives of technological modernization were accompanied by explanations of how new technologies will contribute to the development of society. Home technologies, along with passenger cars and "modern" housing, were central features of the imaginary of the ongoing transformation of Polish society from the era of postwar trauma and frugality into a future with the steady "development of socialist society."

Reid discusses how in the USSR in the Khrushchev era the imaginary of the STR included social progress as a key element of the ongoing changes achieved by the application of new scientific and technological achievements: "The Third Party Programme adopted in 1961—the definitive ideological statement of the Khrushchev period—identified social progress with scientific and technological progress. It was to be achieved through electrification of the whole country, comprehensive mechanization of production, and civilian applications of atomic energy and chemistry."[49]

Similarly, in Poland, the STR was presented as a process that contributed to social progress by fulfilling "social needs." During the PZPR Congress in 1980, which, as quotedpreviously, included the theme of "technology and social goals," the public coverage of this political event included a similar narrative. Among transcripts of policy-makers' speeches, *Przegląd Techniczny* published a photograph of a chemist in a laboratory that did not correspond with any particular development in chemistry but was rather used as a visual symbol of the STR. The caption informed the reader that: "Under the conditions of state socialism, scientific and technological progress gain new social meaning (orig. treść społeczna). New chances to completely harness the Scientific Technological Revolution in the duty of social interests are emerging."[50]

Electric goods played a substantial role in the imagery harnessing the STR for social interests. For instance, a report on the economic aspects of technological development in the 1970s from *Życie Gospodarcze* articulated that "economic planners have an objective of harnessing technological innovation into the improvement of the quality of life."[51]

In the 1970s, policy-makers included this objective as a key element of social policy.[52] Reid characterizes how the social goals relevant to the improvement of the conditions of living were embedded in communist ideology:

> The ultimate global victory of socialism was to be achieved through superior living standards rather than military might. It was an article of faith—and not only of Cold War polemics—that socialism would guarantee the best possible conditions of life for the largest number of people. The Khrushchev regime repeatedly indexed the imminent transition to communism to the achievement

of superabundance and unprecedented prosperity and devoted an extraordinary degree of attention to consumption and everyday, domestic life.[53]

The "social objectives" of the dissemination of consumer electronics can be summarized by a quote from an article by economic expert Andrzej Sikorski, who explained the role of such products: "Still, radio receivers, television sets, audio cassette recorders, and record players, are not common goods and sometimes are still considered a luxury. However, the needs are different. These goods to some extent determine the level of access to information and propaganda and have an impact on the culture of society. We do care about that matter."[54]

This explanation shows how the policy-makers considered media technologies as a means of receiving propaganda content and a massive cultural uplift. They also sought to address the issue of using electric goods as recognizable status symbols. Elsewhere, I have discussed the extensive debate on the problem of using goods as status symbols by juxtaposing the undesired and desirable appropriation of consumer goods according to their use-value.[55]

We can find several claims about the recognition of "social goals" as an objective for the electric goods industry both in official documents and in public communications. The previous quote from PREDOM's founding document includes a statement of the links between social policy and technological development. One of the detailed objectives of the PREDOM's supervision of home appliance manufacturers was: "to fulfill the aims declared in the plan for social and economic development . . . And fulfilling the social needs through the quick development of production of the achievements of new technologies."[56]

When it comes to public communications, here is an example of the reportage on recent trends in UNITRA published in 1974 in *Życie Gospodarcze* in which the author, quoting UNITRA representatives, informs readers that the priority of the UNITRA is the fulfillment of "market and social needs."[57] Here the term "market needs" was rather straightforward, referring to the increase of the production quotas of consumer electronics. The term "social needs" refers to the recognition of postulates on the introduction of technological innovations in the production profile.

Claims of "fulfilling social needs" was a discursive strategy used to claim that the state recognizes the postulates expressed by the society. Here, in the propaganda-laden texts, society has been discursively allocated with the role of an active subject that can express "technological expectations." In the 1970s, the narrative of progress in the electric goods industry was constructed upon the claims of fulfilling the growing, passively named "social needs," more actively expressed as "social demands" for the production of new classes of home technologies.

In a report on the role of durable goods in social policy that was published in *Polityka Społeczna*, a specialist periodical for social policy experts, we can see how "social demands" are formulated as "technological expectations." This report quotes a social survey to explain how under state socialism society expresses some preferences for the development of electric goods and the state apparatus, which should be considered when governmental institutions draft their plans for the production of consumer goods:

> The postulate to take the population's preferences into account while programming the development of durable goods is commonly supported by Polish society. Surely, this is the result of the high level of consumer awareness that has been demonstrated by:
>
> - The pressure of strong public opinion to undertake the production of novelties.
> - Quick advances of novelties in the hierarchy of needs.
> - Significant criticism of the products being offered.[58]

This specific explanation allocates "the population" as an active subject that has an agency in formulating "technological expectations," and the state complies with such expectations.

In my article on the emergence of the program of production of high-fidelity audios, I investigate how the engineering community and economic planners expressed a fulfillment of "technological promise" with claims that the introduction of such an expensive program was a result of the recognition of postulates of a group of music journalists, audio electronics engineers and the intended users of hi-fi audios.[59] In another paper, I discuss the project of "polskie video," or Polish video, one of the most expensive consumer technology-related projects of the 1980s.[60] In the mid-1980s, VCRs became widely acknowledged status symbols of an emerging class of private entrepreneurs. Solving the problem of using VCRs as a status symbol that was unaffordable for ordinary working-class consumers was identified as another "social goal." To achieve such a goal and to fulfill regularly expressed "technological promises," the government introduced a highly expensive project of manufacturing domestic and affordable VCRs.

HOW TO MEASURE MODERNITY?

The editors of *Modernity and Technology* note that their agenda was to challenge the vagueness of the phrase "technological modernity." Thomas Misa in his introduction emphasizes the need for the deconstruction of material objects and infrastructures considered "modernist icons": "If one goal of this volume is to examine modernist icons such as airports, harbors, train stations, mechanical clocks, automobiles, pharmaceuticals, and surveillance and information technologies in the light of social theory, another goal is to consider them at the same time explicitly as technologies."[61]

Misa discusses several technologies that were at some point in time ascribed with the cultural meanings of "modern" artifacts or infrastructures. Still, there is a knowledge gap in the literature of how exactly a host of social actors ascribe technologies with such meanings. Particularly, there are no studies on the cultural logic of narratives in which technologies are used to establish ranking lists with the "most modern" countries that lead in one of the "technological races."

Here, I explore how social actors came up with different methods of measuring modernity and backwardness in the historical setting of the 1970s and 1980s. There were two different yet interconnected ways of quantifying the level of development of modernity in relation to home technologies. The first one was the capacity to design and manufacture new, more advanced products or particular components. The second indicator was the saturation of households with specific appliances used to demonstrate the position of a specific country on the global map of prosperity, the standard of living, and "social progress." Zalewska, drawing from ethnographic interviews, discusses how the increase of the ownership of durable goods became a part of the personal and subjective experience of Polish consumers.[62] However, one of the key elements of twentieth-century modernity was the collection and sharing of data that offers tangible indicators of modernity. Poland in the 1970s and 1980s offers an example of the shifting paradigms of what data was used in public performances of modernity.

The methods of measuring modernity in terms of producing technologies include both quantitative and qualitative elements: how many products of a specific category are made in the country, and is this country capable of designing and manufacturing a product considered as one of the "modernist icons?" The measurements related to the consumption of technologies include census data with specific products per one hundred households and the length of the replacement cycle of a specific product.

Beginning in the early 1970s, economic experts noted that Polish households were already saturated with the most relevant home technologies such as automatic washing machines, refrigerators, and television sets. For that reason, the frequency of the replacement of specific products by households, not their physical presence, should be used as an indicator of "social progress."[63] It is worth noting that Zalewska outlines how the availability of hand-operated washing machines, and their replacement by automatic washing machines, became identified as the cultural postwar "laundry revolution" in Poland.[64]

In Poland in the 1970s and 1980s, the development of the electronic industry became an important symbol used as proof that Poland was a "modern" country. However, at the same time, some elements of this industry were also used to articulate severe problems with the so-called "technology lag," which was the problem that Poland was failing to catch up with the other contenders in the ongoing electronic technological race. I can illustrate the symbolic meaning of the electronics industry by quoting a short remark from *Życie Gospodarcze* from 1974 that reiterated the repertoire of the electronic engineering community: "The electronics industry belongs to one of the most dynamically growing industries. Substantial attention is paid to this industry because it is considered one of the carriers of modernity (orig. nośnik nowoczesności) for the whole national economy."[65]

Similar phrasing was used in the naming of an exhibition of recent developments in the electronic industry from the year 1971 entitled "Elektronika czynnikiem postępu w gospodarce narodowej," or "electronics as the factor of progress in the national economy."[66] These quotes included the regularly used terms "carrier of modernity" and "factor of progress" that indicated that the electronic industry was already "modern." Moreover, it also suggests the role of electronics as a technology whose application significantly contributes to the modernization of other industries, for instance, with the electronic control of the production process.

How exactly did a host of social actors, particularly the electronic engineering community, "perform modernity" through the use of data to support their arguments? The title of the section came from a 1974 article from *Życie Gospodarcze* in which the author asked the question of "how to measure modernity" and noted the problems of providing measurable indicators because of the rapid technological change of the postwar era.[67] He concluded that the most universal indicator would be to measure the number of ball bearings manufactured in a country per capita. He argued that ball bearings are the most essential component of almost every technological object. Unfortunately, I was not able to find any scholarly investigations that explore the use of ball bearings as a twentieth-century "modernist icon." During the era of the postwar STR, ball bearings were replaced as the universal symbol of modernity by electronic technologies: transistors, integrated circuits, and microprocessors. In his monumental history of the electronic industry, Alfred Chandler uses the title "Electronic Century," which grasps the zeitgeist of the era of the 1980s, when electronic technologies symbolized the most significant technological revolution of the twentieth century.[68]

In 1970, the national congress of the SEP included a debate on the role of electronics in the economy and society.[69] The SEP experts concluded that due to the obvious lag in the production of electronic components, the state needed to undertake urgent measures to narrow this gap. This electronic lobby led a campaign that was largely successful, and the government responded with the introduction of a strategic plan for the electronization of the national economy. Also at the congress, SEP experts compared the production of transistors per capita as an illustrative symbol of such a lag. According to the data they provided, in the developed countries, not including those that belonged in the vanguard in electronics (Japan and the United States), production was estimated at four transistors per capita, while in Poland, the production was only 0.6 transistors per capita.[70]

This was the most widely used quantitative indicator of modernity that was regularly used in public debates, but there were also other symbols. Another SEP congress in 1983 used time as a symbol of "the backwardness in the production of electronics," with Poland generally regarded as being around 10 years behind, while in the production of the most modern products, this lag was only six years.[71] This technology gap was calculated as the difference between when a new generation of electronic products was introduced in highly developed countries and the time when such production was initiated in Poland.[72] Stokes discusses similar time-based estimations in the East German chemical industry.[73] Unfortunately, aside from his discussion, despite the wide use of such measurements, there are no other studies on the discursive strategies of measuring different "technology lags" in the Cold War era.

When it comes to such quantitative indicators related to modernity in electronics, I can introduce another rather unique indicator used by an electronics expert to vividly illustrate the potential profitability of the production and export of electronic components. An analysis of the profitability of exports from 1985 includes a table with extensive calculations on the most profitable commodity when it comes to the financial value of exports by weight. As the author notes, exporting a ton of transistors is much more profitable than exporting a ton of steel, grain, or a calculated ton of a ship build in a Polish shipyard.[74] Such "technological promise" of huge profits is rather a curiosity, but its use shows some of the creative strategies employed by the electronic engineering lobby in their struggle for resources with other industries.[75]

Serguei Alex Oushakine notes that one of the tendencies in the commodity culture of the USSR was the development of complex nomenclatures of commodity types. As he argues, this practice was appropriated in the demonstrations of an abundance of consumer products by claiming that consumers are provided with a substantial variety of consumer products from a single category.[76] A similar cultural logic can be seen in a propaganda-laden report on the domestic and foreign successes of the Polish electronics industry which was the result of the NPSG 1971–1975.[77] The author of this report notes that previously, the electronic industry was capable of only manufacturing one or two products from a single category, for instance, two models of radio receivers and black and white television sets. However, after the implementation of the plan and accompanying programs that stimulated the growth of the electronic industry, it managed to design and manufacture thirty-nine different types of radio receivers from all three (popular, standard, luxury) categories, twelve types of television sets, nineteen audio-cassette and video recorders, including one type of a professional video recorder, and twelve types of record players. This is an exact equivalent to the trend discussed by Oushakine. Thirty-nine types of radio receivers and twelve television sets were used to convince Polish consumers that they not only had a choice when making purchases but that Polish engineers are capable of designing such an astounding number of new products in a short time.

The editors of the *Good Life* highlight the role that the indicators related to consumer products played as giving tangible proof of the success of the communist project: "Levels of consumption were considered the primary measure of levels of development, the relative merits of communism and capitalism, and whether one could be considered to belong to 'Europe.'"[78] Elsewhere, I have discussed how the indicators of the ownership of durable goods were used in public debates of the 1980s in arguments on the severity of the economic crisis and as ways of questioning the governmental policy of technological, economic, and social development.[79]

In the 1970s, the concept of electronic technologies became publicly identified as modern, and the consequence was a rise in publicly expressed expectations that the electric goods industry would not only make modern products but that it would also be ready to take part in the "technological race" in electronics, such as miniaturization and the release of new types of consumer technologies. Officials also claimed that the aforementioned ability to design and manufacture VCRs was proof that Poland belonged to a small group of highly developed countries since only a few countries were capable of such an achievement.

Such stories about the ongoing successful modernization of state enterprises also included the discursive strategy of claiming that the postwar development and participation in the global "technological race" took place despite the scale of the war damage and problems with the lack of resources in the frugal early postwar years. We can see such a strategy in a narrative on the history of Polar:

> The production of refrigerators began rather late, in the year 1951. For that reason—despite the increasing supply to the market—it was not possible to shorten the distance that separates us from the highly developed countries. The differences include not only the saturation [of households] in refrigerators but also the quality, quantity, and functionality.[80]

When it comes to comparisons between Poland and other bloc countries, there were two key narratives. The first was a narrative of success that included the claim that Poland was the only socialist state aside from the USSR that was capable of producing some specific technologies. The other was a narrative of failure built on claims that the development of specific technology can be compared to the least-developed countries in the bloc such as Romania, Bulgaria, or the most backward state, Albania. Such voices of failure and the deepening crisis were usually used to express "technological expectation" and appeal for increased investment to avoid further embarrassing comparisons with Albania.

MODERN POLAND IN THE GLOBALIZING WORLD

I previously noted that Polish developments in the production of electric goods, particularly in consumer electronics, were compared with other countries in order to evaluate who was winning the ongoing "technological race." This evaluation was used as a point of reference to illustrate an argument for the success of the modernization policy or to highlight the widening technology gap. The systems of evaluation that were proposed were closely related to the ongoing establishment and fostering of international connections by seeking new trade partners for export goods, purchasing licenses, and establishing OEM agreements. The emergence of trade contacts and their positive impact on the domestic industry and the market became one of the focal points of the socio-technical imaginary of the modernization of the 1970s and 1980s. Such contacts were an instance of establishing multilateral connections that went far beyond the Eastern Bloc.

Public performance on how the Polish electronic industry established such connections was structured by the specific imagery of political geography. Poland was situated in a broader global perspective as a country that was attempting to keep pace in the technological race. The success of such a struggle could result in it joining the advanced countries of the West as being capable of carrying out R&D and designing its own technologies. Failure, on the other hand, would result in Poland descending into being a technologically underdeveloped, Third-World country that could only receive technologies made elsewhere.

The 1970s and 1980s saw the beginning of the economic and cultural globalization that shapes the contemporary world. Despite this, there is a gap in the literature concerning the cultural logic related to the process of how major MNEs, or multinational enterprises, became "multinationals" by shaping networks of contacts with local trade partners and establishing global supply chains. The seminal work that covers such an issue is the study of the emergence of the Sony Walkman as an item that secured the global position of Sony as a household name, a potentate of the electronic industry that leads in terms of technological innovation and product quality.[81] But there are still only few studies on how such processes were accompanied by shaping the "entangled geographies" of power in the postindustrial era that drew on the ability to be at the forefront of the technological race in electronics and other STR-related innovations.[82]

Previous works on consumption in the Eastern Bloc and more broadly on consumer technologies in the postwar era, such as *Cold War Kitchen*, focus on the period of the 1950s and 1960s, an era of establishing cultural and economic contacts with the United States during the postwar economic boom, as Western Europe thrived under the Marshall Plan and the Eastern Bloc moved away from the Stalinist era. As the editors of *Cold War Kitchen* note: "The kitchen debate appeared to be—and so it has been canonized in American historical writing—a fundamental controversy between the two superpowers of the cold war. On closer inspection, the kitchen debate looks more like a transatlantic clash between American corporate and European welfare-state visions of technological development."[83]

This remark highlights two vectors of the cultural and economic clashes of the 1950s. However, in the forthcoming decades, the world changed due to the shift of economic power to the Far East and the expansion of multilateral economic contacts. In the introduction to their edited volume about consumption cultures in post-war Europe, Akira Iriye and Rana Mitter note the recent shift in the scholarly interests in that current: "The conventional literature tends to focus on the Cold War as the overarching framework for the age, but recent scholarship has helped bring into the picture various other themes, for instance, economic globalization."[84]

Łukasz Stanek, in his work on what he calls "global socialism," the collaborations of Eastern Bloc architects and urban planners with the Global South highlight the scale of global contacts that emerged.[85] In addition to Stanek's work on the engagement of the Eastern Bloc in shaping the urban infrastructures of the Global South, there has been recent scholarly interest in "socialist globalization," with two studies on the "socialist sixties" and the emergence of international trade contacts.[86] Yet, the cultural dimension of the emergence of trade contacts beyond the Eastern Bloc is mostly overlooked in the scholarship.

In his work, Stanek focuses on how the Eastern Bloc states were capable of exercising agency to achieve what he calls "socialist worldmaking."[87] For the electronics industry, however, the focus was on making international contacts related to global supply networks in electronics instead of "socialist world-making." Thus, Polish policy-makers and industrial managers with limited resources, production, and R&D capabilities sought to create a small niche in the globalizing world in which the leading force was the Japanese *zaibat-sus*. To paraphrase Stanek, they sought to be somehow recognized as active subjects in the worldmaking process that was being driven by the globalizing market economies. In particular, the consumer electronics industry played a pivotal role in this process through the expansion of global supply chains.[88]

In a section on design in the postmodern era 1967–2006 in *The Design History Reader*, Rebecca Houze provides a quick summary of Frederic Jameson's classic work on postmodernism. As she summarizes, Jameson described the 1970s and 1980s "as a simultaneously seductive and alienating period of late capitalism in which global commerce enabled the fluid distribution of an enormous range of manufactured objects."[89] For two decades, the Eastern Bloc existed concurrently with such currents that marked the beginning of economic and cultural globalization. Stokes in his work on East Germany discusses the notion of technological autarky as one of the dominating forces in East German policy toward technological development.[90] In Poland, as well as in other Eastern Bloc states, there were of course tendencies for technological autarkies as well, but the case of the electric goods industry shows a clear trend of opening borders and establishing foreign trade contacts.

The governmental policy in the 1970s toward the pursuit of technological innovation driven by Western licenses had the objective of securing Poland's position in foreign markets. Poznański notes one of the macroscale economic policies in that era:

> In its effort to mobilize exports, Poland was helped by the fact that its investment policy enabled it to supplement a number of traditional exports with more sophisticated products (e.g., cars and trucks, consumer electronics, construction machinery), while at the same time purposely reducing expansion of some of the less promising product areas, including a large part of the machine tool building sector.[91]

The introduction of new designs and the pressure to improve product quality and reliability were at the same time driven by internal factors and the need for the capability of making products that were suitable for export. Kotowicz-Jawor notes the pressure on domestic manufacturers to fulfill "increasing expectations from the foreign markets both the COMEOCM and in the West."[92] An interesting phrase that demonstrates the qualitative change between foreign contacts and Polish state enterprises can be found in correspondence from France from the year 1972 related to the establishment of the direct partnership between UNITRA enterprises and Thomson, a French potentate in consumer electronics. As the author notes, the establishment of such a partnership shows a substantial change from "współpraca handlowa," or trade cooperation, to "współpraca przemysłowa," or industrial coopera-tion.[93] This phrasing illustrates the significance of the establishment of new, closer, and more profitable geographies of collaboration between the Polish manufacturers and Western potentates.

Poznański notes how Polish industrial managers shifted their attention from COMECON to the West, both through seeking the purchases of foreign licenses and subsequently by seeking a market for their products.[94] He dis-cusses several products identified as major recipients of Western technology, in the years 1970–1978, that "were found to experience a dramatic shift from the CMEA and other non-Western markets to the West."[95] That list includes washing machines, refrigerators, sewing machines, cars, ships, television sets, tape recorders, and nitrogen fertilizers. Poznański mentioned washing machines as one of the most significant export products. Polar began manu-facturing automatic washing machines in 1972, and these products became one of the symbols of Gierek's technological modernization and prosperity. In the report on the successful development of Polar, we can find an ele-ment of the narrative of success that regularly appeared in media, a some-how exotic list of destinations for Polar washing machines exports: West Germany, Sweden, Austria, the UK, the Canary Islands, the United States, the GDR, Yugoslavia, Bulgaria, and Hungary.[96] Such lists regularly appeared in the media to highlight the export successes of Polish industries.

The notion of entering the world of global commerce with electric goods was used as one of the key elements of the performance of modernity with narratives on the "modernization of production" and the steady pace of the introduction of technological innovation at the level of state enterprises. Media coverage of this expansion shared the narratives of progress pro-vided by state enterprises. This imagery can be interpreted as the strategy of intermediary actors to support manufacturers by helping them to express their technological promises. An example of this is the production profile of Tonsil, the largest loudspeaker manufacturer, from the early 1980s, which shows the common narrative about the purchases of technology licenses as a successful strategy that widens the range of manufactured products and secures market expansion:

After 1974 [the state] purchased technology for producing loudspeakers from Japan and an assembly line for manufacturing headphones and microphones from West Germany for Tonsil. Currently, Tonsil manufactures eighty-two basic types of loudspeakers with one hundred and eighty different subtypes. Loudspeakers are exported to West Germany, France, the USA, Spain, Greece, the GDR, Bulgaria, and Czechoslovakia.[97]

This point is again demonstrated in an interview with Jerzy Auerbach, the director of the COBRESPU, on the need for the constant improvement of electronic products designed for foreign markets:

Q: Is it worth investing in such research in our current economic situation and with such an unclear prognosis for the future?

A: We have to make it if we want to keep the export of audio electronics. Foreign trade partners demand products with the most novel functions and of the highest quality . . . This means that such products won't be available on the domestic market, although such products are already manufactured by some state enterprises. This is the case of an excellent audiocassette recorder from Diora that is still unknown in the domestic market. If we find an importer for our color television set, he will surely demand that it has to be provided with Teletext.[98]

Auerbach also noted a significant trend in the production of electric goods, the clear prioritization of foreign trade partners over domestic trade organizations. I will briefly discuss this issue in the next section on the imagery of "technological novelties."

A key element of this narrative concerning Western trade partners was the claim that Polish manufacturers can successfully cope with the "technological expectations" expressed by foreign trade partners. This narrative on technological progress can be illustrated by a lengthy report on the history and current trends for the manufacturer ZRK from the year 1980:

For years there has been an ongoing battle for the modernity and reliability for the products of ZRK. Cooperation with Western and highly demanding partners has provided an excellent lesson in that matter . . . After moving away from the production of popular class products the enterprise aims the production of higher classes [that is "standard class" and "luxury class" products]. The guarantee for such an endeavor is the sum of almost thirty years of experience, the stabilization of the work crew, and new management that came from the ranks of ZRK's employees. The weakest chain of all of [Polish] electronics are components that lack much in terms of modernity and quality. It [the growth of Polish audio electronics production] has begun in Kasprzak and currently, we are the leading manufacturer of the audiocassette recorder in the COMECON. It is not only worth it but rather necessary to keep that position. Otherwise, we will cease to matter and that means a lack of good quality products for the domestic market and hard current income.[99]

On the one hand, the Polish state media regularly communicated developments in high technologies from the United States, Japan, and Western Europe. This seductive imagery of robots, fiber optics, videotelephones, television sets with huge color kinescopes, hi-fi audios, microcomputers, and CD players reinforced claims by the electronic engineering lobby that these achievements proved that Poland was being left behind by the developed world. Thus, these descriptions were accompanied by the question, "When will we catch up with the world?" in high technologies.[100] The only solution was that the state should offer much more support with more investment. On the other hand, such imagery included an elaborate repertoire of explanations of how state enterprises were already taking measures to catch up with the world and avoid being left behind even with their limited resources. An example of this can be found in the previous quote from the producer ZRK.

Most media narratives that referred to the establishment of collaboration between Polish manufacturers and global potentates emphasized that this collaboration was a result of the competencies and capabilities of Polish manufacturers. One of the reports on the trajectory of the development of the ZRK-Grundig collaboration highlights the role that ZRK played in helping Grundig outcompete Philips by improving the technological standard of their audiocassettes. According to this story, Grundig offered ZRK the license for manufacturing the highly popular series of ZK 100 audiocassette recorders as a reward for their role in the Grundig-Philips rivalry.[101] This narrative presented Polish electronics manufacturers as almost equal partners to Western potentates. My interpretation of the sources on these policies of the 1970s shows that most narratives included a similar statement. Yet, I also found a single claim that Grundig established collaboration with ZRK as an OEM primarily because ZRK was simply the cheapest subcontractor apart from an unspecified electronics company from Portugal.[102] Claims that Western potentates established partnerships with Polish manufacturers because they offered the cheapest production costs are rare and appeared only in the 1980s. It is plausible that this reason for establishing OEM partnerships could not be expressed publicly in the 1970s, when Polish technological capabilities in electronics were one of the key features of the performance of modernity.

THE RACE TO INTRODUCE NEW DESIGNS

Here, in the final section of this chapter, I discuss the core element of the imaginary of technological innovation in home technologies, which is the capability to steadily introduce, design, and manufacture new, improved, and more "modern" models of appliances. In the section on the cultural logic of the STR, I discussed the centrality of the assumption that this revolution was not a single leap forward from one technology to another but rather a continuous state of constant change. As a result, only those who were capable of adapting and constantly carrying out R&D and releasing new products could survive and thrive in the market. The electric goods industry is an instance of an industry that is under substantial pressure to design and manufacture new products with improved technical parameters and new features that have been recently popularized by the industry leaders. It is also worth noting that this industry illustrates a feature of "modern" consumer culture. As Slater notes: "Consumer culture is about continuous self-recreation through the accessibility of things which are themselves presented as new, modish or fashionable, always improved and improving."[103]

One of the first attempts in the 1960s to stimulate the constant attention to introduce new technological products was the establishment of a nomenclature of three categories, which can be applied to a new technological product to evaluate its "poziom nowoczesności," or level of modernity. In 1966, the economic planners introduced the system of "ABC" categories applied to consumer products, where A was the highly innovative product, B was a product that was neither innovative nor obsolete, and C was an obsolete product.[104] This categorization was followed by some economic incentives to state enterprises that released products that were evaluated as being in the A category.

In the previous section, I highlighted two central "technological expectations" that lie behind the need to constantly modernize the industry and release new products. The first was the need to secure a steady increase in the standards of living enjoyed in Polish society, with home technologies perceived as tangible indicators of such an increase. The second reason was the need to expand trade contacts and seek new foreign markets. Of course, in state socialism, the most significant expectation about consumer goods production was to make more products to overcome domestic shortages. However, at the same time, there was another policy for improving the quality of manufactured products, and this trend was visible in Poland in the 1970s. In a 1972 paper that outlined the new governmental policies toward consumer products and the complexities of fixing prices for newly released products, economist Lech Miastkowski notes the ongoing economic policy referred to as "the process of improvement of consumer goods." As he notes, this policy included three focal points that he refers to as the elements of the ongoing "progress":

1. The improvement of production quality
2. Undertaking the production of new, modern products
3. When justified, the differentiation of products and the expansion of available assortment.[105]

This is an instance of socialist "projectness," an attempt to introduce a new "program" to make the desired change in terms of quality and innovativeness of consumer goods.

In chapter 1, I discussed the most typical means of communicating the release of new products with the "novelties from . . . " format, accompanied by claims on improved "modern" design by the state media. I will continue that exploration by introducing more elaborate examples of the narratives that present how state enterprises fulfilled the technological expectations by constant self-reflective improvement. I will discuss two types of media formats used to publicly perform the "modernization" of production profiles: a press report and a self-published chronicle of a state enterprise that documents its history and successes.

The first source is an excerpt from a published commemorative chronicle of Zelos enterprise, which was tasked with making black and white kinescopes for WZT. Zelos played a significant role in the founding of Polkolor, which will be discussed in chapter 4. The chronicle of Zelos was written by its employees, and it offers an insight into how an enterprise shapes its identity based on the constant "walka," or struggle with problems and obstacles, to take part in the technological race in the design of television sets:

> The history of the enterprise [Zelos] is full of human struggle and coping with technological, organizational, and personnel issues. A narrative on technological change from the late 50s to the 80s. During the period [1956–1986] there was a constant struggle to build further objects, assemble machinery, improve the electricity supply, for materiel, and finally master new technologies and introduce the design of new products.[106]

> The introduction of the production of kinescopes and the assemblage of color television sets was a significant achievement for that time [the late 1950s]. After the USSR we were the first country in the socialist bloc that pursued this difficult objective with our inexperienced personnel . . . Shortly after [in the 1960s] further development of production of kinescopes became necessary particularly if we consider that at that time there was the chance of joining the leading European manufacturers.[107]

Further, the chronicle notes the key achievements of Zelos. First, over the thirty-year period, the plant had manufactured thirty million kinescopes. Second, a substantial part of this production had been exported to Czechoslovakia, Bulgaria, India, and West Germany.[108] Both achievements illustrate the different rhetoric of success under state socialism. First, the successes were measured in quantitative terms, such as the number of produced items. Such evaluation was grounded in the Stalinist era with its rapid industrial growth. The second achievement was measured not in terms of the production capability but rather the ability to successfully find trade partners and buyers, desirably foreign ones, for their product.

Trade contacts with foreign partners were brought into the narrative that at the same time included a statement on the increasing technological expectations and a subsequent promise that such expectations are fulfilled. A typical example of such a narrative is a lengthy report from *Magazyn Rodzinny* on Zelmer. This article aimed to perform Zelmer's propaganda of success, but *Magazyn Rodzinny* had its own agenda of presenting industrial plants as attractive places for potential employment of young adult readers (cf. chapter 4). This narrative at the same time presented stories on the modernity, efficiency, and skilled and attentive workforce on the Zelmer factory floor:

> First, there are parts, details, and components. They are placed next to the moving assembly line. The young female workers are stuffing colorful chassis of vacuum cleaners with them. A single vacuum cleaner is assembled from more than thirty elements [for that reason] female workers have full hands of work. Due to their precision and diligence, quality control is merely a formality.[109]

> The successes didn't come themselves. They were built upon the effort of the whole work crew which improved its qualifications during all these years. The success is also caused by the concept of investment in modernity [orig. postawienie na nowoczesność].[110]

Later, the report explained, the key decision relevant to the undergoing of Zelmer's modernization was to move away from the production of vacuum cleaners with a metal chassis and replace them with a chassis made of plastics. Such a story corresponds with the agenda of Zelmer by showing that Zelmer's management and workers understand the necessity of constant self-improvement. It also corresponded with the agenda of *Magazyn Rodzinny* of offering the young, positively valued imagery of being a part of the workforce in a state-owned enterprise.

Like the textile labels discussed in the aforementioned paper on the mediation junction, product manuals are also similar bodies of knowledge and offer a narrative on progress and modernity.[111] Manufacturers used this material to communicate the technological innovation of a newly released product. Here, I discuss the manual of the radio tuner Radmor 5102, which was considered to be a symbol of Polish modernity in consumer electronics products (cf. chapter 4). The manual informed its readers that the tuner was designed by Radmor, the consumer electronics department of the Przemysłowy Instytut Telekomunikacji, or Industrial Institute for Telecommunications, and Unitech, an enterprise that specialized in industrial design.[112] The technical details of the tuner were also used to perform the modernity of Radmor production. First, it informed readers that this is a "Luxury audio tuner of the HI-Fi class." The term "luxury" informed that this is a product that belongs to one of three official classes of consumer electronics (popular, standard, luxury class), based on the number of product features and production quality.[113] Later, the manual lists its key features:

> The tuner includes several modern electronic components such as noise reduction, the automatic frequency control board, gauge illuminations, soft-touch buttons, and internal memory for tuning to eight different radio stations. The tuner has been built with modern components, circuit boards, and ceramic and hybrid filters which guarantee the reliability of use.[114]

This is a microscale level performance of modernity in a document as mundane as a user's manual with a list of highly desired features considered novelties in 1970s audios.

This section has demonstrated how the ongoing process of moving toward the future with the regular release of new and more "modern" products became a central element of the public imagery of the electric goods industry. The declared willingness of manufacturers to constantly improve the innovativeness of products corresponds with the aforementioned central feature of the STR, the constant need to introduce new technologies to replace older ones that instantly become obsolete.

SUMMARY

This chapter has presented several different aspects of the performance of modernity that were built with narratives about the ongoing steady modernization of the electric goods industry. Josephson, while discussing grand-scale technological projects in the Stalinist-era USSR presented how such performance can include claims that the successful use of technology can conquer nature and other utopian aspects of technological development.[115] The case of late state socialist Poland shows a more pragmatic approach. While the utopian performance of technology in state socialism included some claims that socialist engineers can use large dams to reshape river systems, modernity in the 1970swas instead performed with enthusiastic news about the establishment of new trade agreements with consumer electronics potentates beyond the Iron Curtain.

Instead of focusing on the utopian aspects of technological innovation, except possibly of the notion of electronics as a technology of the future, there were rather more down-to-earth discussions on the economic and social aspects of technological modernization. Such topics included the need for exportable high-added-value products and establishing trade contacts with Western consumer electronics giants to incorporate Polish electronics manufacturers in their supply chains as OEMs. It also included debates on the need to secure "modern" products to provide new possibilities for consumption by the emerging state socialist middle class.

This is also an instance of how the ruling elite used the public performance of modernity and the state capability of undergoing modernization and achieving related economic successes in foreign trade to sustain the political status quo.[116] The shaping of identities of domestic manufacturers as those who make "modern products," introduce "modern" methods of production, and understand the rules of the STR-related "technological race" was a tangible form of the public reaffirmation of the state's social and economic order.

NOTES

1. The most significant discussion on the interconnection of technology and imaginary modernity can be found in Thomas J. Misa, Philip Brey, and Andrew Feenberg, eds., *Modernity and Technology* (Cambridge and London: MIT Press, 2003). For a contemporary debate on the notion of obsolescence as an element of sociotechnical imagery of electronic technologies, see: Giles Slade, *Made to Break. Technology and Obsolescence in America* (Cambridge and London: Harvard University Press, 2006); Babette B. Tischleder and Sarah Wasserman, *Cultures of Obsolescence: History, Materiality, and the Digital Age* (New York: Palgrave Macmillan, 2015).

2. van Lente and Rip, "Expectations."

3. Louisa Schein, "Performing Modernity," *Cultural Anthropology* 14, no. 3 (August 1999): 361–95, here 361.

4. Kjetil Fallan, "Culture by Design: Co-Constructing Material and Meaning," in Kjerstin Aukrust, ed., Assigning Cultural Values (Frankfurt: Peter Lang Publishing, 2013): 135–63.

5. Law, *Aircraft Stories,* 8–9.

6. Slater, *Consumer Culture.*

7. Slater, *Consumer Culture*, 1.

8. Slater, *Consumer Culture*, 9.

9. Per Lundin, "Mediators of Modernity: Planning Experts and the Making of the 'Car-Friendly' City in Europe," in *Urban Machinery: Inside Modern European Cities*, ed. Mikael Hård and Thomas J. Misa (Cambridge, MA: MIT Press, 2008): 257–79.

10. Bren and Neuburger, *Communism Unwrapped*; Scarboro et al., *The Socialist Good Life.*

11. Mary C. Neuburger, *Balkan Smoke: Tobacco and Making of Modern Bulgaria* (Ithaca and London: Cornell University Press, 2013).

12. Josephson, *Would Trotsky,* 4.

13. Cf. Augustine, *Red Prometheu*; Kristie Mackrakis, Dieter Hofman, eds., *Science under Socialism, East Germany in Comparative Perspective* (Cambridge,

MA: Harvard University Press, 1999); Benjamin Peters, *How Not to Network a Nation: The Uneasy History of the Soviet Internet* (Cambridge and London: MIT Press, 2016).

14. Stokes, *Constructing Socialism.*

15. Zalewska, "Consumer revolution."

16. Philip Brey, "Theorizing Modernity and Technology," in Thomas J. Misa, Philip Brey, and Andrew Feenberg, eds., *Modernity and Technology* (Cambridge and London: MIT Press, 2003): 33–71, here 34. For a previous debate on the notion of technological progress, see: Daniel Sarewitz, *Frontiers of Illusion: Science, Technology, And the Politics of Progress* (Philadelphia: Temple University Press, 1996).

17. Brey, "Theorizing Modernity," 35.

18. Josephson, *Would Trotsky,* 12.

19. Cf. Zalewska, "Consumer revolution."

20. James R. Beniger, *The Control Revolution: Technological and Economic Origins of the Information Society* (Cambridge, MA: Harvard University Press, 1986); Leonard Dudley, *Information Revolutions in the History of the West* (Cheltenham: Edward Elgar, 2008); Tom Forester, *High-Tech Society: The Story of the Information Technology Revolution* (Cambridge: MIT Press, 1987); Gerald W. Brock, *The Second Information Revolution* (Cambridge and London: Harvard University Press, 2003).

21. Carlota Perez discusses how "technological revolutions" are embedded in economic currents: Carlota Perez, "Technological revolutions and techno-economic paradigms," Cambridge Journal of Economics 34, no. 1 (2010): 185–202.

22. For a discussion on notions of "races" and "competition" in the Eastern Bloc, see: Katalin Miklóssy and Melanie Ilic, eds., *Competition in Socialist Society* (London and New York: Routledge, 2014).

23. Slava Gerovitch, *From Newspeak to Cyberspeak: A History of Soviet Cybernetics* (Cambridge and London: MIT Press, 2002).

24. Reid, "The Khrushchev Kitchen."

25. Reid, "The Khrushchev Kitchen," 290.

26. Reid, "The Khrushchev Kitchen," 290.

27. Woodall, *The Socialist Corporation,* 43.

28. Wasiak, "VCRs, Modernity."

29. Joanna Kotowicz-Jawor, *Presja inwestycyjna w latach siedemdziesiątych* (Warszawa: Państwowe Wydawnicwo Naukowe, 1983).

30. Kotowicz-Jawor, *Presja,* 62.

31. Kotowicz-Jawor, *Presja,* 61.

32. Kotowicz-Jawor, *Presja,* 61.

33. Kotowicz-Jawor, *Presja,* 103–14.

34. Emil Antoniszyn, "Unowocześnianie struktury organizacyjnej gospodarki," *Życie Gospodarcze*, September 22, 1974, 8. Cf also: Andrzej Karpiński, ed., *Problemy nowoczesności w gospodarce* (Warszawa: Państwowe Wydawnictwo Ekonomiczne, 1974).

35. Kotowicz-Jawor, *Presja,* 11.

36. Karol Mieczykowski, "TVC—opium dla mas?" *Przegląd Techniczny*, January 2, 1983, 14–16, here 14.

37. van Lente and Rip, "Expectations," 217.

38. "Uchwała Nr 97/75, Rady Ministrów z dnia 30 maja 1975," 1, Ministerstwo Przemysłu i Handlu, Archiwum Akt Nowych.

39. "Uzasadnienie do Uchwały Nr 97/75, Rady Ministrów z dnia 30 maja 1975," 12, Ministerstwo Przemysłu i Handlu, Archiwum Akt Nowych.

40. "Uchwała Nr 97/75," 2.

41. Arjun Appadurai, ed., *The Social Life of Things: Commodities in Cultural Perspective* (Cambridge: Cambridge University Press, 1986).

42. Woodall, *The Socialist Corporation,* 80.

43. Andrzej Werblan and Zbigniew Sufin, "Technika a cele społeczne," *Przegląd Techniczny*, February 3, 1980, 10–12.

44. Vincent Mosco, *The Digital Sublime: Myth, Power, and Cyberspace* (Cambridge and London: MIT Press, 2004).

45. "TechCrunch," https://techcrunch.com/.

46. Sheila Jasanoff, "Ordering knowledge, ordering society," in Sheila Jasanoff, ed., *States of Knowledge: The Co-production of Science and Social Order* (London and New York: Routledge, 2004): 13–45, here 39.

47. Gille et al., "The Pleasures," epub.

48. "Konstytucja Polskiej Rzeczypospolitej Ludowej z dnia 16 lutego 1976 r," http://libr.sejm.gov.pl/tek01/txt/kpol/1976-01.html.

49. Reid, "The Khrushchev Kitchen," 290.

50. *Przegląd Techniczny*, February 3, 1980, 10.

51. Michał Borowy, "Innowacje a jakość życia," *Życie Gospodarcze*, October 27, 1974, 8.

52. This policy resembles the policy of the Khrushchev era with the attention to the term "byt," roughly translated as the "conditions of living." Cf.: Victor Buchli, *An Archeology of Socialism* (Oxford and New York: BERG Publishers, 1999): 138–57.

53. Reid, "The Khrushchev Kitchen," 290.

54. Andrzej Sikorski, "Bariery dźwięku," *Życie Gospodarcze*, April 1, 1974, 4.

55. Patryk Wasiak, "Debating consumer durables, luxury and social inequality in Poland during the system transition," *Zeitschrift Für Ostmitteleuropa-Forschung* no. 4 (2015): 544–65.

56. "Status Zjednoczenia Przemysłu Zmechanizowanego Sprzętu Domowego PREDOM," 1976, 2, Ministerstwo Przemysłu i Handlu, Archiwum Akt Nowych.

57. Janusz Dąbrowski, "Dlaczego nie kochamy elektroniki," *Życie Gospodarcze*, December 15, 1974, 5.

58. Mirosław Haffer and Tomasz Skąpski, "Sprzęt trwałego użytku w gospodarstwach domowych," *Polityka Społeczna*, June 1980, 13–16, here 14.

59. Wasiak, "The Production of High Fidelity."

60. Wasiak, "VCRs, Modernity."

61. Thomas J. Misa, "The Compelling Tangle of Modernity and Technology," in Thomas J. Misa, Philip Brey, and Andrew Feenberg, eds., *Modernity and Technology* (Cambridge and London: 2003), 1–30, here 2.

62. Zalewska, "Consumer revolution."

63. I have discussed the practices of using such indicators to evaluate the actual progress and the acuteness of the economic crisis of the 1980s in Wasiak, "Debating consumer durables."

64. Zalewska, "Consumer revolution."

65. Aleksander Kopeć, "Polski przemysł radioelektroniczny," *Życie Gospodarcze*, February 24, 1974, 10.

66. *Radioamator*, Issue 6, 1971, 2.

67. Lech Froelich, "Znak znany już na świecie," *Życie Gospodarcze*, June 2, 1974, 7. Cf. also: Karpiński, *Problemy nowoczesności.*

68. Alfred D. Chandler, *Inventing the Electronic Century: The Epic Story of the Consumer Electronics and Computer Industries* (Cambridge et al.: Harvard University Press, 2005).

69. *Radioamtor*, Issue 1, 1971, 1.

70. *Radioamtor*, Issue 1, 1971, 1.

71. Stanisław Stępień, "Imperatyw rozwoju—albo wizja upadku," *Przegląd Techniczny*, January 2, 1983, 18–20, here 20.

72. Stępień, "Imperatyw," 20.

73. Raymond G. Stokes, "Autarky, Ideology, and Technological Lag: The Case of the East German Chemical Industry, 1945–1964," *Central European History* 28, no. 1 (1995): 29–45.

74. Stanisław Stępień, "Kiedy dogonimy?" *Przegląd Techniczny*, January 6, 1985, 12.

75. Cf. Woodall, *The Socialist Corporation.*

76. Oushakine, "Against the Cult."

77. "Dzień jutrzejszy krajowego rynku sprzetu elektronicznego," *Radioamator*, Issue 7/8, 1975, 162–64, here 163.

78. Gille et al., "The Pleasures."

79. Wasiak, "Debating consumer durables."

80. "Chłodziarki i zamrażarki z Polaru," *Veto*, July 18, 1982, 13.

81. Paul du Gay, Stuart Hall, Linda Janes, Hugh Mackay, and Keith Negus, *Doing Cultural Studies: The Story of the Sony Walkman* (London, Thousand Oaks, and New Delhi, SAGE, 2003 [1997]); Partner discusses the emergence of the Japanese electronic zaibatsus on foreign markets: Simon Partner, *Assembled in Japan: Electrical Goods and the Making of the Japanese Consumer* (Berkeley, Los Angeles, and London: University of California Press, 1999).

82. Here I refer to the term "entangled geographies" that was used to discuss the political and military-related transnational interactions during the Cold War: Gabrielle Hecht, ed., *Entangled Geographies: Empire and Technopolitics in the Global Cold War* (Cambridge and London: MIT Press, 2011).

83. Ruth Oldenziel and Karin Zachmann, "Kitchens as Technology and Politics: An Introduction," in *Cold War Kitchen: Americanization, Technology, and European Users,* ed. Ruth Oldenziel and Karin Zachmann (Cambridge and London: MIT Press, 2010), 1–29, here 8.

84. Akira Iriye and Rana Mitter, "Series Editors' Preface," in *The Making of European Consumption: Facing the American Challenge*, ed. Per Lundin and Thomas Kaiserfeld (Houndmills: Palgrave Macmillan, 2015), x–xi, here x.

85. Łukasz Stanek, *Architecture in Global Socialism: Eastern Europe, West Africa, and the Middle East in the Cold War* (Princeton and Oxford: Princeton University Press, 2020), 1.

86. Anne E. Gorsuch and Diane P. Koenker, eds., *The Socialist Sixties: Crossing Borders in the Second World* (Bloomington and Indianapolis: Indiana University Press, 2013); Oscar Sanchez-Sibony, *Red Globalization: The Political Economy of the Soviet Cold War from Stalin to Khrushchev* (Cambridge and New York: Cambridge University Press, 2014).

87. Stanek, *Architecture*, 29–34.

88. For a discussion on globalization of IT markets and the restructuring the modern world, see: Jeffrey Henderson, *The Globalisation of High Technology: Production, Society, Space and Semiconductors in the Restructuring of the Modern World* (London and New York: Routledge, 2003 [1989]).

89. Rebbeca Houze, "Introduction," in Grace Lees-Maffei and Rebecca Houze, *The Design History Reader* (Oxford and New York: BERG, 2010): 175–77, here 175. Cf. also Fredric Jameson, *Postmodernism, or, The Cultural Logic of Late Capitalism* (Durham: Duke University Press, 1991).

90. Stokes, *Constructing Socialism*.

91. Poznanski, *Poland's Protracted Transition*, 21.

92. Kotowicz-Jawor, *Presja*, 117.

93. Anna Kuszko, "Francja zmienia oblicze," *Życie Gospodarcze*, July 30, 1972, 11.

94. Poznanski, *Poland's Protracted Transition*, 56.

95. Poznanski, *Poland's Protracted Transition*, 56.

96. Danuta Mąkowa, "Polar ze znakiem Q," *Magazyn Rodzinny*, Issue 6, 1975, 47–50, here 49.

97. *Przegląd Techniczny*, February 17, 1980, 7.

98. *Przegląd Techniczny*, August 15, 1982, 12.

99. Jerzy Waglewski, "Zaczęło się od Melodii," *Przegląd Techniczny*, June 8, 1980, 34–35, here 35.

100. Stępień, "Kiedy dogonimy?" 6.

101. Waglewski, "Zaczęło się," 34.

102. "U 'Kasprzaka' i w elektronice," *Przegląd Techniczny*, September 19, 1982, 25.

103. Slater, *Consumer Culture*, 10.

104. Michał Jadczyk, "Zamiast ABC ocena jakości," *Życie Gospodarcze*, April 16, 1972, 4.

105. Lech Miastkowski, "Ceny a jakość wykonawcza wyrobów," *Życie Gospodarcze*, September 24, 1972, 3.

106. *30-lecie Zelos. Kronika wydarzeń* (Piaseczno: Zakłady Kineskopów Monochromatycznych Zelos/Unitra Polkolor, 1986), 3.

107. *30-lecie Zelos*, 5.

108. *30-lecie Zelos*, 15.

109. Danuta Mąkowa, "Zelmer 03 na taśmie," *Magazyn Rodzinny*, Issue 1, 1974, 19–20, here 19–20.

110. Mąkowa, "Zelmer 03," 19–20.

111. Oldenziel et al., "Europe's Mediation," 112.

112. *Radmor 5102 Manual* (Gdynia: Zakłady Radiowe Radmor, 1977), 3, author's collection.

113. *Radmor 5102 Manual*, 3.

114. *Radmor 5102 Manual*, 3–4.

115. Josephson, *Would Trotsky.*

116. Jasanoff, "Ordering knowledge," 39.

Chapter 3

Categorizing the Quality of Socialist Home Technologies

INTRODUCTION

This chapter investigates how manufacturers and intermediary actors ascribed newly designed home technologies with properties related to the broad category of "quality," especially to their reliability. While doing so, I explore how a host of social actors attributed some technological artifacts with the attribute of "high quality" through epistemic procedures. Later, I continue this investigation by demonstrating how other actors challenged these attributions and articulated some flaws in these procedures. At the same time, they problematized the issue of the quality of these technological artifacts, or the lack thereof, as a problem that could have severe economic and social consequences.

The authors of the article on the mediation junction note that the lack of attention paid to the quality of consumer goods is one of the key elements of the cultural logic of the state socialist economy: "the Soviet-style emphasis on production and planning resulted in consumer goods that de-emphasized quality, diversity, and service."[1] This was a side-effect of the prioritizing of production output in quantitative terms and the pressure to fulfill the production plans. In the 1970s and 1980s, one of the most important structural features of the mediation junction in state socialist Poland was the increased attention paid by the state apparatus to these aforementioned three factors: product quality, the diversity of production profile, and customer service. Under the broad slogan of "poprawa jakości," or the improvement of quality, the state apparatus attempted to increase the reliability of products, expand the range of products offered to consumers, and improve the quality of related services such as retail trade and warranty claim systems.

This chapter also considers the experience of backwardness and the public articulation of both the human and nonhuman obstacles to the ongoing modernization project. An obstacle could be an unreliable subcontractor who delivers delayed shipments of poor-quality electronic components that hinders "unowocześnianie produkcji," or the modernization of the production profile, as well as the lack of resources and procedures to implement an efficient quality control system on the factory floor. While examining this area, I pay attention to how social actors identified "successes" and "failures" related to the quality of products.[2]

Firstly, I deconstruct how the notion of "success" in terms of the improvement of the quality of production in the electric goods industry was embedded within broader sociotechnical imaginaries. Secondly, I investigate the social construction of several failures and organizational problems related to the notion of product quality. As we will see, the issue of the reliability of electric goods was frequently brought up in public communications as a central problem related to their "quality." This issue was articulated by manufacturers who emphasized the ongoing implementation of technological and epistemic procedures to enhance the reliability of their products, and by intermediary actors who supported such narratives or challenged them by raising the issue of the lack of reliability and, in some instances, the inefficiency of such procedures.

This investigation provides insight into a broader perspective of the postwar pursuit of reliability in high technologies. The Cold War era was a period of extensive "projectness" in terms of carrying out projects whose successes greatly depended on technologies that had to be designed to be reliable and perform exactly as intended due to the enormously high political stakes.[3] Historian of technology Edward Jones-Imhotep uses the insightful term "disciplining technology" to investigate the core strategy of the social actors involved in these designs.[4] Successful examples include the Manhattan and Apollo projects in which "disciplined" technologies performed exactly as intended, and their successes had significant political consequences. However, as the case of the Strategic Defense Initiative project proposed by Ronald Reagan in 1984 shows, it was not always possible to "discipline technology" even with the allocation of vast resources.[5]

Cold War military technologies, particularly nuclear weapons delivery systems, depended on the reliability and precise functioning of electronic technologies. Historians of technology have already paid attention not only to the politics of the design of Cold War–era technological artifacts but also to the establishment of the procedures for measurement and the technological standards of accuracy, reliability, and durability. For instance, Donald MacKenzie studied the "projectness" related to the design of the highly accurate targeting systems of US ballistic missiles.[6] He discusses how interest groups not only designed "accurate" ballistic missiles but also engaged in a debate over the epistemology of the term "accuracy."

Studies of Cold War technologies offer numerous examinations of the notion of reliability when used in large-scale technological projects. In his essay on space science, Jones Imhotep discusses "deep immersion in the material and epistemic dimensions of a military 'culture of reliability,' elaborated during the design and construction of the 'electronic material culture of the Cold War.'"[7] He investigates the development of a system of evaluation of the reliability of electronic technologies through the production of bodies of "reliable" and "accurate" data received from research satellites. In this chapter, we will see a similar development of a system for evaluating and improving the quality and reliability of technological consumer goods, and a related system for the production of the relevant knowledge and epistemic categories.

This chapter has been inspired by the aforementioned works. I intend to investigate an "epistemic culture of reliability," and equally, an "epistemic culture of unreliability." Testing the quality of stereos and washing machines sounds much more mundane than testing research satellites or ballistic missiles, but such an investigation offers insight into an unexplored topic of the social lives of technologies in the Eastern Bloc. Moreover, the notion of the quality of electric goods was one of the central controversies raised in public debates on the politics of consumption in state socialist Poland. Although historians of consumption in the Eastern Bloc have discussed various types of consumer goods regularly, they only briefly note their poor quality, which is a feature that is taken for granted. Aside from Oushakine's work on the epistemic categories of consumer products in the USSR, little attention has been paid to the politics of using the terms "good quality" and "poor quality" by actors in socialist-style mediation junctions.[8]

A literary example of the elaborate state socialist nomenclatures of the types and qualities of consumer goods was the famous "sturgeon of the second freshness" served in a Soviet restaurant in Mikhail Bulgakov's *The Master and Margarita* novel.[9] "The second freshness" was an ingenious euphemism used to serve clients spoiled fish. In this chapter, we will see similarly ingenious attempts to convince Polish consumers that they were receiving "products of world quality" despite some widely recognized flaws.

The key interpretative framework used in this chapter is an article by Callon, Cécile Méadel, and Vololona Rabeharisoa on the economy of qualities.[10] One of the sections of that article is entitled "The product as a variable: conflict and negotiation around the qualification of goods," which summarizes the authors' argument.[11] Such a negotiation is the central theme of this chapter. The authors' approach corresponds with Igor Kopytoff's proposition of the concept of "the social life of things."[12] Such conflicts and negotiations are intermediate states of the social life of consumer products that take place between production and consumption. Callon and colleagues note that in their investigation of the economy of qualities, they are primarily concerned with the practices of economic agents that operate in market economies and ascribe their products with specific qualities through the system of marketing:

> The product (considered as a sequence of transformations) describes . . . the different networks coordinating the actors involved in its design, production, distribution and consumption. The product singles out the agents and binds them together and, reciprocally, it is the agents that, by adjustment, iteration and transformation, define its characteristics.[13]

This chapter also draws inspiration from Oushakine's investigation of the "commodity transmission network" since the evaluation of a products' quality through the imposition of a quality testing regime built on a set of epistemic categories was a significant element of such a network.[14] Another point of reference is Gooday's aforementioned paper on the controversies over defining technological successes and failures.[15] To what extent can the poor reliability of a television set be perceived as a "technological failure?" This chapter does not intend to offer an answer to such a question but instead provides insight into how historical actors defined successes and failures and used these definitions in the politics of consumption.

This chapter is structured as follows. First, I discuss the emergence of organized systems of quality control in the electric goods industry, which were established under the frequently used term "system sterowania jakością," or the quality steering system. The next section outlines the emergence of consumer tests that were carried out by several organizations. In the next section, I discuss the process of the epistemic qualification of consumer goods through the establishment of several quality certificates and awards for products of "the highest quality." Next, I highlight the key obstacles that hindered the improvement of quality, particularly problems with supply chains and unreliable subcontractors. Finally, I investigate how the consumer protection movement articulated problems with the quality of electric goods as a symptom of an acute conflict between producers and consumers. This campaign was organized under the slogan of "bubel," which can be roughly translated as "failed product."

"THE QUALITY STEERING SYSTEM"
FOR ELECTRIC GOODS

As previously stated, Oldenziel and colleagues note the issue of prioritizing quantities over qualities of consumer goods as a side-effect of the cultural logic of state socialism. The same issue was regularly brought up in public debates beginning in the late 1960s over the need for the government to reform the production of consumer goods. For instance, an economic expert noted this issue in his discussion of the implementation of the "policy of consumption" on the pages of *Polityka Społeczna* (*Social Policy*), a professional journal for social policy experts from the year 1980: "The issue of preference for quantitative results is closely correlated to the fulfillment of [Five Year] plans. Remarkably, the qualitative criteria in all socialist countries play a much lesser role than they should."[16]

To understand the cultural logic behind the campaign for improving the quality of consumer products, it is necessary to highlight the significance of the term "quality" used in the "quality of life" phrase in public discourse in Poland of the 1970s during the Gierek era. Starting in 1971, the government paid closer attention to the issue of domestic consumption than in the frugal Gomułka era of the previous decade. In a 1974 article in *Magazyn Rodzinny*, which had an agenda of delivering a normative model of "social values" and delivering propaganda-laden narratives on the "social aims" of governmental policy, we can find the following statement: "An income is only one side of the conditions of living and particularly, the quality of life. The production of relevant machines [electric goods] and the establishment of services also contribute to such a condition."[17]

From the 1970s onward, several factors influenced the implementation of a host of reforms concerned with improving the quality and reliability of consumer products made in state socialist industries. The Eastern Bloc governments paid more attention to their policies for consumption, stimulating not only an increase in the production quota for consumer products but also a greater focus on product quality. Such policies included the production of a broader range of products within a specific category, more attention to the visual appearance and ergonomics of the products through the employing of industrial design, and more focus on the reliability and durability of the products.[18] The last category was particularly significant for electric goods, as complex technological products were prone to failure if any of the components were of poor quality or had some defects.

The key factor that provided an incentive to improve the quality of electric goods was the establishment and steady expansion of trade contacts with Western manufacturers and the steady increase of such goods.[19] I have

discussed this policy in detail in chapter 2 as a key element of the modernization strategy of the Gierek era. Foreign partners for whom Polish state enterprises worked as OEMs required that delivered products had to meet their
technical requirements and pass their quality tests. In state socialist Poland,
there was a tacit understanding that state enterprises paid much more attention to the quality of their products when they manufactured them for export
rather than for the domestic market. In chapter 4, I will discuss the knowledge
that accompanied the category of "export goods."

The expansion of foreign trade contacts and the reformed domestic consumption policy resulted in manufacturers setting up new quality standards
to comply with new demands (cf. chapter 2).[20] Porter-Szűcs explains how
improving the quality and reliability of export products became a significant
issue for industrial managers responsible for designing products attractive for
foreign trade partners:

> First of all, it was hard to get decent prices for Polish goods because of all
> the disincentives against rigorous quality control in the communist system.
> Industrial managers in the PRL had not previously needed to worry much about
> pleasing customers, and almost no one in Poland had any experience in market-
> ing or sales. Polish products that were sold abroad had a notorious reputation
> for shoddy workmanship, and an unsustainably high percentage were returned
> because of defects. This wasn't because Polish workers were incompetent, but
> because they lived within an economic order that systematically de-emphasized
> consumer satisfaction. This became a major problem when the "consumer" was
> a foreign firm buying industrial goods.[21]

Still, in the public communications on electric goods in the 1970s and
1980s, the issues of problematic quality, the shortages of products, and price
increases were seen as key issues. These debates were identified in terms
of "technological expectations/promises." First, expert groups such as the
KGD and the FK, and consumers submitting their angry letters to the press,
particularly *Veto* magazine, expressed the expectation that the industry should
improve the technical quality of its products. Later, representatives of the
industry in virtually all public interviews expressed relevant "technological
promises" regarding their constant improvement of the reliability and durability of their products at the design stage of new models and the constant
improvement of the quality control procedures on the factory floor.

We can interpret the issue of the quality of electric goods by using
Appadurai's insights about the significance of the production of knowledge
and the knowledge sharing that goes into the production and consumption of
commodities.[22] The increased attention paid to the issue of quality can be first
interpreted as an increase in the production of quality-related knowledge that

goes into the design and manufacturing of products. Such knowledge includes the know-how required to manufacture a reliable product through the use of specific components and materials and the application of production techniques. One of the most widely discussed examples of this knowledge was the technique that averted the frequent problem of improper soldering, the so-called "cold solder" joint that causes failure in electronics.

The second form of this knowledge was the development of elaborate testing techniques and their use in evaluating the performance and reliability of products at various stages of the production process. This testing and evaluation were significantly expanded in the 1980s as a response to the critical voices from both intermediary actors, particularly the FK, and angry consumers. Another form of this knowledge was the development of a new quality-related epistemic category: several quality certificates and awards usually given during the biannual Targi Krajowe, or the Domestic Fair. These practices are discussed in a subsequent section of this chapter.

The relevant social actors addressed the problem of product quality at two levels. First, state enterprises attempted to cope with this issue by introducing new procedures and practices, including additional inspections of the quality of materials and components from subcontractors, the introduction of new soldering techniques to cope with common soldering defects and improve cleanliness regimes, and the extensive testing of assembled products. Second, they sought recognition for the quality of their products by encouraging other actors to award their products with the designation of "high quality" through some form of a quality certificate or an award. The pursuit of this recognition could also have a more mundane dimension, for instance, as a response by the enterprise's chief engineer to an unfavorable article on the quality of a newly released product. Another important trend was the formation of a coalition that undertook some collaborative actions, defined as the means of achieving a commonly defined goal for the improvement of quality that was supposed to benefit all participants of the mediation junction.

In a similar way to how images of Citroen, Vespa, and the TSR-2 and the accompanying descriptive texts in catalogs or official documents were used (cf. chapter 2), a public statement by a representative of a Polish state enterprise that manufactured electric goods was also such a "story" about a technological product. Such a "story" could be based on an announcement that the manufacturer would soon release a new type of audio-cassette recorder or a television set, or a claim that the enterprise was already paying close attention to improving the quality of the specific product.

Intermediary actors played a significant role in mediating the issue of quality by communicating their own "stories." Although they regularly criticized the industry, all three major journals, *Przegląd Techniczny*, *Życie Gospodarcze*, and *Veto*, had a similar strategy of confronting knowledge obtained from the manufacturers with feedback from consumers themselves or the institutions that conducted tests on consumer goods (cf. chapter 4). The editors criticized the manufacturers by referring to letters sent to their editorial board by frustrated consumers who were not able to purchase the desired product, or if they had managed to do so, described their disappointment with some technical problems with it. *Veto*, the unofficial press organ of the FK that built its identity as an organization that represented actual consumers instead of treating them as "implicated actors," regularly gave them a public voice.[23] *Veto* did this by publishing customers' letters which discussed how exactly their product had failed and, usually, the inefficiency of the warranty. These complaints about the quality of electric goods were examples of the knowledge produced by, with reference to Appadurai, consumers "alienated" from products because of the lack of availability of a particular product in retail stores, a technical malfunction, or simply an unsatisfactory performance. These issues can be perceived as acts that alienated consumers from specific electrical goods.[24]

It is important to note the wider context in which this occurred, namely the cultural logic of state socialist "projectness" in terms of designing elaborate "projects" that were supposed to herald the desired future of an abundance of high-quality consumer products. These projects were accompanied by the establishment of epistemic cultures that were constructed from the phrases "quality" and "quality control." The establishment of such an epistemic culture in the 1970s can be illustrated by the dedication shown to the new economic and technological management practices, both at the level of *zjednoczenia* and specific state enterprises, under the slogan of "system sterowania jakością produkcji," or the system for the steering of product quality.[25] Beginning in the early 1970s, the economic planners also implemented the project of "quality steering" that took place at the level of the central economic planning, *zjednoczenia*, and at the scale of a single state enterprise that could voluntarily impose its own "campaign for steering the quality."

I do not discuss in detail the complexity of the government incentives that sought to encourage *zjednoczenia* and state enterprise managers to pay attention to improving the quality of their products. However, later in this chapter, we will see several practices related to the shaping of epistemic culture related to product quality. This culture included a widely reproduced sloganized phrase that was used to articulate the key elements of a new epistemic category of "good quality products." This policy was interconnected with the increased interest paid by industrial designers, economists, and commodity knowledge experts to the user's experience of a product. We can see an example of a phrase relevant to user experience in a commodity knowledge report published in *Handel Wewnętrzny* with the elaborate title: "Shaping of the products for mass consumption during the preproduction and post-production phases (with particular attention to the social and psychological elements of the use-value of consumer goods)."²⁶ This title itself demonstrates the shift from a quantitative approach to the production of commodities to one that emphasizes the need to consider the subjective experience of users who will evaluate the practicality, ergonomics, and reliability of the product during its use.

In the consumer electronics industry, the most significant attempt to impose a system of quality control in the 1970s was the establishment of the COBRESPU in 1978. The establishment of this institute under the direct control of the UNITRA management was an expansion of the previous regimes of quality control that were situated at the level of state enterprises. In 1977, Jerzy Auerbach, who was appointed as the director of the COBRESPU in the following year, explained that the UNITRA had its internal quality control system carried out by Ośrodek Badawczy Jakości i Normalizacji (OBJN), or the Research Center for Quality and Normalization, which was tasked with "search and implementation of the methods of quality control" and "providing the *zjednoczenie* management with information about the product quality and quality control in the state enterprises that belong to the *zjednoczenie*."²⁷ Aside from COBRESPU, another governmental research institute—Instytut Tele-i Radiotechniczny (ITR), or the Institute for Radio and Television Technologies—was responsible for testing new technologies for radio and television broadcasts. In 1977, it established its own Branżowy Ośrodek Sterowania Jakością i Normalizacji, or the Industry Center for Steering Quality and Normalization.²⁸

After Auerbach had later been appointed as the director of COBRESPU, he regularly emphasized the need for a steady increase in product quality in consumer electronics. In an interview with Auerbach, we can see the narrative on the positive role of the COBRESPU as an institution that significantly contributed to the improvement of the quality of consumer electronics: "I think that we were the catalyzer in the process of the improvement of the quality and reliability of products. Quality is not only related to goodwill and consciousness [of manufacturers] but it is also an economic category linked with the economic situation."²⁹ In that interview, Auerbach did not mention any problems and challenges faced by the COBRESPU as an institution responsible for disciplining state enterprises, but the interviewer brought up the issue of such tensions in the industry caused by the emergence of the COBRESPU as a new intermediary actor:

There was a time when the center [the COBRESPU] was considered the leading promoter of the better quality and reliability of audio electronics. However, it was identified as an institution that represents the interests of the [UNITRA] *zjednoczenie*. And that did not bring it any praise. State enterprises frowned upon it since they were obliged to verify their product [with the COBRESPU], and the retail trade [that is retail trade organizations] didn't like you either because you have pointed out several different frauds which had an impact on the statistics of the quality of audio electronics.[30]

Here we can see how the magazine editor uses the interview to openly articulate some of the informal currents in the industry such as how the UNITRA management used the COBRESPU as a tool for disciplining insubordinate state enterprises and the conflicts related to its attempts to impose external product quality control. This is an instance of a broader practice of magazine editors who publicly discussed tensions and conflicts of interest between state enterprises, trade organizations, and governmental institutions that ultimately harmed consumers. This practice became particularly common in the 1980s when there were many more possibilities to openly articulate the flaws of Polish centrally planned economy (cf. chapter 1).

While in the 1970s propaganda-laden narratives presented a vision of a steady increase in product quality, there was a substantial decrease in product quality after the economic crisis in 1980–1981. This was because of the economic crisis, which was mainly the result of the introduction of martial law, which resulted in economic disruption that limited the availability of resources. As a popular weekly *Polityka* commentator noted in 1982: "I have to admit that I do not believe in any coherent economic and financial system influencing the quality [of consumer goods] and obligatory requirement for quality seals in the NPSG."[31]

This doubt in the established "epistemic culture" of consumer goods' quality was regularly expressed by economic experts, social critics, and FK activists. The emergence of a discussion about the quality of electric goods in public debates and its problematization as an issue that had a tangible economic and social cost can be interpreted as an instance of, referring to Callon and colleagues, the reflexive role of social actors in "the qualification of products."[32] One of the elements of this problematization was the argument that the lack of attention paid to product quality not only led to some additional costs for the state enterprises but also had a tangible impact on society. The editor of *Przegląd Techniczny* noted that there were significant "społeczne koszty złej jakości produkcji," or social costs of the poor quality of the production. As he noted, such costs "include the stress of consumers who have to cope with product failures."[33] Later in this chapter, we will examine the peculiarities of the system of quality seals and how criticism of the inefficiency of this system were articulated.

THE EMERGENCE OF CONSUMER TESTS

In this section, I will examine the procedure for testing electric goods that were carried out as consumer tests to publicize the results of a test to potential consumers. This section is inspired by Trevor Pinch's seminal article on the sociology of testing technological artifacts.[34] Pinch sees the emergence of procedures of testing as an element of modernity that accompany the dissemination of new technologies: "In addition to playing a role in the development of technologies, testing and the discourse of the test are increasingly prevalent in modem societies."[35] The consumer tests discussed here belong to the category of tests that are designed and performed in order to be communicated to other social actors. Pinch discusses this category of tests: "Many tests are performances that can be witnessed by others. For instance, a new aircraft or a boat may be demonstrated to prospective purchasers, as was the case for the Turbina—the first turbine-powered boat . . . The witnesses or audience to a test may themselves have different interests in the outcome."[36] There is a considerable amount of consumer culture literature on consumer tests, understood as testing consumer behavior, preferences, and tastes. Surprisingly, it seems that there are no comprehensive studies of the history of testing consumer products.[37]

When it comes to STS, there are several studies on testing as an element of scientific discovery and how a technological invention includes testing to prove that the invention works. For this section, I refer to Pinch's study and another paper by Noortje Marres and David Stark. They offer a useful conceptual framework for studying the social construction of testing. As they note, their agenda is to understand "testing as a way of knowing, valuing and intervening."[38] Later, they note the importance of asking what exactly has been produced during a test: "We argue that tests should be studied not on the basis of what they resolve but by what they generate."[39]

Later in this chapter, I will discuss the significance of the procedure of testing products on the factory floor through quality control procedures, but here I want to discuss how publicly communicated electric goods testing emerged as a way of circulating knowledge that was driven by the agenda of the relevant interest groups. Three major interest groups carried out electric goods consumer tests: the KGD, the electronic engineering community, and the FK. At the most abstract level, in all cases, their agenda for conducting tests was to entrench their power as an expert group capable of producing and sharing technical knowledge. There were two types of tests. The first type of test sought to reveal differences between different products in comparatives tests. The second category is a test of a single product that sought to reveal the properties of a single product during an interaction between a tester and the product itself.

First, KGD activists carried out extensive comparative product testing to evaluate the usefulness and efficiency of products offered by the home appliance industry. The results of these tests were usually published in *Gospodarstwo Domowe*, or, less frequently, in women's magazines. Usually, *Gospodarstwo Domowe* published an overview of several models of home appliances available on the market with relevant information: technical parameters, capabilities, and power usage. However, this was not a result of any test but rather a collection of data on available products that could be used during a course organized by the KGD.

Tests, whose results were published in *Gospodarstwo Domowe*, were usually carried out by the female KGD activists who specialized in carrying out instructional courses on using home appliances. Their position was represented in the design of their tests, and the testing process usually included an extensive collection of detailed data collected during a real-life test, for example, cooking, baking, washing, or processing fruit or vegetables. The primary agenda of these tests was to inform not the housewife but rather female instructors, who were the audience of the *Godpodarstwo Domowe* with some tacit knowledge about practical aspects of using such products and how they fit into the household economy, for example, how a juice extractor processes available fruits.

The second, and much more complex form of testing was the testing of consumer electronics by the *Radioamator* editorial board and associates. Here the testing was carried out within the electronic engineering community by reviewers who had engineering degrees and belong to the same social world as the designers of the products being reviewed. The editors of *Radioamator* had both the technical expertise and the facilities to disassemble and extensively inspect the internal construction of consumer electronics.

Beginning in the 1960s, *Radioamator* regularly provided not only information about the recent products by the electronics industry but also published product reviews and the occasional test. Apparently, at the end of the 1960s and start of the 1970s, some critical comments in their reviews and the publicized test results led the senior management of UNITRA to temporarily ban the editors of *Radioamator* from being provided with products for testing and reviewing.[40] The ban was temporary, and after a while, *Radioamator* was permitted to once again review products. This is an example of how the practices of testing can cause tensions between different parties. As Marres and Stark note: "The relation of testing agents and tested subjects is unstable and to an extent reversible, sometimes leading to a test ban."[41]

Initially *Radioamator* published information about the products under the headline "przegląd konstrukcji," or the review of the product's construction, and this included technical information and some basic evaluation of the design that was based on a cursory inspection. Then, starting in 1972, the magazine began publishing the results of full-scale tests under the headline "badania exploatacyjne," or an actual use test.[42] These tests included not only an evaluation of how a product behaved during its use but also a detailed evaluation of the components and materials used to build the product. This is an instance of testing that according to Pinch focused on the "pure technical realm" of a tested technological artifact: "Test data are usually thought of as providing access to the pure technical realm, a means whereby the immanent logic of a technology can be revealed."[43]

As mentioned, reviewers and designers belonged to the same social world, and that connection had a substantial impact on the format of the reviews. After writing a review, the editorial board would submit it to the manufacturer, and the published version of the review included feedback from the manufacturer, frequently written by the chief engineer responsible for the design of the tested product, who delivered some explanations concerning the problems mentioned in the review. A similar form of testing was carried out by the *Przegląd Techniczny* editorial board in the late 1970s. With this form of testing, the institution that conducts tests allocates other actors as silent or as actors that can somehow be enrolled with the possibility of expressing their voices. As a result of these connections, the reviewers asked the manufacturers to respond to the critical results of the tests.

Until 1988, the FK did not conduct consumer tests, but from the beginning, the organization built its identity as a mediator between the electric goods industry and consumers and used discussion on the performance of home technologies in such a process. On the one hand, the FK activists in the pages of *Veto* weekly expressed their will to protect the interests of the consumers by, for instance, publishing guidelines on how to successfully submit a warranty claim for a broken product. Yet, *Veto* editors also gave voice to the manufactures and enabled them to explain two key controversies about consumer goods: the pricing and the quality of products. Representatives of the manufacturers were able to explain in detail how a specific enterprise sets a price and what costs were included in it. When it came to issues of quality and reliability, the representatives offered explanations for some widely known problems with electric goods, usually explaining that a specific issue was caused by problems with "kooperacja," such as the poor quality of components and materials delivered by subcontractors.

In 1983, *Veto* organized a short-lasting attempt to more directly facilitate the mediation between the manufacturers and the consumers under the slogan "Akcja Venus," or the Venus campaign, from the name of the model of a color television made by WZT with the kinescope from Polkolor, which was about to be released in early 1984.[44] The editorial board published a special voucher that could be cut off and sent to WZT to reserve one of the 250 newly released televisions. These early users would be able to submit their feedback about the product to the manufacturer.

Veto was an informal press organ of the FK, and in 1988, the organization began to publish its own official (1988–1989) periodical, *Atut*. The content of this monthly publication mostly included the published results of detailed consumer tests which were carried out by the FK's own recently established Ośrodek Testowania Jakosci Produktó in Kraków.[45] The short-lived magazine regularly published tests of home appliances and consumer electronics for both products manufactured domestically and a growing range of imported products. However, in 1989, the magazine ceased to exist due to financial difficulties.

QUALITY CERTIFICATES AND AWARDS

In this section, I will outline the epistemic categories that were employed to formally identify a specific product as an object of "good quality" based on its performance during an evaluation or a test. Aside from testing, there were a number of additional steps in the social life of electric goods when a product would have to pass some form of judgment of its technical qualities through the process of obtaining a certificate or award.

This process can be interpreted as the production of additional knowledge that accompanies the release of a new product onto the market. In state socialist Poland, these certificates and awards were artifacts of knowledge that certified the fulfillment of a specific "technological promise" related to the product's quality and the fulfilling of the specifications of a previously defined technological standard.[46] Once again I return to the comments of Oldenziel and colleagues on the role of knowledge artifacts, such as a standardized textile label, in the mediation junction.[47] The quality certificates for electric goods were similar artifacts that were established to mediate the social life of a product on its journey from the manufacturer to the consumer. Callon and colleagues discuss an instance of how a car undergoes such procedures:

> Its road-holding, engine capacity, consumption and comfort, the resistance of its paint to corrosion and its delivery time are all parameters that, to be appreciated, evaluated and objectified, need a battery of tests, test benches, approved measurement instruments, documents guaranteeing traceability, etc. The characteristics of a good are not properties which already exist and on which information simply has to be produced so that everyone can be aware of them. Their

definition or, in other words, their objectification, implies specific metrological work and heavy investments in measuring equipment.[48]

The "projectness" as an intrinsic feature of the cultural logic of state socialist modernity can be illustrated with a long list of epistemic systems. Such systems were established to examine commodities and identify them as products of either low or high quality. These are also instances of the trend in state socialist commodity cultures noted by Oushakine, who discussed extensive categories of consumer goods in the USSR.[49] Oushakine primarily focuses on showing how "the commodity transmitting network" sought to prove that consumers have access to a large variety of products. My discussion on testing and awarding products with one of several quality certificates shows another tendency of differentiating products. This process transformed products that had been selected from the ordinary world of products and without any formal quality-related identity and remade them into "high-quality products."

In chapter 2, I noted the use of the ABC system in the evaluation of the modernity of consumer products. This was only one of several forms of evaluation that a product could undergo during its social life, from its design to the moment it was sold to the consumer. It is worth noting that from the early 1970s onward, governmental institutions initiated a policy of extensive evaluation of not only modernity but also the quality of consumer goods that was widely communicated in the media.[50]

There were two basic forms of quality testing of consumer products. First, every state enterprise that manufactured industrial and consumer products had to have an internal branch of Służba Kontroli Technicznej, or the technical control service, which was responsible for controlling the quality and the safety of machinery on the factory floor and the manufactured products.[51]

The second stage of the quality control process took place when the product was delivered to a warehouse of a retail trade organization. Such organizations had their local branches named Zakłady Odbioru Jakościowego Towarów, or ZOJT, the service for the quality reception of products. These institutions, established in the 1960s, hired commodity science experts who specialized in inspections of specific types of products such as durable goods, clothing, or staples. Such an inspection was referred to as "odbiór jakościowy," or quality reception, during which an expert would evaluate the product and mark it as an object that belonged in one of three categories named "gatunek," or type, along with the Roman numeral of I, II, or III, which was based on the quality of the manufacturing and the standards of a specific industry. After this evaluation, a relevant number was stamped on the price label that was attached to the product.[52]

If a specific product had a severe flaw or an obvious malfunction, the quality control expert would simply reject the product and return it to the manufacturer. *Handel Wewnętrzny* regularly published materials relevant to "odbiór jakościowy" and reports from these inspections, including statistics concerning rejected products. One of the types of products notorious for problems with poor quality was electric goods. A report in *Życie Gospodarcze*, for example, explained the functioning of the quality reception system by quoting ZOJT data from the late 1960s on the percent of washing machines rejected during such an evaluation due to malfunctions: 1968–13.5 percent, 1969–14.7 percent. For refrigerators, it was: 1968–6.7 percent, 1969–7.31 percent.[53]

There was also an additional obligatory testing procedure for some newly released products that could potentially have an impact on the consumer's safety or health. Komitet Normalizacji i Miar (KNiM), the Committee for Normalization and Measures, carried out such tests, and if a product was safe to use, it received a "B" certificate, a stamp with the letter B (B stands for "bezpieczeństwo," or safe in Polish) in a reversed triangle.[54] With electric goods, KNiM tested if a product's electrical circuit was safe and could not cause, for instance, a short circuit. If a product was safe, it received a B stamp on a nameplate.

Beginning in the 1960s, Polish governmental institutions imposed the policy of "normalization" of the production of industrial and consumer products and established a range of normative and unified standards for all manufactured goods.[55] This policy was partially a result of the establishment of international trade contacts, as foreign partners expected that Polish products would comply with some international standards such as the ISO system (cf. chapter 2). Under the auspices of Polski Komitet Normalizacyjny, or the Polish Normalization Committee, this standardization included obligatory technical norms for industrial products particularly involving voltage and safety related to the B certificate.

Additionally, all consumer electronics had to obtain a certificate from Państwowa Inspekcja Radiowa, or Polish Radio Inspection, the Polish counterpart of the US Federal Communications Commission, to prove that they do not cause any interference to radio and television transmissions.[56] This was not a serious issue, but there were publicized cases when television sets were prone to receiving random transmissions from short-wave radios.

Aside from such an orchestrated system of obligatory standards, beginning in the 1970s, the Polish government actively pursued the policy of stimulating the increase of the quality of consumer products through the use of "znaki jakości," or quality certificates that were linked to some economic incentives for state enterprises.[57] When it came to the standards of testing products, the guidelines for such tests were taken from the principles introduced by the European Organization for Quality Control and the system of testing used in the West German *TEST* magazine published by the NGO Stiftung Warentest.[58]

The main institutional body responsible for carrying out such tests and providing quality certificates was Biuro Znaku Jakości, or the Office for Quality Certificates (est. 1958), which was one of the branches of Centralny Urzędu Jakości i Miar. In the early 1980s, this institution was renamed Centralne Biuro Jakosci Wyrobów, or the Central Office for the Quality of Products, and it provided two different certificates for state enterprises interested in undergoing the verification process. These certificates were not compulsory, but they provided some economic incentives for the manufacturers. These incentives were the source of some manufacturers' practices considered by the press as somehow misleading consumers on the actual quality of their products.[59]

The first type of certificate, "Q," from "quality" in English, was granted to the products that demonstrated "the highest world-class level," and the second "1" certificate was awarded to "products that are equal to the quality of products manufactured by foreign producers."[60] It is worth noting the use of the letter Q. The use of this letter and the phrase "highest world-class level" showed that the Polish government was interested in establishing a specific epistemic category of high-quality products easily recognizable to foreign buyers.

The imposition of the system of "Q" and "1" certificates received substantial propaganda-laden media coverage, which sought to demonstrate that the production quality in Poland could be equal to the products that were judged to be "world-class." The peak of such coverage was the period of the mid-1970s, a short period of export successes, particularly of high-added-value products, as well as a period of domestic prosperity and a steep increase of the "quality of life."

The second system of product evaluation was imposed during both Międzynarodowe Targi Poznańskie, or the Poznań International Fair, and Targi Krajowe, or the Domestic Fair, which was held every spring and autumn. One of the key objectives for the organizers of these fairs was to provide manufacturers with an incentive to pay attention to good design and quality of offered products. The fairs were supposed to demonstrate that the manufacturers competed for the attention of the retail trade organizations and consumers. Several initiatives during the fairs were referred to as "konkursy jakości wyrobów," or product quality contests. An evaluation of Targi Krajowe from 1970 in *Życie Gospodarcz*e highlighted the positive role of the recently established contests on the consumer culture:

[new practices]such as product quality and aesthetics contests, exhibitions of industrial design, quality evaluations, etc. have a significant impact on the development of the production in the direction of the expansion of the assortment and increase of the quality of market products. As a result of such actions undertaken by the industry, retail trade, and institutions that supervise the development of quality, obsolete designs have·been eliminated and replaced by new products with improved values of functionality, usage, and aesthetics.[61]

The name of the most prominent contest held during Targi Krajowe—"Dobre—ładne—poszukiwane," or Good—aesthetic—desired—tells us about the key values required from the commodities and key problems with domestically manufactured consumer goods. In this particular context, the term "good" referred to the category of "good quality." If we look at the establishment of this contest as an emergence of a new epistemic category, it reveals the acuteness of the issues with quality, poor design, and the making of products for which there was no demand.

Indeed, the most common image of state socialism is the shortage economy, which is linked with the assumption that all the available products in retail trade were desired because of the imbalance between demand and supply. Indeed, Oushakine makes the important observation that in the Soviet consumer culture, there was a widely recognized category of "unwanted" products made by manufacturers that were ordered to make such products due to the requirements of FYP, not because there would be demand for such products.[62]

Another contest, established in the early 1980s, was "Mister Konsumpcji," a reference to a beauty contest. In 1988, this title was awarded to, among other products, a food processor exhibited by Zelmer. The coverage for this award included a narrative about the recent modernization program of Zelmer despite the harsh economic conditions of the mid-1980s.[63] This coverage demonstrated how the stories about modernization emphasized the resourcefulness and ingenuity of engineers and managers who were still capable of designing and introducing new attractive products despite the severity of the problems faced by the industry.

Like other issues discussed in this book, there was a difference between the public coverage of quality certificates in the 1970s and the 1980s. In the first decade, this system was generally welcomed as an important incentive for the industry and was seen as one of the indicators of the actual improvement of quality production. But in the 1980s, along with the general experience of stagnation not only in terms of the shortages but also the diminishing quality of consumer goods, the consumer protection movement, economists, and technological experts regularly claimed in the media that these systems of product qualifications were insufficient. Later in this chapter, I will discuss in detail the establishment of a discursive category of a flawed product that was referred to as the "bubel," which was used not only to condemn the practices of manufacturers but also to articulate the inefficiency of the existing quality certificate systems.

In press reports about consumer electronics, engineers from Diora, ZRK, and WZT provided interviewers and audiences with detailed acknowledgments of the problems with product quality, the methods for coping with the poor quality of electronic components, and the systems of quality testing. Moreover, when they were accused of making products that frequently failed, they questioned the definition of "failure." The representatives of the industry, intermediary actors, as well as consumers dissatisfied with the quality of the products, were also, to paraphrase Jones-Imhotep, deeply immersed in the material cultures of electronic reliability and unreliability.[64] Such an immersion was one of the key features of the state socialist consumption mediation junction.

THE GAME CALLED "KOOPERACJA"

"Kooperacja," or cooperation, became a buzzword in the public communications of the governmental economic reforms from the years 1979 to 1981 that sought to provide a solution to the ongoing economic crisis.[65] First, the government introduced several reforms that enabled and even forced state enterprises to pay more attention to making tangible profits and that limited the "soft-budget constraints" policy.[66] Second, policy-makers attempted to improve the efficiency and the profitability of the cooperation between state enterprises that were obliged to collaborate, usually when one enterprise that made some material or component supplied its products to another enterprise for its production process. The public acknowledgment of the tensions between enterprises that were supposed to collaborate, and the economic and social costs of these tensions, was an admission that the Polish planned economy was not working as efficiently as had previously been claimed during the peak of the "propaganda sukcesu" in the mid-1970s.

In chapter 1, I introduced Porter-Szűcs' comments about the conflict of interests between state enterprises from the same industry as one of the intrinsic elements of the Polish centrally planned economy.[67] This issue was regularly raised in the public debates on the quality of electric goods, as it was seen as a major problem that had a significant negative impact on the quality of the manufacturing of electric goods. Porter-Szűcs insightfully explains how these tensions and inefficiencies were intrinsic elements of the state socialist centrally planned economy. I will now employ his explanation of how the "unplanned socialist economy" differed from the "industrial modernity" in the Western market economies:

There are many myths about communism that need to be dispelled. The most important involves the concept of a "planned economy," which is misleading if taken to imply a contrast with an *unplanned* economy, because no such thing existed. Planning was a general feature of industrial modernity more broadly, and in the West, it usually took the form of "vertical integration," which brought everything from the extraction of raw materials through manufacturing to sales into one massive firm.[68]

In the market economy, the policy of establishing vertical integration not only impacts the ability of mass-scale efficient production but also enables the imposition of quality control regimes during all stages of design and production. In the state socialist economy, the system of *zjednoczenia* led to the horizontal integration of several state enterprises from the same industry. However, there was little vertical integration between the manufacturers of the materials and components and the manufacturers of the products that obtained these materials and components from the subcontractors.

To give an insight into the problems with cooperation in a state socialist economy, which was particularly acute for the production of technologically complex products, I quote an excerpt from Sergei Khrushchev's monograph on his father's rule. Khrushchev gives an anecdote about the Soviet special committee that sought to investigate the poor quality and performance of a Soviet-made copy of an American air-to-air missile:

> The committee met for a long time, made a thorough investigation of the technology, and listened to dozens of proposals and hundreds of complaints. Electronics experts blamed machine builders for the lack of the equipment they required. When the machine builders were asked for their explanation, they complained about the poor quality of metal. They couldn't do any better with the metal they were given. Metallurgists simply threw up their hands. The quality of the ore they were given was so bad that the machine builders should be thankful for what they got. The mining industry in turn referred to the poor quality of equipment supplied by the machine-building industry for processing ores. That closed the circle. Everyone gradually got used to the unbelievable percentage of defective parts, which slowly decreased as people mastered production techniques. The situation was considered satisfactory, so the committee disbanded itself and was soon forgotten.[69]

This anecdote reveals one of the key elements of the cultural logic of the planned economy. This same issue, that is the lack of reliable materials and components for production, was an acute problem in the Polish electric goods industry, which was particularly prone to that problem due to the specificity of the manufactured products and the need for a substantial variety of components that had to be ordered from external contractors over whom they had very little direct control. My analysis of the press articles on the production of UNITRA and PREDOM enterprises shows that in a definitive majority of these articles where the authors have raised the issue of the quality of the manufactured products, they, or quoted representatives of state enterprises or *zjednoczenia*, referred to the problems with the quality of subcomponents.

The scale of this problem can be illustrated with an example from an article from 1971 that outlined the problems encountered with the quality of products from Diora and offered some quantitative data.[70] The enterprise had about 200 contractors that delivered components. Of that number, 120 contractors had signed a "umowa kooperacyjna," or cooperation agreement, that specified the quantities and the qualities of products to be delivered. From the rest of the circa eighty subcontractors, Diora routinely purchased components without any formal agreement. From the list of contractors with cooperation agreements, only forty belonged to UNITRA, which sought to guarantee some level of quality control and had the ability to order these enterprises to deliver their products on time.

This report also noted two anecdotes that illustrated some acute problems related to the cooperation of Diora and subcontractors. There were some cases when an enterprise competed with another enterprise for the same component manufactured by a single producer, hence participating in a zero-sum game. The report gave the example of when Diora had to "steal" telescope antennas for radio receivers from a small production cooperative that was about to deliver these antennas to Eltra, which also manufactured radio receivers and needed these antennas. This is an example of the notion of the unplanned economy that Porter-Szűcs discussed earlier. The report on Diora also noted its need to import some components from the West, and so spend its very scarce reserves of a convertible currency, because it was impossible to find a domestic manufacturer of such a component. Usually, these were complex electronic components or high-quality materials that were simply not manufactured by a domestic enterprise. However, Diora had to spend its reserves of convertible currency on importing something as banal as small hexagonal Allen screws from West Germany, which were much superior to flat head screws for securing the casings of consumer electronics. At that time in Poland, simply no one was manufacturing suitable Allen screws.

It is worth emphasizing the level of control over the distribution of the available convertible currency since even the decision to import such trifles as Allen screws had to be accepted at the central level. A former UNITRA manager, in his memoir about UNITRA's privileged position and the electronics industry in the 1970s, noted that the industry was allowed not only to import components for consumer electronics but also such products such as glue and gaskets.[71] That was an exception, since usually, decision-makers did not allow these precious dollars and West German marks to be spent on the import of such things.

One of the side effects of the poor quality of components and the difficulties in finding reliable replacements was, as the UNITRA director noted in
a public speech during the PZPR meeting, a steep decrease in the morale of
engineers and work crews.[72] They were fully aware of the poor quality of
the components from which they manufactured consumer electronics. I have
previously referred to Appadurai's note on how consumers can be alienated
from consumer goods.[73] Here we can see how the workers who manufacture consumer goods can also be alienated from such products due to their
understanding of the flaws in the organization of the production system and
"kooperacja."

Most of the aforementioned issues included in the repertoire of the public performance of the development of the electric goods industry can be
identified as instances of "technological promise/technological expectation."
However, the issue of poor quality or simply the lack of subcomponents was
raised as a structural problem that could not be easily resolved. For this reason, I call it a "technological excuse," a public explanation for the reasons
behind the poor quality of manufactured products and an articulation of a deep
flaw in the economic system. If we look at the content of the technological
and economic press in state socialist Poland, we can find abundant examples
of these "technological excuses" for every sector of industrial production.

The issue of "kooperacja" can be considered as an example of Callon's
work on the sociology of qualities as an element of a sequence related to the
production of a product:

The product (considered as a sequence of transformations) describes,
in both senses of the term, the different networks coordinating the actors
involved in its design, production, distribution and consumption. The
product singles out the agents and binds them together, and, reciprocally,
it is the agents that, by adjustment, iteration, and transformation, define its
characteristics.[74]

The problems with the "kooperacja" showed the severe inefficiency
of the network of actors involved in the production process. In the early
1980s, "kooperacja" became a fashionable word used in the discourse on
the large-scale economic reform that sought to improve the efficiency and
profitability of the state economy. As a part of that reform, the principles of
cooperation between state enterprises had to be organized more rationally.
The postulates for this reform presented the opportunity for several debates
and the chance for different voices to articulate the problems and tensions
caused by the way the interactions between state enterprises were organized.
The aforementioned debate among the directors of state enterprises that
manufactured some technological products, published as "The Game Called
Kooperacja," revealed that most of them had problems with subcontractors
that manufactured mundane components such as piping, rubber hoses, and

most notoriously, "uszczelki" (in Polish, "uszczelka" refers to both gaskets and o-rings).[75]

Similarly, two lengthy press articles on the situation at Polar, a symbol of Polish modernity in the 1970s, revealed the scale of this problem. Polar had about 150 subcontractors. In 1980–1981, the enterprise experienced problems with "uszczelki" and the rubber hoses that connect a washing machine with the indoor plumbing, along with the complex programs for automatic washing machines.[76] As the solution to the problem with these hoses, Polar managers came up with the idea of ending their cooperation with the unreliable subcontractors and purchasing their own machine for manufacturing these parts on their own. This machine had to be purchased in the West, however, for $120,000, an eye-popping price for a Polish state enterprise.

In a memoir of an engineer from Radmor published in the exhibition catalog from the recent exhibition of Radmor history and industrial design (cf. chapter 4), we can see how the imposition of martial law in December 1981 negatively affected the quality of products and more generally limited the capability of the pursuit of technological innovation:

> Martial law which was introduced in 1980 harmed the company. The Forced Administrator liquidated the Testing Unit. The staff's activity decreased significantly, and international cooperation was blocked. Imports of sub-assemblies were limited significantly. All of the above led to a decrease in production and the technological level of the products.[77]

The aforementioned report on Polar from 1982 noted even the most basic problems, such as the inability to make an international telephone call to a trade partner in West Germany to discuss the future shipments of components to Poland.[78] In the 1980s, the most common way to deal with the problem of obtaining Western components was to seek a domestically manufactured replacement, which was of a lower technical standard and poorer quality. The use of such replacements was widely discussed in the debates on the practice of making consumer electronics in the era of the crisis. This particular issue is an example of the professional users' strategy of coping with limited access to products needed for their manufacturing. As the Tensions of Europe intellectual agenda document notes: "Professional users, too, developed novel innovation strategies when faced with poor distribution and shortages. The elaborate system for substitution and recycling—and the technologies developed to support them—is the final focus of this research area."[79]

Not only did Polish electric goods manufacturers establish complex strategies for coping with these aforementioned issues, but this system was openly discussed in public. In the next section, we will see how this open discussion on the inefficiencies of state socialist manufacturing was accompanied by the establishment of a new epistemic category.

THE SOCIAL CONSTRUCTION OF "BUBEL"

In this section, I will explore the cultural significance of the term "bubel" that was used in the 1980s to articulate the severity of the conflict between producers and consumers. Like the textile labels discussed by Oldenziel and colleagues and the quality certificates that I discussed in the last section, "bubel" was a knowledge artifact that intermediary actors ascribed to a consumer product during its social life.[80] However, the difference is that the ascription of "bubel" referred not to the achievement of any quality standard but the opposite: its failure to achieve even a standard of usability.

As I have discussed, the issue of poor quality of electric goods regularly appears as a topic for technology mediation in the 1970s. But at that time, the public sphere was dominated by the "propaganda sukcesu" discourse, and the poor quality of goods was presented in media as a problem that was being successfully addressed by state enterprises, *zjednoczenia*, and governmental institutions. This changed with the crisis of the years 1979–1981, which saw a steep decrease in the quality of consumer goods due to the limitation of available resources and also allowed, indirectly, as discussed in chapter 1, for explicit criticism of the flaws in the consumer culture orchestrated by governmental institutions, manufacturers, and retail trade organizations.[81] Along with the increasing shortage of consumer goods and steep price increases, the problem with the quality of consumer goods was the third key topic of mediation in the mediation junction in Poland in the 1980s.

Here I argue that the introduction of the epistemic category of "bubel," a single easily recognizable phrase, was a central strategy of social actors that problematized the poor quality of consumer products and the accompanying structural conflict between manufacturers and consumers, in which the latter were at a significant disadvantage. In Polish, "bubel" is defined as "a product of low quality that has defects."[82] Paraphrasing Jones-Imhotep, the notion of "bubel" was used as a key element in the public articulation of the "epistemic culture of unreliability" of domestically manufactured products.[83]

This term is still used in contemporary Polish language, but its original introduction to Polish is not clear. My research suggests that this term became widely used with the significant decrease in the quality of consumer goods during the turn of the decade of the 1980s. I could not find any information on the etymology of this word, and the only plausible explanation is that this is a loanword from archaic English use of the word "bubble." The popular internet Wiktionary website notes the archaic use of "bubble" as a verb "to cheat;

deceive; swindle."[84] Economic journalist Ben Zimmer in an article on the history of using "bubble" in finances, as in, for instance, "speculative bubble," refers to the *Oxford English Dictionary*, which traces down the meaning of "bubble" in English from the sixteenth century as a noun: "anything fragile, unsubstantial, empty, or worthless; a deceptive show."[85]

It is unclear when "bubel," or the plural "buble," were used in Polish for the first time before they regularly appeared in the press in the 1980s. However, during my research, I have found that to some extent in the 1970s, social critics used the term "knot" with the same meaning. "Knot" in Polish is a noun, that literally means a candlewick, but there is also the verb "knocić," which means "to do something in an inattentive and unprofessional manner."[86] So in this context, "knot" as a noun had a meaning similar to "bubel." However, there is a nuanced difference, since "knot" simply means something that was poorly made, possibly by an unskilled or inattentive worker, but not necessarily with an intrinsic defect that renders it unusable.

In contrast, "bubel" refers to a product that has an intrinsic flaw in the design that will be present in all, or at least in several, products of the same design. There is also a difference in using this term; in the 1970s, "knot" was used in the ritualized rhetoric of complaints about the quality of consumer goods. In the 1980s, however, the term "bubel" was regularly used as a slogan that was supported by a body of knowledge produced by intermediary actors to illustrate the acuteness of the poor quality of consumer goods and its social impact. "Bubel" was also frequently used in the press beginningin the 1980s, particularly in the pages of *Veto*, which included frequent presentations of a diverse range of failed products marked as "buble." Such complaints were regularly supported by examples from the personal experience of FK activists or letters from readers, who shared their stories on failed and flawed consumer goods.

These critical voices on "buble" were supported by qualitative or quantitative data on product defects. Baczyński, the UNITRA manager, in his memoir noted that in 1979–1981, there was a steep decrease in the quality of the products visible to anyone familiar with the consumer electronics industry.[87] The same problem was experienced by the whole consumer culture. In 1982, a *Polityka* columnist noted that the central elements of the experience of being a consumer in the early 1980s were a significant price increase for most consumer products, accompanied by an equally significant decrease in the quality of those products.[88] In the 1970s, debates on the poor quality of consumer products were presented in a somewhat abstract way as primarily a macroeconomic problem due to the costs of warranty claims. But from the early 1980s on, this approach changed, and the problem of quality became ascribed with a new context not only as an economic but also as a social issue.

This excerpt from *Polityka Społeczna* articulates the poor quality of consumer products as an acute social problem:

> The quality of our products, those intended to be distributed on the domestic market, frequently leaves much to be desired. This problem is too frequent to get along with. Plausibly the reason for it is an insufficient application of criteria of quality during the manufacturers' appraisement of their obligations. This issue has severe social consequences: it absorbs consumers' time that has to be spent on submitting warranty claims, generates additional costs for both consumers and producers, it causes social unrest.[89]

The last comment on the social unrest caused by the poor quality of products is particularly important and worthy of further discussion about the category of "bubel." Mazurek and Hilton discuss how the emergence of the FK was a channeling of the unrest caused by both the shortages of consumer products and the price increases in 1979–1981.[90] Here I focus on "bubel" as an indication of the unrest that was not simply the result of the poor quality of consumer goods but also a reaction to manufacturers' negligence and their disregard for consumers. Mazurek and Hilton note that the aim of the struggle against the negligence of manufacturers who made "buble" was one of the central objectives declared by the FK in their manifestos.[91]

Magazine articles that represent consumers' anger about products offered long lists of the most acute problems with consumer goods, which they identified as instances of the category of "buble." Remarkably, virtually all articles that addressed problems of "buble" in detail included some remarks about electric goods, for instance, two articles from *Razem,* a magazine that represented the ideology of communist youth organizations. In addition, to the propaganda-laden content on the need for "the political and social engagement of youth," the magazine extensively addressed the problems faced by young adults that were starting families and establishing their households with limited resources.

A magazine issue with several pages dedicated to the quality of consumer goods included two lists of products described as typical "buble": "Furniture that breaks apart, scary dolls, shoes without soles, pantyhose with only one leg, ovens, refrigerators, bicycles, . . . the list of buble is very long," including, "television sets with no picture, washing machines that do not wash."[92] The ultimate form of "bubel" was a product that put its user's health or even life in peril. For that reason, the most famous "bubel" of the 1980s was unquestionably the domestically made color television set that could explode or spontaneously combust due to the kinescope overheating. This spectacular failure and the related *Veto* collaborative campaign for the improvement of the quality of color television sets is discussed in the case study about domestic television set production in chapter 4.

One of the most interesting studies of "buble" was given by a columnist of *Razem* in the same thematic issue. The columnist, Bożena Wiktorowska, noted the possible impact of "buble" on the lives of their users. As an example of a "bubel" home appliance, she notes an unnamed gas oven whose knobs that regulate the gas flow had unreadable and misleading signs, a flaw that could have tragic consequences for its user. This is an instance of an intentionally introduced element of design that became a safety hazard, rather than a flaw introduced by a single inattentive worker on the assembly line.[93] Further, Wiktorowska grasped the essential feature of "bubel," the fact that someone intentionally designed a product with a feature that causes the product to be practically unusable: "Everything can be bubel, a building that freezes, an unfashionably made dress, uncomfortable shoes. However, before bubel appear on store shelves, someone actually designed it, manufactured, and what is the strangest part, ordered it during a trade show."[94]

This definition is central to understanding the "bubel" as a special category of products. As Wiktorowska noted, the central feature of "bubel" is an element of design that makes it unusable or that causes a plausible failure after only a short period of use. Wiktorowska based her aforementioned article on data from the FK, an informal survey with a list of about two thousand products offered in domestic retail trade identified as "buble," including virtually all major types of electric goods.[95]

In several magazine articles that elaborated on the problems with "buble," the authors not only drew their conclusion from their observations but also referred to some quantitative data quoted from representatives of the FK or the Ministry of Domestic Trade and Services. Here are two articles in *Razem* that provide insight into the construction of "stories" about "buble." In a report from 1984, the authors quoted Kazimierz Waszuk, an economist and the secretary of the Domestic Council, the governing body of the FK. Drawing from an unspecified source of data, he noted that generally, about 10 to 20 percent of industrial goods have some defects that qualify them for repair. Further, he quoted data obtained from an inspection of Państwowy Komitet Normalizacji Miar i Jakosci from 1983 which revealed that 61 percent of refrigerators, 156 percent of black and white television sets, and 223 percent of color television sets sold in domestic retail trade had to be repaired.[96] The reason why the percentage given is above 100 percent indicates that some products had to be repaired multiple times. This is one of several sources that noted color television sets, the flagship product of the nationwide technological modernization project of the 1970s, as the most publicly visible, and possibly hazardous, "bubel" produced by the electric goods industry.

Wiktorowska also quoted data from the Ministry of Domestic Trade and Services that collected data from its internal organization of the "policja jakościowa," or the quality police, which estimated that 30 percent of all products that underwent its inspection had some defect.[97] Furthermore, she quoted Zbigniew Klarner from the FK, who noted that in 1985, there was a steep increase of about 100 percent in warranty claims. According to the FK activists that collected this data, cars, furniture, washing machines, and refrigerators dominated the list of products under warranty claims. According to this data, for the first half of 1986 alone, consumers returned more than ten thousand television sets, five thousand refrigerators, and about thirty thousand other electric goods. Articles that were published in *Razem* sought to raise public awareness about the massive scale of this problem. Both just-mentioned cases illustrated how the FK became an intermediary actor that collected detailed quantitative data from governmental bodies and shared them in public with social commentary on the severity of this problem.[98]

In *Przegląd Techniczny*, which was addressed to the engineering community, we can find more specialized campaigns against "buble" as an instance of a campaign against the inefficiencies of technological quality control measures during the process of the manufacturing and retailing technological products. One of the *Przegląd Techniczny* columnists published an article with detailed information about the structural flaws in the system of obtaining quality certificates that was taken from data provided by Najwyższa Izba Kontroli, the Highest Council for Control, the institution responsible for external accounting of activities of governmental institutions.[99] As the author took the most important facts from the highly critical NIK report, he concluded that an inefficient and corruption-prone system of quality certificates is a "bubel" itself.

Wiktorowska emphasizes that someone decided to purchase these products during fairs, hereby accepting that these products would be further distributed to consumers in retail stores.[100] Another author of a report in *Przegląd Techniczny*, a member of the Naczelna Organizacja Techniczna (NOT), or the Main Technical Organization, the dominant professional association for engineers, provided minute details of the struggle by the local engineering community that was tasked with the Sisyphean challenge of the "elimination of buble from the fairs."[101] He noted that the side effect of the crisis of the year 1981 was the suspension of the "Dobre—ładne—poszukiwane" contest and the inadequate supervision of the commission that controlled and accepted products to be exhibited at the fairs in Poznań.

This absence of a quality control system during the fairs led to the local initiative by two groups within the Poznań NOT branch structure, the Scientific-Technological Committee and Poznański Klub Jakości, or the Poznań Club for Quality, a group of engineers that were interested in increasing the quality standards for technological products. Both organizations were engaged in a grass-roots initiative of "the social control of the quality" of products offered during fairs and published data collected during their surveys in unspecified periodicals or brochures or appealed directly to manufacturers to remove poor-quality products from the fairs. Such a form of control existed in the years 1982–1983, and then in 1984, NOT successfully appealed to the Ministry of Domestic Trade and Services to establish an official Komisja Kontrolno-Weryfikacyjna, or the Control and Verification Commission, during the fairs. In the same year, as a result of joining the NOT-FK initiative, the fair's organizers returned to "Dobre—ładne—poszukiwane" contest, which was held that year.[102]

With reference to the interpretative frameworks, the coining of the term "bubel" and the formation of the campaign against poor quality can be interpreted as an instance of a stage in the sequence of transformation which discursively transforms product characteristics from a usable product into a category of failed products.[103] The public articulation of the notoriety of "bubel" in the retail trade was the result of a coordinated action by actors that built and shared a body of knowledge by gathering data on various product failures and who claimed their authority as those who represent consumers and their interests. For Appadurai, "bubel" would be an instance of "mythology" that accompanies the alienation of consumers from products.[104] This alienation could take place in a store when they see a child's toy that could scare children or unfashionable and ugly clothing. However, in the case of electric goods, alienation usually took place at another step in the social life of the product, when it broke down during use and the consumer had to find a way to repair it. If we refer to van Lente and Rip, previously discussed orchestrated programs of "steering the quality of products" were "technological promises." The campaign against "buble" was a mostly unsuccessful method of expressing "technological expectations" from the industry, retail trade, and governmental institutions.

SUMMARY

This chapter has investigated two interconnected issues related to the shift of attention from quantitative production quota to the quality of electric goods, and more broadly, all consumer goods, in late state socialist Poland. First, I have outlined an instance of a "projectness" whose aim was to establish an orchestrated system for "steering the product quality" through several institutional bodies, procedures, and standards that were supposed to achieve the nationwide and long-term goal of a tangible increase of the quality of electric goods. The quality of electric goods had particular relevance for the

economy since these products were identified in the 1970s as both a key category of export goods and goods that could provide an observable increase
in the standard of living or, to use the frequently used term from the public
discourse from the 1970s, "quality of life." Finally, I discussed the emergence
of a range of problems with the quality of electric goods as an example of the
mediation junction.

The notion of the improvement of "the quality of life" was one of the
key elements of the policy of modernization of Poland in the 1970s. In this
chapter, I first discussed how the improvement of the quality of technological
products was embedded in this policy and later discussed how the inefficiencies of this policy became articulated as an indication of the deterioration of
the quality of life in the 1980s. This investigation offers insight into a specific sociotechnical order that was established within a state-socialist-style
consumer culture.

This chapter has demonstrated the connection between the notion of "the
quality of life" under state socialism and the qualities of material culture
artifacts. One of the most fascinating yet mostly unexplored aspects of state
socialism was the creation and negotiation of complex epistemic categories.
The "sturgeon of the second freshness" in *The Master and Margarita* is an
insightful example of such a culture. The introduction of a complex systems of testing and the attributing to appliances with some sort of quality
certificates, separating them into popular, standard, and luxury categories
or naming them illustrates how the authorities attempted not only to control
the economy through the planning system, but also control the qualities of
domestically manufactured consumer products. The emergence and the popularity of the epistemic category of "bubel" show us that social actors sought
to challenge the official epistemic culture.

NOTES

1. Oldenziel et al., "Europe's Mediation," 122.

2. For a discussion on the notion of "technological failure," see: Gooday,
"Re-writing."

3. Law, *Aircraft Stories.*

4. Edward Jones-Imhotep, "Disciplining technology: Electronic reliability, Cold-
War military culture and the topside ionogram," *History and Technology* 17, no. 2
(2000): 125–75.

5. Cf. Edward Tabor Linenthal, Symbolic Defense: The Cultural Significance of the
Strategic Defense Initiative (Urbana: University of Illinois Press, 1989).

6. Donald MacKenzie, *Inventing Accuracy: A Historical Sociology of Nuclear Missile Guidance* (Cambridge and London: MIT Press, 1990).

7. Jones-Imhotep, "Disciplining," 127. See also: Edward Jones-Imhotep, *The Unreliable Nation: Hostile Nature and Technological Failure in the Cold War* (Cambridge and London: MIT Press, 2017).

8. Oushakine, "Against the Cult."

9. Mikhail Bulgakov, *The Master and Margarita* (London: Penguin Books, 2001 [1967]).

10. Michel Callon, Cécile Méadel, and Vololona Rabeharisoa, "The economy of qualities," *Economy and Society* 31, no 2 (2002): 194–217, here 197.

11. Callon et al., "The economy," 197.

12. Igor Kopytoff, "The Cultural Biography of Things: Commoditization as a Process," in *The Social Life of Things: Commodities in Cultural Perspective,* ed. Arjun Appadurai (Cambridge: Cambridge University Press, 1986), 64–91.

13. Callon et al., "The economy," 197.

14. Oushakine, "Against the Cult."

15. Gooday, "Re-writing."

16. Andrzej Tymowski, "Rozważania o jakości spożycia," *Polityka Społeczna,* Issue 4–5, 1980, 8–10, here 9.

17. "Jakość, wygoda i uroda życia," *Magazyn Rodzinny,* Issue 1, 1974, 16–17.

18. Cf. Oushakine, "Against the Cult"; Krisztina Fehérváry, "Goods and States: The Political Logic of State-Socialist Material Culture," *Comparative Studies in Society and History* 51, no. 2 (April 2009): 426–59.

19. For a broader discussion on the establishment of cultural, economic, and technological contacts across the Iron Curtain, see: Sari Autio-Sarasmo and Katalin Miklóssy, eds., *Reassessing Cold War Europe* (London and New York: Routledge, 2011).

20. Miklóssy and Ilic, *Competition.*

21. Porter-Szűcs, *Poland,* 280.

22. Appadurai, "Introduction," 41.

23. Callon, "Some elements," 82. Cf. Adele E. Clarke, Carrie Friese, and Rachel Washburn, eds., *Situational Analysis in Practice. Mapping Research with Grounded Theory* (Walnut Creek, CA: Left Coast Press, 2015), 16; Nelly Oudshoorn and Trevor Pinch, "Introduction: How users and non-users matter," in How users matter: The co-construction of users and technology, ed. Nelly Oudshoorn and Trevor Pinch (Cambridge and London: MIT Press, 2003), 1–25, here 6.

24. Appadurai, "Introduction," 48.

25. For instance, see: Andrzej Kostrzewa, *Ekonomiczne podstawy sterowania jakością produkcji* (Warszawa: Państwowe Wydawnictwo Naukowe, 1974).

26. Zofia Andrykiewicz, "Kształtowanie jakości towarów powszechnej konsumpcji w sferze przedprodukcyjnej i poprodukcyjnej (ze szczególnym uwzględnieniem psychospołecznych elementów wartości użytkowej towarów)," *Handel Wewnętrzny,* Issue 1, 1981, 62–64.

27. Jerzy Auerbach, "Elektronika na cenzurowanym," *Przegląd Techniczny,* April 6, 1977, 10–12, here 10.

28. For the history of ITR, see: "History," Instytut Tele- i Radiotechniczny, https://itr.lukasiewicz.gov.pl/historia.

29. "Czy zapomnimy o Hi-Fi?" *Przegląd Techniczny*, August 15, 1982, 12–13, here 12.

30. "Czy zapomnimy," 13.

31. Jacek Poprzeczko, "Bylejakość," *Polityka*, August 28, 1982, 4.

32. Callon et al., "The economy," 196.

33. Marek Samotyj, "Do czego służy jakość?" *Przegląd Techniczny*, September 15, 1976, 6.

34. Trevor Pinch, "Testing—One, Two, Three . . . Testing!: Toward a Sociology of Testing," *Science, Technology, & Human Values* 18, no. 1 (Winter 1993): 25–41.

35. Pinch, "Testing," 27.

36. Pinch, "Testing," 27.

37. Oldenziel et al. offer some remarks on the history of testing and standardization of consumer goods: Oldenziel et al., "Europe's Mediation."

38. Noortje Marres and David Stark, "Put to the Test: For a New Sociology of Testing," *The British Journal of Sociology* 71, issue 3 (2020): 1–34, here 3.

39. Marres and Stark, "Put to the Test," 4.

40. *Radioamator*, Issue 9, 1971, 203.

41. Marres and Stark, "Put to the Test," 15.

42. *Radioamator*, Issue 7, 1972, 177.

43. Pinch, "Testing," 25.

44. Marek Hauszyld, "250 telewizorów dla czytelników "Veto," *Veto*, December 18, 1983, 2.

45. Andrzej Żmuda, "Nasz start—nadzieje i obawy," *Atut*, Issue 1, 1988, 3.

46. For the discussion on the social role of the technological standards, see: Lawrence Busch, *Standards: Recipes for Reality* (Cambridge and London: MIT Press, 2011).

47. Oldenziel et al., "Europe's Mediation," 112.

48. Callon et al., "The economy," 198–99.

49. Oushakine, "Against the Cult."

50. Jadczyk, "Zamiast ABC," 4.

51. Jerzy Jaworski, "Reklamacje jakościowe temat nadal aktualny," *Życie Gospodarcze*, April 4, 1972, 2.

52. Jan Waliszewski, "Gdzie sprawdzać jakość wyrobów," *Życie Gospodarcze*, August 15, 1971, 4.

53. Marian Sikora, "Za czyje grzechy cierpi konsument?," *Życie Gospodarcze*, September 13, 1970, 3.

54. "Znak bezpieczeństwa," https://znak-b.pl/.

55. Jerzy Stępiński, "Normy i normalizacja a jakość produkcji," *Życie Gospodarcze*, May 24, 1970, 10.

56. For a history of institutions responsible for regulating radio broadcasting and later all electronic media, see: "Historia," Urząd Komunikacji Elektronicznej, https://www.uke.gov.pl/o-nas/historia/.

57. Janusz Nowastowski, "Ocena jakości wyrobów przemysłu elektrotechnicznego w Polsce," January 24, 2014, "Elektroonline.pl," http://elektroonline.pl/a/6946,Ocena-jakosci-wyrobow-przemyslu-elektrotechnicznego-w-Polsce,,Elektrotechnika.

58. Maciej Matuszewski, "Zasady kwantyfikacji jakości środków konsumpcji," *Zeszyty Prawnicze*, no 63, 1974, 71–81.

59. Poprzeczko, "Bylejakość," 4.

60. "Polskie Centrum Badań i Certyfikacji," https://www.pcbc.gov.pl/pl/wazne -informacje/znak-q-wzor-jakosci.

61. "XXVI Targ Krajowe "Jesień 1970," *Życie Gospodarcze*, September 20, 1970, 3.

62. Oushakine, "Against the Cult."

63. Mieczysław Starkowski, "Jesień'88," *Veto*, October 23, 1988, 4.

64. Jones-Imhotep, " Disciplining," 127.

65. "Gra zwana kooperacją," *Przegląd Techniczny*, January 20, 1980, 8–12.

66. Kornai, "The Soft Budget."

67. Porter-Szűcs, *Poland,* 264.

68. Porter-Szűcs, *Poland,* 263.

69. Sergei N. Khrushchev, *Nikita Khrushchev and the Creation of a Superpower* (University Park: Pennsylvania State University Press, 2000), 272.

70. Andrzej Sikorski, "Rozwiązania częściowe czy systemowe?" *Życie Gospodarcze*, June 13, 1971, 5.

71. Jerzy Baczyński, "Ciche granie," *Polityka*, April 28, 1984, 5.

72. Lucjan Jaskólski, "Jesteśmy krytykowani," *Przegląd Techniczny*, February 2, 1977, 17.

73. Appadurai,"Introduction," 41.

74. Callon et al., "The economy," 197–98.

75. "Gra zwana kooperacją."

76. Andrzej Wróblewski, "Pod presją," *Polityka*, February 21, 1981, 7; Jacek Poprzeczko, "Samodzielność z rozdzielnikiem," *Polityka*, February 27, 1982, 1, 6, here 6.

77. Stanisław Kosicki, "Technika i Technologia Radmor S.A.," in Agnieszka Drączkowska and Paweł Gełesz, eds., *Legenda Radmoru/The Legend of Radmor* (Gdynia: Muzeum Miasta Gdyni, 2020), 65–77, here 75.

78. Poprzeczko, "Samodzielność," 6.

79. "Tensions of Europe Intellectual Agenda," 18.

80. Oldenziel et al., "Europe's Mediation," 112.

81. Mazurek and Hilton, "Consumerism."

82. "Wiktionary.org," https://pl.wiktionary.org/wiki/bubel; "Słownik Języka Polskiego," https://sjp.pwn.pl/sjp/bubel;2446480.html.

83. Jones-Imhotep, "Disciplining," 127.

84. "Wiktionary.org," https://www.dictionary.com/browse/bubbling.

85. Ben Zimmer, "The 'Bubble' That Keeps on Bubbling," August 27, 2013, "Vocabulary.com," https://www.vocabulary.com/articles/wordroutes/the-bubble-that -keeps-on-bubbling/

86. Andrzej Nałęcz Jawecki, "Nowości rynkowe na huśtawce," *Życie Gospodarcze*, September 23, 1973, 11.

87. Baczyński, "Ciche," 5.

88. Krystyna Cholewicka-Goździk, "Ceny a jakość," *Polityka*, February 27, 1982, 4.

89. Tymowski, "Rozważania," 9.

90. Mazurek and Hilton, "Consumerism."

91. Mazurek and Hilton, "Consumerism," 335.

92. Bożena Wiktorowska, "Super bubel," *Razem*, December 14, 1986, 7; Grażyna Woźniczko, Andrzej Wolin, and Paweł Wyrzykowski, "Jego wysokość bubel," *Razem*, November 30, 1984, 3, 6.

93. Wiktorowska, "Super bubel," 7.

94. Wiktorowska, "Super bubel," 7.

95. Wiktorowska, "Super bubel," 7.

96. Wiktorowska, "Super bubel," 7; Woźniczko et. al., "Jego wysokość," 6.

97. Wiktorowska, "Super bubel," 7.

98. For an overview of the FK activities related to the improvement of the quality of consumer goods, see: Krystyna Wójcik, "Oddziaływania Federacji Konsumentów na jakość dóbr konsumpcyjnych," *Handel Wewnętrzny*, Issue 4, 1985, 6–12.

99. Stanisław Frankowski, "Bubel?" *Przegląd Techniczny*, July 27, 1987, 8.

100. Wiktorowska, "Super bubel," 7.

101. "Eliminacja targowych bubli," *Przegląd Techniczny*, January 20, 1985, 33.

102. "Eliminacja," 33.

103. Callon et al., "The economy," 197.

104. Appadurai, "Introduction," 41.

Chapter 4

Case Studies

INTRODUCTION

The final chapter of this book presents six case studies that provide detailed illustrations of some of the main themes discussed in the previous chapters. As a sociologist, I consider supplementing any large-scale scholarly investigation with case studies as a prerequisite for a multifaceted and comprehensive historical study. With these case studies, I would like to move between the meso- and microscale perspectives. As Phillip Brey notes in his paper in *Modernity and Technology*, "the major obstacle to a future synthesis of modernity theory and technology studies is that technology studies mostly operate at the micro (and meso) level, whereas modernity theory operates at the macrolevel, and it is difficult to link the two."[1] In this chapter, I aim to develop a historical explanation of some mesoscale/microscale cases that correspond with the macroscale analysis that was presented in chapters 1–3. With these case studies, I intend to bridge these scales and offer some examples of how to connect them in the study of technological innovation.

In her contribution to *Competition in Socialist Society* on the slogan "To catch up and overtake the West," Jutta Scherrer notes that detailed case studies also offer a valuable insight into how the cultural logic of technology transfer in state socialist states was embedded into the ideological framework: "Neglected by Western as well as Russian scholarship, the relationship between ideology and technology transfer, if based on particular empirical case studies, would be of the utmost importance for our knowledge of the construction of socialism in the Soviet Union."[2]

Although only some parts of my book are dedicated to technology transfer through exports, licenses, and OEM partnerships, Scherrer's remark is, of course, relevant to the broader issue of technological innovation not only in the USSR but also for the whole of the Eastern Bloc. It also corresponds with

Brey's remark on the need for more extensive studies that connect macro- and microscales.

This chapter is structured as follows. The first case study explores how the public imagery of modernization and the improvements made to the quality of electric goods extensively employed visual and textual narratives about the role of factory crews and work culture. The second case demonstrates the application of the practices of industrial design to the design of electric goods. The third case presents the public life of Polkolor, the most expensive electric goods industry investment of the 1970s. The fourth and fifth case studies discuss the stereotypes of domestically made products intended to be distributed to both the domestic retail trade and foreign markets. The last case study investigates the construction of the cultural memory of Polish audio electronics from late state socialism, particularly from the late 1970s, and how this memory is connected with a nostalgic vision of unfulfilled alternative modernity.

In addition to the case studies included in this volume, I can point to three different publications that are also case studies from my research project on technology and modernity in late state socialist Poland. These cases include an article about the design and manufacturing of video-cassette recorders in the late 1980s; the emergence of a audiophile culture in the 1970s, a cultural and social trend closely connected to technological innovation in consumer electronics; and the project to design and manufacturing a microcomputer.[3] The last paper includes a comparison of the Polish and Czechoslovak pursuit of producing microcomputers and discusses how the microcomputer was an artifact ascribed with the ideology that computers would be revolutionary educational tools.

THE IMAGE OF AN ELECTRIC GOODS
FACTORY IN STATE SOCIALISM

In chapters 2 and 3, while discussing the stories on the modernization of the production process and efforts to improve the quality of the products, I regularly introduced narratives that emphasized that it was important to pay attention to the role of the human factor in this process. The contribution of the managers of state enterprises, engineers, and factory floor workers was identified as a key element of the modernization project. Here, I go further and investigate the textual and visual imagery of the work culture of electric goods factories. I argue that one of the most significant objectives of the public performance of electric goods production and the related technological innovations was to highlight the role of workers and their contributions not only to the process of production of modern, high-quality products but also to the macroscale technological, economic, and social development of state socialism.

Unfortunately, there are no comprehensive and theoretically informed works that investigate the repertoire of publicly shared imagery of the production of consumer goods in state socialism. This is surprising due to the centrality of the imagery of work and figures of workers in the textual and visual ideologically laden narratives and how it was connected with progress in the Eastern Bloc. Similarly, the history of technology scholarship also lacks any examinations of the public imagery of the work culture related to the manufacturing of technological artifacts. However, despite this gap in both scholarly fields, I have found two relevant papers that provide a suitable investigative framework for this case study. Hebdige in his essay on the commercial imagery of Italian scooters explores how images of factories and the production process accompany the images of scooters themselves and how they are embedded in the marketing and advertising strategies.[4] As he notes:

> This image of the Innocenti works in Milan appeared as a logo on many of the early Lambretta ads. The image of the factory itself is the final mediation—the moment of production recalled at point of sale. The photograph, taken from an aeroplane, reduces an entire industrial complex to the status of a diagram (the reduction is a display of power in itself). We are left with an abstract "modern" pattern signifying progress, technology, resources: an echo of the image of the scooter.[5]

Thus, an aerial photograph of a large manufacturing plant is used in the performance of modernity through the communication of the carefully planned design of the factory itself, the scale of its infrastructure, and a suggestion of available resources for the production of scooters and the pursuit of technical innovation. Such an image had a strictly commercial purpose: it was intended to communicate a message to potential trade partners and consumers. But later Hebdige outlines how such imagery with the idealized visual narratives of factory floors and workers have been used in Italy in previous eras to show the social role of factories:

> The idealization of production and production processes and the related image of the factory-as-microcosm are not of course confined to Innocenti's publicity campaigns. The same motifs can be found in the tradition which led to the development of Italian corporatism under Mussolini and to the "progressivism" of Giovanni Agnelli, head of Fiat during the period immediately after World War I. They lay behind Adriano Olivetti's attempts to establish "factory communities" and worker welfare schemes after World War II; they provided the moral and aesthetic basis for Olivetti's concept of "integrated design."[6]

The second work that I refer to is Clarke's investigation of the history of French appliance manufacturer Moulinex and its network of manufacturing plants in the region of Normandy. Clarke's agenda is to connect the field of studies of consumption from cultural history and studies of the history of labor. As she explains:

> Like much of the cultural history that emerged in this period, however, these studies paid little attention to what had long been the privileged objects of social history: labour, the workplace and the working class. As historians of twentieth-century France turned their attention towards consumption, they seemed—with some notable exceptions—to turn their gaze away from the world of work.[7]

Clarke's agenda corresponds with the aforementioned "mediation" shift in design studies and STS and other works that emphasize the need to investigate the connections between manufacturing and the consumption of commodities. While working on the cultural history of Moulinex manufacturing plants, she highlights the need to study the connections between productivism and consumerism as social values. Later, she notes how the marketing of Moulinex appliances included imagery of the workers' contribution to the national technological development: "I will first trace some of the meanings ascribed to Moulinex appliances in the company's marketing and promotional discourse from the end of 1950s to the late 1970s and will demonstrate that, during the postwar boom years, the Moulinex consumer was sold not just a product, but an ethos of national productive effort."[8]

Polish work culture under state socialism has been studied by Małgorzata Mazurek and Małgorzata Fidelis.[9] Another study of the work culture in a state enterprise before and after the year 1989 can be found in the work of Elizabeth Dunn on baby food production.[10] However, like other Eastern Bloc states, there are no scholarly investigations dedicated primarily to the cultural logic of the repertoire of the visual and textual narratives for work culture.

One of the elements of public discourse in state socialism was the constant public communication about the culture of work and workers in their workplaces. In Poland, the work culture was performed in the state media with narratives about occupations identified as being a constitutive part of the industrial workforce: coal miners, iron-workers, welders, lathe-operators, foundry workers, construction workers, automotive factory workers, ship-builders, and state farm employees.

In addition to these groups, another group which received prominent exposure were workers at electric goods manufacturers, since, as I outlined in chapter 2, this industry was identified as being the producers of key commodities that produced tangible increases in the standard of living and that provided badly needed high-value-added exports. Working at these plants was also presented as a particularly prestigious occupation due to the skills required to work in the industry that manufactures precision components that had to satisfy demanding foreign buyers. It is also necessary to mention the issue of gender because of the substantial number of women in the workforce in this industry. This is in contrast to the imagery of the aforementioned industries, which were male dominated.

There is an abundance of texts that communicate such imagery, but here I would like to focus on two reports about the workforce in Zelmer and ZRK published in *Magazyn Rodzinny* by Danuta Mąkowa that I quoted from in chapters 2 and 3, and that can be considered as representative of the whole genre.[11] *Magazyn Rodzinny* represented the ideology of a nexus of communist youth organizations, and the editors' agenda was to publish content that would provide its young readers with role models consistent with "socialist values."

As Clarke found in her study, when publishing content about attractive career paths in different occupations, the editors aimed to help to build attractive identities of employees by presenting the staff of these industries as an elite workforce. Mąkowa's three articles about Polar, Zelmer, and ZRK can be interpreted as a "technological promise" for young readers. The plants are presented as highly attractive places that offer both high salaries and good working conditions, and a place where the youth could forge highly attractive social identities by pursuing careers in engineering and by becoming a member of a skilled workforce who works on a "modern" factory floor and makes products considered attractive enough to satisfy a range of Western trade partners.

One of the most significant elements of the repertoire of these articles was the lengthy descriptions of the workers involved in quality control procedures. In chapter 3, I discuss how these narratives were used as a "technological promise" addressed to consumers, who should expect an improvement in the quality of products. However, we can also read such articles as a way to discipline the workforce through the expression of "technological expectation" from the audience that was both consumers and workers. Such articles included normative models of work ethics by emphasizing that all the factory-floor workers were obliged to pay attention to the quality of their work. In these narratives, the employees are presented as responsible workers who carefully assemble or inspect the quality of the products. This message sought to communicate both the solidity of the product as well as the solidity of the work culture at the manufacturing plant.[12]

Having studied art history, I was particularly interested in the visual language employed by the press photographs used in the "novelties from . . ." genre. The central feature of virtually all photographs taken by Centralna Agencja Fotograficzna photo reporters, which were used in the

communication of technological innovation, was that the technological artifacts presented in the photographs were accompanied by workers engaged in
some work-related activities. There were three major conventions for presenting the interaction between people and technological artifacts.

The first convention, and the mostly commonly portrayed, can be stylized as Western-style commercial photographs. A smiling young female
employee, who is wearing make-up, holds or sits next to an appliance with
a neutral background, a blank wall, or in an office space. Sometimes, in the
case of portable radios, the photograph includes a female sitting on the grass
while holding the radio. Importantly, the caption that accompanies the photograph does not provide the name of the employee. Although the young female
appears to be an employee of the enterprise, this genre does not include any
performance of the work culture since it includes only a consumer product
and the sexualized image of an anonymous female used as a model.

The second type was a photograph of a design team that was almost exclusively all men. They proudly show their product with the names of all team
members included in the accompanying caption. But this convention does
not include references to the work culture, and such photographs were usually published in *Przegląd Techniczny* or other magazines addressed to the
engineering community. The third convention was a photograph from the factory floor that showed workers assembling the products or a smiling female
worker proudly holding a completed product in her hands. Importantly, most
of these photographs included the name of the worker pictured.

These photographs not only demonstrated technological artifacts but also
communicated to the readers the efficiency of the network that included
humans (designers, workers) and nonhuman agents such as machinery that
had been used to assemble the products and maintain quality. In the advertising of the market economy, the imagery of young females, who usually
accompanied the technological artifacts, were more or less sexualized, or they
were presented as idealized housewives. In contrast, in state socialist Poland,
the context was very different, as the photographs of the smiling female
workers, who were depicted in their workplaces, holding their high-tech
products, were a public performance of gendered roles in a production system that sought to emphasize the important role played by the young highly
skilled female workforce to the system.

The most comprehensive repertoire of the performance of the culture of
work can be seen in the published histories of specific state enterprises. Here,
I will refer to the published histories of Zelos and EDA.[13] Although the history of EDA was published in 1969, it includes similar content and narrative
to the materials from both later decades. Other enterprises also published
such commemorative books, but such books were published only in small
quantities and distributed to the work crews. Both publications document the

successes in the development of production, and they include the repertoire of the modernization of production, the constant improvement of the quality of products, and successes with exporting products. But the largest part of both publications is dedicated to commemorating the effort of the work crew.

In chapter 2 in the section on "social objectives," I introduced a quotation from the published history of Zelos that highlighted the role of the plant as an attractive employer that could transform the lives of the peasantry from an overpopulated and infertile southern part of the Mazovia region. It documents the role of the plant in its remaking of the peasants into a skilled industrial workforce, who live in modern housing projects in Piasaczno, and who have access to modern infrastructure: hospitals, schools, kindergartens, and retail stores. The same narrative can be found in the published history of EDA, but here the success of EDA was even more spectacular, as before the building of EDA, the Poniatowa region located circa 45 km south-west of Lublin had only overpopulated villages. The story of the development of the town was closely interconnected with the development of EDA.[14]

The published history of Zelos highlights the social and economic role that this manufacturing plant played in the development of the local community in the town of Piaseczno and, more broadly, for the whole impoverished rural region of Southern Mazovia:

- An industrial plant that provides a tangible economic impact for the country, that provides employment, and the opportunity for professional and social upward mobility for thousands of people.
- The enterprise has contributed to the development of the mass culture in Poland.
- A center for education, a specialist in the electronics industry, which enabled the undertaking of the construction of the Enterprise for Color Kinescopes in the 1970s.
- A factor that contributed to the integration of the community that lives in the area of Piaseczno because at that time [1956–1986] employment in Zelos, the biggest industrial plant in the area, was the element of pride.[15]

The public imagery of the electric goods manufacturing plant in state socialist Poland closely resembled the sociotechnical imagery of the French Moulinex plant discussed by Jackie Clarke. She discusses the role of the "industrial imagery" of Moulinex: "A vision of the factory as a harmonious space of technological achievement and contented collective effort, a message reinforced by the gendering of the production line as a feminine space."[16]

Despite the differences between the economic systems, we can see the similarities in terms of the manufacturing of electric goods, the focus on the factory as a site that plays both significant economic and social roles, and the focus on the workforce. All the aforementioned sources show how different forms of source material can be used to investigate the public performance of the work culture in state socialist Poland. While the "industrial imagery" of Hebdige primarily had commercial purposes, it also referred to the social role of the factory as an important component in the attempt to create a welfare state in Italy.

In terms of the examples I have presented, the imagery of the work culture was propaganda-laden communication about the successful development of the production of consumer electric goods and a tool for disciplining the workforce. Thus, I have provided a short example of how productivism in the technological sector under state socialism was socially constructed through the use of textual and visual narratives.

INDUSTRIAL DESIGN AND AESTHETICS

Apart from the key issues of modernity and the quality of electric goods, there is a third epistemic category of aesthetics that is relevant to this category of consumer goods. The issues of aesthetics and industrial design regularly appeared in the sociotechnical imaginary related to electric goods. The social role of the industrial design of consumer products can be summarized by the outline of the agenda for the Festival of Britain:

> Diffusing knowledge through popular education, encouraging people to partake in "culture" in their leisure time, improving their material surroundings, stimu-lating the arts, broadly fostering an enlightened citizenry "rich in culture," these were all goals shared by the 1951 festival and the postwar Labour Party.[17]
>
> This wide-ranging education in "good design" sought to educate young people about more aesthetically orientated consumption. The explicit intention was to encourage modernist tastes through the prioritization of functionality and through the use of high-quality materials. The Festival of Britain's modernist agenda in design, art and architecture sought to encourage people of all ages to learn about and, when available, consume well-designed modern artefacts.[18]

Several authors discuss design as a body of aesthetic values as they are related to commodities, architecture, and interior design in the Eastern Bloc, for instance, *Style and Socialism*, an edited volume, and works by David Crowley and Victor Buchli on design as a body of normative principles embedded within an ideological framework.[19] Design historian Bernhard Bürdek provides a brief overview of the establishment of an organized system of design in the USSR:

The initiatives of the 1960s to develop industrial design as an integral system attempted to connect with these longstanding traditions (VNITE 1976). Following a decision by the Council of Ministers of the Soviet Union, work began in 1962 to set up a unified system the activities of which were to be based on scientific methodology and closely meshed with the manufacturing industry. To this end the All-Union Research Institute for Technical Aesthetics was established in Moscow.[20]

However, despite the interest in design in general, there has been little interest in the history of the industrial design of technological products in the Eastern Bloc. Eli Rubin investigates the industrial design of the Trabant car, and Stokes offers more general remarks on the history of designing technologies in the GDR.[21]

In 1970s Poland, along with the attention that was paid to the qualitative aspects of consumer goods, we can also observe an interest in their aesthetic qualities. This trend can be illustrated by the name of the competition "Dobre—ładne—poszukiwane" from Targi Krajowe. In publicly shared narratives on the development of electric goods, we can see similar attention to the industrial design in this era.

In the case of home appliances, the basic form of the imposition of aesthetic qualities, to paraphrase a historian of design Regina Lee Blaszyk's work on color in design, there was a "color revolution" that took place primarily at Zelmer, the main manufacturers of small appliances.[22] Here is an excerpt from a narrative on what constitutes modernity in Zelmer: "Modern injection molding machines . . . manufacture all the details necessary for the production of plastics . . . that guarantees high durability and aesthetics of the products."[23] The directorate of Zelmer organized a permanent exhibition of Zelmer's previous products in an administrative building to demonstrate the process of modernization. Mąkowa in her report summarizes this exhibition: "Here one can see the substantial difference in products manufactured currently from products made twenty years ago. [This difference] primarily concerns esthetics, external design, and functionality. Heavy and blocky casings [made from metal alloy] have been replaced by color plastics that are pleasing to the eye."[24] Thus, plastic was used instead of metal in the design of small appliances, enabling a wider range of colors. This innovation was consistent with global trends in the production of home appliances from that era.

Usually, this category of home appliances is also referred to as "white goods" because this is the conventional color of most of these products, particularly larger products such as refrigerators and washing machines. However, Mąkowa in her report on Polar in the 1970s notes an experimental short series of automatic washing machines that had different colors.[25]

If we think back to the discussion about product testing by the KGD that was raised in chapter 3, the functionality and ergonomics of the appliances were the primary concern for the reviewers. Thus, while commentaries about the aesthetics of the appliances were scarce, we can see one example of this subject in the rather banal sounding problem of the discoloration of a tested juice extractor: A KGD reviewer complained that a juice extractor from EDA Poniatowa, made from plastic, had after some use become permanently discolored by the pigments from dark-colored fruits, which caused "obniżenie wartości estetycznej wyrobu," or a decrease in the aesthetic value of the product.[26]

When it came to the industrial design of consumer electronics, a somewhat different course was taken. First of all, we can see the attention to detail even in the Unitra logo itself, a stylized letter "U." An author of one of the studies of the industrial design of Radmor products notes how this logo fits into the principles of graphic design, and how this change was emblematic of the application of a broader policy for industrial design in home technologies.[27]

In the 1950s and 1960s, the prevailing materials used in the chassis of television sets, radio receivers, and record players were plywood, veneer, and brushed aluminum. In the 1970s, the dissemination of plastics also brought a color revolution, which was later superseded by the abundance of black plastics. One of the tests carried out by the *Radioamator* editorial board can be employed to provide an example of the role of industrial design and the positive evaluation of the use of plastics. Here is an excerpt from a review of the Mister Hit record player released by Fonica: "The Tested WG-400 Mister Hit record player has an aesthetic external design and modern lightweight construction made from plastics."[28]

A commentary on recent developments in the design of audio electronics from *Przegląd Techniczny* from the year 1980 noted that the Polish manufacturers were not following the recent trends in the industrial design of audio electronics:

> While browsing the catalogs of renowned companies one can easily see the escape from black and plastics. There are more and more details finished with a gloss, matte silver, and colors. [. . .] We propose to manufacture at least a part of the production of Lena [the discussed radio receiver model] with different colors.[29]

It is worth noting that Jerzy Auerbach, aside from his prominent role in the design of audio electronics as an engineer and as a propagator of the audiophile culture, also promoted the application of industrial design principles to audio electronics. One of his papers in *Przegląd Techniczny* on this subject was entitled, "The industrial design is the fashion dictator in the consumer electronics."[30] Later, COBRESPU under his directorship would both design technical features of audio electronics and hire industrial designers to improve the design of products manufactured by UNITRA enterprises.

In recent years, we have witnessed a revival in interest in the Polish industrial design of the state socialist era. In addition to architecture and interior design, we can also see the public coverage of industrial design in consumer electronics. I will address this issue in the last section of this chapter on cultural memory, but here I would like to note the recently held (2020–2021) exhibition about the history of Radmor and its dedication to the principles of good industrial design. The exhibition was organized by the Muzeum Miasta Gdyni.[31]

According to current notions of cultural memory, the pinnacle of the industrial design of consumer electronics in state socialist Poland were two Radmor radio receivers, Radmor OR 5100 and 5102 (OR stands for odbiornik radiowy, or radio receiver), which will be also discussed in the last section.[32] We can see the attention that was paid to industrial design in the "technological story" in the product's manual: "The Radmor radio receiver has a modern, aesthetic look, and the sound reception quality can satisfy even the most demanding music-lovers."[33] I will now present an overview of the design of that product by a historian of industrial design:

> To understand the style of OR-5100, we must refer to what was happening in the West a decade earlier. In the 60s, Dieter Rams, the chief designer for the Braun company, proposed a radical change in style when it came to commercial technological products like radios or record players. Technical character was desired. Radios which were a sort of furniture in a wooden French-polished casing before, now became rectangular solids with ordered knobs and buttons for clear information. Dieter Rams reduced the number of control instruments and made the form as simple as possible. He was one of the most influential designers of the second half of the 20th century. Grzegorz Strzelewicz was inspired by these tendencies but as he designed over ten years later, he also based his work on other trends. This kind of product was supposed to communicate technological advancement and professionalism. This was noticeable in the large number of switches, the lit sensor buttons or strongly emphasized gauges.[34]

Such an overview provides insight into the social construction of the memory of technical innovation in state socialist Poland, particularly the capability of pursuing the latest global trends in industrial design by industry leaders such as Braun.

In addition to this study of the history and the context of the design of this product, in the catalog, we can also read a memoir of a popular music journalist and radio host Piotr Metz, who offers an insightful remark about the cultural history of the industrial design of Polish audio electronics from the 1970s:

> Real audio equipment should look like a brown and copper-coloured 9000 series Technics. The more segments the better. More knobs? Better still. Handles were a must too—just like those of a professional rack . . . And here we are approaching the moment when our audio market decided to really bring us closer to the rest of the world . . . And then came RADMOR 5100. It was different from the very first sight. After all, it had touch-sensitive diodes for changing stations. As it turned out later on, its guts were world class, compared to everyday life in Poland. And now I also know why I liked it so much too. It was designed by the awesome Grzegorz Strzelewicz—the expert and a student of Lech Tomaszewski from the Department of Industrial Design at the Academy of Fine Arts. It was beautiful and unique, with a clear reference to Radmor's roots—professional radios for communication.[35]

Another paper on Radmor's design also highlighted the impact of the economic problems of the1980s, which resulted in a decline in product quality and reliability (cf. chapter 3). This also had an impact on product design:

> The 80s were the hardest period for the Polish economy and they were twice as hard for design. Admittedly, there was the Governments directive of 1977 that an industrial designer should take part in all the phases of a design process but in reality, complying with it was impossible. Agnieszka Wroblewska, in her article from, 1987, discusses Ryszard Hoga's output and the work conditions in Radmor. She mentions a decrease in production which resulted from material and sub-assembly shortages. At the same time, she mentions deteriorated quality "in the details on the outside, texture of the surface, which is far from the desired, worse print on the front panel. To save money and make it simpler, [it] will be completed based on a long-lasting license agreement concluded with the military electronics tycoon, the French company Thomson."[36]

The author is quoting from an article from the 1980s that was published in an IWP magazine with a narrative typical of the decade, the "technological complaint" about the stagnation in the Polish electronics industry from the 1980s. If we return to Law, we can see how such testimonies dedicated mostly to a single artifact, RADMOR 5100, are instances of retrospective "performance of progress."[37] Like the TSR-2, this radio receiver became a symbol of an unfinished and ultimately lost project of Polish modernity of the 1970s.

These quoted testimonies about Radmor's legacy correspond with a shift in the sociotechnical imaginary of Polish home technologies in the 1970s and 1980s. These memories about the application of industrial design show a short-lasting period in which industrial design procedures and designers were included by the network of social actors that took part in technology production. According to Appadurai, at that time, the industrial design process became included as an additional part of the production stage in the social life of consumer electronics. The later abandonment of this stage became part of the bitter memory that resulted from the decline of the technology-related modernization project in the 1980s.

THE PYRAMIDS NEAR PIASECZNO.
THE POLKOLOR STORY

The Polkolor manufacturing plant and the project to domestically produce color kinescopes was the largest and most costly investment in home technologies in the era discussed in this book. The scale of this project, as an instance of shaping Polish modern consumer culture of the 1970s, can only be compared with the project of manufacturing the Fiat 126p, an affordable passenger car on a license from Italian Fiat.[38] The Polkolor project promised new technology that would supposedly substantially improve the quality and aesthetical aspects of accessing television broadcasts. We have to remember that black and white television had been introduced on a mass scale in Poland in the 1960s, and so the promise of color broadcasting was imagined as the next media revolution. The public imagining of color television was that of the next technological sublime.

Thus, color television was a key element of the public performance of the "technological race" in electronics of the 1970s. In an article titled "Wojna w kolorze," or the war in color, the author mentioned the recent oil crisis from 1973 and then discusses the recent trade war between the United States and Japan and accuses Japan of using price dumping to get rid of its US competitor. He argued that the capability to produce television sets is one of the requirements to participate in the ongoing high stake technology race in consumer electronics.[39] In the early 1970s, Polish policy-makers and the consumer electronics industry were faced with the question of how to cope with the ongoing process of introducing color television. The national broadcaster Telewizja Polska began the color broadcasting of selected programs on December 7, 1971.[40] At the time, the demand for color television sets was fulfilled with large shipments of Rubin sets from the USSR, which were supplemented by small shipments of Western televisions that were distributed through the Pewex hard currency stores. Thus, the obvious question was whether Poland was capable of making its own color television sets.

The most important and the most-difficult-to-make component of a color television set is the kinescope. There is a substantial difference in terms of the required precision, resources, and quality control between manufacturing black and white and color kinescopes. For this reason, the most important issue of technological success in the early 1970s was the capability of making Polish color kinescopes. This debate was concluded with the decision to invest substantial resources into building a manufacturing plant for color kinescopes. The project for the domestic manufacturing of color television sets was accompanied by a "technological promise": "Telewizor kolorowy w każdym domu," or "a color television set in every home."

This decision was fueled by the Gierek regime's licensing policy, and the Polkolor plant was supposed not only to help to fulfill the domestic demand for color television sets but also help to build Poland's strong position as an OEM exporter of kinescopes. The Polkolor project also was influenced by another trend of the 1970s, the expansion of the economic contacts with the West and, where possible, the limiting of such contacts with the USSR. Poznanski discusses the impact of this decision on Poland's trade relations with the USSR:

> At that time [the late 1970s], the Soviet regime had lost much of its initial enthusiasm for Poland's energetic efforts to build up Western ties. This was because many specific choices made by Gierek ran directly counter to Soviet priorities. From the Soviet point of view, Gierek's strategy was detrimental to long-lasting Soviet-Polish cooperation agreements (e.g., in the tractor industry), to sales opportunities for Soviet plants (e.g., colour television), and to certain specialization efforts sponsored by the Soviet leaders (e.g., the regional programme for computers, called RIAD).[41]

The first series of five hundred domestically manufactured color television sets were made by WZT in 1972. Later, WZT began making a licensed version of the Rubin 707 model and shortly after that, the WZT engineers came up with their design based on the licensed product.[42] The first technical report, which was authored by Auerbach, about the first series of domestically manufactured television sets with color kinescopes offers an example of the performance of modernity since COBRESPU collaborated with Polkolor to design this product.[43] Moreover, in 1974, a widely publicized conference titled "Today and tomorrow of color television in Poland" was held.[44] Its press coverage can be interpreted as the performance of modernity built on the central "technological promise" that soon Poles would be able to purchase domestically manufactured television sets.

After some experiments with color television technology, the next step was to look for Western partners. The construction of television sets was licensed by Thomson, a French company, while the construction of the kinescope was licensed by the American potentate RCA. This was a key political decision, for in Gierek's era, France and the United States were Poland's key western trading partners. Polkolor established a long-lasting collaboration with the

French Thomson, and the first series of television sets was manufactured as a licensed copy of a model of the Thomson set with several changes and improvements introduced by Polish Polkolor engineers. In Auerbach's communication, he claimed another "technological promise" that the television set had passed a "rigorous examination" by Thomson's engineers.[45]

The Polkolor plant was built in 1976 in Piaseczno and used some of the infrastructure of the Zelos kinescope manufacturing plant. This investment became one of the flagship projects of the Gierek decade, and it regularly appeared as part of the repertoire of "propaganda sukcesu." A detailed description of the construction of the television set provides us with an insight into what constituted modernity in electronics in the late 1970s. The television set was built solely with transistors, with no vacuum tubes except for the kinescope, which is a large vacuum tube itself. As was mentioned in chapter 2 in the section on the indicators of modernity, moving away from vacuum tubes was a symbol of the modernity of the 1970s. It was also substantially lighter than the Rubin, but at the same time, it had the same diameter of 22 inches. While the Rubin weighed 57 kg, the first Jowisz with the same-sized kinescope weighed only 32 kg; the presentation of the Jowisz included a remark that when it comes to weight, the Jowisz can be compared with the same-sized Sony model. This comment illustrates the tendency of seeking any possible favorable comparisons between domestically made technologies and Western products.

Conversely, in the 1970s, with the introduction of electronic transistor-based technologies, we can see how discursively vacuum tubes became considered a symbol of technological obsolescence. Unfortunately, as far as I am aware, very little scholarly attention has been paid to the shifting cultural values related to technologies from symbols of modernity into symbols of obsolescence.

In the 1970s, Polkolor, a newly established major electronics plant, and the production of Jowisz were presented in media narratives as major successes. However, some issues with the technology were raised, with the editors of *Przegląd Techniczny*, who carried out a test of the model, raising some "minor concerns." These problems included issues with the ergonomics, the spontaneous changing of channels, and low-power short circuits which manifested as flashes on the screen. But these were minor problems when compared with the later much more severe problems, which had their own public life in the 1980s.

Thus, as was discussed earlier, the narrative on modern technologies changed in the early 1980s, and this was accompanied by a critical revision of Gierek's policies of modernization and a deepening economic crisis. The early 1980s marked a halt in the further development at Polkolor. A series of planned assembly lines for components other than kinescopes were never built. In 1983, *Przeglad Techniczny* published an extensive evaluation of the recent troubles with Polkolor.[46] This article was framed by a broader narrative that critiqued several of the policies of the so-called "miniona dekada," or the past decade, an extensively shared slogan that was used to criticize the shortcoming of the Gierek era's policymaking.

The title of the evaluation was "Color television sets, the opium of the masses," which paraphrased Marx's famous quote about religion and clearly corresponded with the popular image of Polkolor as the way to provide Polish society with a product that claims to demonstrate technological and economic success in order to hide the truth about the growing economic tensions. The article also employed the phrase "Piramidy pod Piasecznem," or the pyramids near Piaseczno, which seemed to portray Polokolor as a grandiose monument, built on the personal order by Gierek in order to commemorate his successes as the First Secretary of the PZPR.[47]

The author of the article, Mieczykowski, also includes as evidence the conclusions of Najwyższa Izba Kontoli, the Highest Office for Control that criticized the establishment of Polkolor itself as being much too expensive and as an "incorrect choice from the point of view of the social needs." This conclusion includes the specific phrase "social needs" that was discussed in-depth in chapter 2. The NIK report concluded that a more viable alternative for the project of manufacturing color television sets would have been to have continued the collaboration with the USSR to build a licensed product and "uzupełniajacy import," or to import supplementary products from Japan.[48]

According to this alternative plan offered in the report, licensed Rubin television sets would have provided the majority of consumers with affordable color television sets. At the same time, the importation of a specific Sony television set priced at $365 from Japan that would have been sold in hard currency stores would have fulfilled the need of affluent consumers.[49] Despite this critique, until the early 1990s, Polkolor was manufacturing a large number of color kinescopes which were used both in domestically manufactured television sets by WZT and were exported to Thomson since Polkolor still had an OEM agreement with the French company. Thomson would ultimately acquire Polkolor in the early 1990s.

In the 1980s, in addition to the economic problems of WZT, the media also discussed the more or less serious problems of the Jowisz's reliability. The most serious issue with the Jowisz was that it could in some extreme cases spontaneously combust, resulting in potentially fatal consequences.[50] Marek Hauszyld, an editor of *Veto,* provided extensive evidence of the problems with the Jowisz, and he was the first to describe this product as possibly being not only an ordinary "bubel" (cf. chapter 3) but a "superbubel" due to the long list of technical problems, as well as the negligence of WZT in contacts with consumers seeking warranty claims.[51] However, as he notes in a second article that accompanies his analysis of the problems with the Jowisz, he was directly contacted by the director of WZT, who provided explanations for these problems and promised to help the consumers who experienced these issues during their use of the product.[52] Among other declarations concerning improving the quality of the next series of Jowisz sets, the director claimed that WZT was implementing a coherent "system sterowania jakością" (cf. chapter 3).

Polkolor was the most visible instance of the "projectness" of the Gierek era. A single enterprise that manufactured highly sought after products for the domestic market and Western trade partners demonstrates how the sociotechnical imaginary of technological innovation of the Gierek era was embedded in a specific political, social, and economic context. In the 1980s, Polish color television sets moved to another stage of their social life and became "super-bubel." The blazing Jowisz television set became a symbol of the problems of the domestic electronics industry.

MADE IN POLAND AND EXPORT
PRODUCT STEREOTYPES

In these next two case studies, I discuss how the stereotypes connected with the country of origin (COO) played an important role in the evaluation of electric appliances by consumers and how intermediary actors attempted to strengthen or reevaluate them. In this section, I analyze two distinctive COO stereotypes that were relevant to the most popular sources of electric goods available for Polish consumers: domestically made products and export goods (dobra eksportowe) that were occasionally available for domestic retail. Stereotypes about the place where an electric appliance was made were ascribed with a meaning that was related to the broader social imagery about the technical and societal differences between countries and geopolitical regions.

I argue that the way different societies are perceived and the perceptions that inform the knowledge about the manufacturing practices of different economic systems and cultures play an important role in how the quality of the product is estimated in the public discourse and by consumers. Thus, these cases investigate how representatives of manufacturers, experts, social critics, and consumers, when speaking about the COOs, situated both products and themselves on the global map of modernity in the 1970s and 1980s.

The COO is a conceptual framework extensively used in consumer research as one of the key components of knowledge about consumer goods, and it is a crucial extrinsic product cue in addition to the brand name.

Michael Chatallas, a marketing studies scholar who publishes extensively on this topic, notes that the stereotype associated with the COO refers to the information about the country where a product is made, which is usually operationalized and conveyed with the phrases "made in" and the country name.[53] As Chatallas argues in his PhD thesis, research shows that information about a product's country of origin activates a rich associative network of associations about the origin nation, its culture, and its people's perceived traits.[54] Similarly, Celia Lury, while discussing the "brand as a place" category, emphasizes that the country of origin can play a role similar to notions of brand in how a consumer evaluates a product.[55]

In contemporary consumer research, the COO framework is regularly used to explain positive and negative attitudes toward industrial goods, which are manufactured and distributed through global commodity chains. In this case study, I show how this framework can be particularly useful for studying the evaluation of electric goods. Ingrid M. Martin, and Sevgin Eroglu argue that knowledge about political, economic, and technological dimensions ("the level of industrialization" and "the level of technological research") of the COO significantly contributes to the consumers' evaluation of the quality of a product.[56] Chatallas elaborates that the stereotypes associated with the COO are particularly important for building estimations of technologically complex durable goods:

> Country of origin information may be more important for a durable product with more complex features (e.g., television sets) than a common non-durable product with simpler features (e.g., shirts).[57] Specifically, the magnitude of the country of origin effect was found to be larger for technically complex products, fashion-oriented products, and expensive products than those for products that are low in technical complexity, inexpensive, or not fashion-oriented.[58]

If we connect this framework to Appadurai, we may view the stereotypes associated with the COO as a consumer's estimation of "the knowledge (technical, social, aesthetic, and so forth) that goes into the production of the commodity." which has "technical, mythological, and evaluative components."[59] Here, I particularly focus on the notions of technical ingenuity and prowess that went into the process of manufacturing, the innovativeness of the product, and its design, and aesthetics.

Understanding the process of evaluating stereotypes associated with the COO that are related to electric goods that require complex technological knowledge helps us to grasp the everyday meanings of the global race for technological modernity in the 1970s and 1980s, as well as the early 1990s. As I will show, the political and economic boundaries of the late Cold War and the lowering of these barriers shortly after the year 1989 strengthened the role of the COO as an important criterion in product evaluation. Appadurai points out that one of the most significant elements of the social life of commodities is the "peculiarities of knowledge that accompany relatively complex, long distance, intercultural flows of commodities."[60] These case studies show how the production and sharing of these "peculiarities of knowledge" are connected with the symbolic meanings that social actors ascribe to commodities.

The emergence of the stereotypes associated with the COO was stimulated by both the physical availability of products on the local market and the flow of information about how they are produced. Here it is necessary to note an important specificity about Polish consumer culture in the context of the Eastern Bloc. David Crowley, while writing about the Thaw, notes that a specific feature of Poland at that time was that the availability of consumer products increased at a slow rate while knowledge about the possibilities of consumption expanded significantly due to the circulation of images of consumption and the existence of goods elsewhere.[61] Similarly, as I showed in previous chapters, beginning in the early 1980s, while access to foreign products was limited, the Polish media provided extensive information about the manufacturing of electric goods elsewhere.

The most important way to categorize consumer products on the basis of knowledge about their origin was the phrase "made in the West." While discussing the "brand as a place" category, Lury discusses the example of "the West" as such a category.[62] Fehérváry outlines the meanings of the West as a brand and shows how the inhabitants of Central Europe used "made in the West" products to construct their everyday mythologies.

Emblematic goods of state-socialist production as well as their settings came to be seen as evidence of the failure of a state-socialist-generated modernity, but more importantly, of the regime's negligent and even "inhumane" treatment of its subjects.

In contrast, select commodities imported from the West (including socialist goods produced solely for export) were encountered as prized valuables and icons of a different world. The properties of these goods—designed, it seemed, to make life easier and more pleasurable—were not just evidence of a better production system but served as icons of a more humane political and economic system, a place where living a "normal" life was possible.[63]

The cultural impact of the imaginary West on the commodity culture of the Eastern Bloc both before and after 1989 has been extensively discussed in studies on postwar material culture in the Eastern Bloc. Here, I intend to enrich the scholarship by investigating the public perception of two categories of domestically made products and how they were compared with Western electric goods.

MADE IN POLAND

Until the 1970s, most of the electric appliances available in Polish retail trade were manufactured domestically. These products were generally referred to as "produkt krajowy," or a domestically made product, which can be viewed as a sort of COO stereotype. The only exceptions were small quantities of appliances imported from the Soviet Union and to a lesser extent products from other COMECON countries. From the 1970s in media texts, we can find regular acknowledgments that there were shortages of domestically made industrial goods, and that the products that were available were of low quality and were crudely designed. Such admissions were embedded in a staged debate on the politics of consumption as well as in the narrative on the ongoing process of modernization of the Polish electric goods industry.

We can see such a narrative in the television series *Dyrektorzy* (*The Directors*), one of the most popular television series of the 1970s, which was set at Fabel, a fictional large state enterprise that manufactures industrial goods.[64] This show was an attempt to soften the image of the *nomenklatura* cadre of directors through their fictional depiction. *Dyrektorzy* was an equivalent of the Socialist Realism "production novel" which embodied a set of propaganda messages from Gierek's era. Two episodes of the series show the ongoing modernization of the manufacturing of washing machines, one of Fabel's main products. In Episode Four, one of the state enterprise managers admits to the current problems with manufacturing by using the phrase "poor quality and modernity of products" ("niska jakość i nowoczesność wyrobów"), which was a part of the normalized vocabulary regularly used in the staged debate about consumption.[65] The next episode shows the implementation of a reform that sought to improve the quality of products and to "start manufacturing products of world standard" ("rozpoczęcie produkcji wyrobów światowej jakości"), another excerpt from the pages of *Trybuna Ludu* and *Życie Gospodarcze*.[66] Similar remarks about the poor quality and modernity of domestic products can be found in dozens of state media sources from the 1970s and 1980s. We can read such phrases as a highly normalized element of political communications and as a discursive strategy of governmental agencies that sought to communicate their devotion to increasing the quality of domestically made products.

As Mazurek and Hilton show, the rise of the consumer movement in the 1980s significantly opened up new possibilities for articulating opinions about and evaluations of domestically made products.[67] In *Veto* as well as *Polityka*, *Życie Gospodarcze*, and *Przegląd Techniczny*, we can find regular explicit opinions on the poor organization of the manufacturing processes of state enterprises, the lack of a positive work ethic, and quality control, as well as the low quality of the materials and parts that were provided by domestic subcontractors (cf. chapter 3). These voices are consistent with the consumer movement campaigns for structural changes in the system of manufacturing consumer goods, particularly the introduction of efficient quality control.

At the same time, Poles became extensively exposed to products that had been imported from the West. Both through private import and Pewex hard currency stores, these Western products significantly contributed to the shaping of hierarchies between domestic and foreign products and the strengthening of consumer's conviction that domestic products were inferior. This apparent difference in the evaluation of domestic and Western products was so obvious that such products were incomparable. In media texts from this time, I was unable to find any direct comparisons between both the utilitarian and hedonistic elements of the evaluation of domestic and Western products. It is worth emphasizing that before 1989, *Veto* and the KGD, who regularly carried out tests of consumer products, mostly only compared Polish products. The exception was for a few products made in the COMECON area, which were available from the state-owned retail trade. In the press articles from before 1989, I have not found any tests in which Polish products were directly compared with appliances that were available in Pewex shops or Western products from private import. They simply belonged to two different cultural categories and were in completely different price ranges. For this reason, no one even tried to directly compare their design and qualities in a consumer test.

Only after 1989 did domestic products start to be routinely compared with imported appliances in consumer tests. Analysis of these comparisons show an important reconfiguration of the Polish consumption mediation junction. Shortly after 1989, the consumer movement attempted to encourage Polish manufacturers to pay attention to the design and quality of their products by pointing out the most notorious flaws of Polish products, but the authors of these texts avoided identifying any specific manufacturer, instead referring to a general category of "product krajowy." For instance, I can quote a typical comparison between foreign and Polish household appliances in a report about market trends from *Veto* published in 1991:

> Several appliances made by Western companies have arrived in our market. [author lists manufacturers such as Moulinex, Bosch, Philips, Hoover, Candy, Ocean, Zanussi, and Eurotech]. Their products work noiselessly. All components fit together. They are not corroded by rust. The plastic doesn't stink, as it frequently occurs in Polish refrigerators and deep freezers.[68]

At the same time, the columnists of *Veto* regularly appraised specific state enterprises that managed to design and manufacture new products that could compete with imported appliances. The aforementioned complaints, primarily referred to the general category of "product krajowy," but appraisals indicated the name of a manufacturer, who underwent a transformation and managed to establish a new relationship with consumers. In these narratives, the products of a company that underwent a successful transformation stand out and are distinct from the general category of "product krajowy." Here is an instance of such a narrative from a note from the Poznań Autumn Fair in 1991 with an appraisal of Zelmer:

> Electronics manufacturers from the Far East don't give any chances to Polish manufacturers. The relationship between the price and quality of their products is unrivaled. However, some of our manufacturers, for instance, Zelmer, . . . don't have to be ashamed since they showed products on the world's level.[69]

In the early 1990s, market researchers identified consumers' distrust of the quality of domestically made technologically complex products, particularly electric goods and cars, compared with the trust in foreign products as one of the most distinctive differences in evaluations of domestic and foreign products.[70] Polish sociologist, Anna Giza Poleszczuk, who in the early 1990s pioneered market research states that: "When we conducted our research, we came up with the conclusion that the more 'technological' category of product, then—according to consumers' opinions—this category requires more *know-how*, quality control, etc., and their Western brands performed much better than domestic ones."[71]

After 1989, the nature of the Polish consumer was redefined by the intermediary actors, evolving from a passive beneficiary of the state distribution system into an active market actor who could determine if Polish electric appliance manufacturers were to flourish or disappear by making deliberate choices between competing domestic and foreign technologies. This sovereign consumer became a recipient of an orchestrated campaign that sought to change their beliefs about the quality of domestic products.

This campaign was supported by a host of governmental and nongovernmental organizations as well as the mass media. There were many proposals for more or less drastic means of limiting the massive flow of commodities to Poland, but due to the *laissez-faire* policy of the decision-makers, the only active measure to help Polish manufacturers to compete on the market was an active long-term campaign of nation branding.[72] This nation branding is carried out under the auspices of the "Teraz Polska" ("Poland Now") campaign, and it continues to this day. The official history of the "Teraz Polska" concept shows how nation branding is embedded in the narrative of the successful transition to a postsocialist system:

The Foundation for the Polish Promotional Logo (Fundacja Polskiego Godła Promocyjnego) dates back to the year 1991, which is the beginning of the system transformation and the rise of the free market in Poland. The opening of borders to imported products enabled society to get to know the new possibilities of consumption. At the same time domestic manufacturers, due to investments in new technologies, started to manufacture products that could compete with counterparts available in Western Europe. Then the initiative of the Polish Promotional Program [Polski Program Promocyjny] appeared. The idea of this program was to promote Polish companies and support them in terms of marketing in the increasingly competitive market.[73]

The story of the "Teraz Polska" campaign, which was organized by an NGO with the support of governmental agencies, shows how the national branding campaign was perceived as providing substantial assistance to enterprises so that they could successfully pass through the most difficult stage of the post-socialist transition. This campaign offered help to Polish manufacturers that showed their willingness to start competing in the new economic environment. By awarding specific companies that passed the selection process with the "Teraz Polska" seal of approval, the foundation helped them to generate symbolic capital that could boost sales.

The mass media enthusiastically supported the "Teraz Polska" campaign by providing regular coverage about which manufacturers were nominated for the certificate and by publishing success stories about those who obtained the "Teraz Polska" certificate. Among them were Polar (see chapter 5), Zelmer, and WZT (rebranded as Elemis). Furthermore, all three manufacturers extensively used the "Teraz Polska" logo in their advertising campaigns.

The positive shift in consumer attitudes to "made in Poland" products in the middle of the decade were welcomed by the mass media as a positive change, as this was seen as the next stage in the successful transition of the system. However, these attitudinal changes were most pronounced in the FMCG market. As a survey from 1995 shows, while Poles preferred domestically produced groceries, soap, clothing, shoes, cigarettes, and alcohol over Western products, they still preferred Western consumer electronics (41 percent) over domestic products (28 percent).[74]

Before 1989, a host of intermediary actors who spoke about the poor quality of domestically made products spoke on behalf of nonsovereign consumers. They attempted to influence the practices of the producers toward the manufacturing and distribution of their products. After 1989, these actors realigned their position and started focusing on the high quality of domestic products on behalf of Polish manufacturers in order to influence sovereign consumers to make a specific choice between competing technologies. For example, here is a quote from *Przegląd Techniczny* from 1992. Its title, "Let's promote Polish products!" clearly shows the author's agenda of supporting domestic manufacturers: "There is no lack of domestically made products on our market, which are equally good and sometimes even better and cheaper than foreign products which lure with color packaging and persistent advertisement."[75]

Here, the claim about the "persistent advertisement" used by foreign manufacturers provides another clue to understanding the specificity of the "made in Poland" nation branding. The "persistent advertising" refers to the massive use of localized global television commercials, full-page color adverts, which were a normalized standard, and large neon billboards in the city centers of Polish cities. By contrast, Polish manufacturers in the early 1990s used informative adverts and lengthy advertorials which covered in detail both the successful restructuring of a manufacturer and provided extensive technical data about its products.[76]

Furthermore, the author states that the high quality of Polish technologically complex consumer goods was primarily achieved through the introduction of meticulous quality control systems, and thus manufacturers were eliminating poor quality products. She also provided two instances of imported products that were unsafe. The first was an unnamed VCR that combusted due to a short circuit. The second was an imported television set, which had not passed the interference test, from which a viewer could also hear short-wave radio conversations. She warned that buying Western products was a pig in a poke.

It is important to note the different outcomes for the Polish manufacturers of white and brown goods. The successes of both Zelmer and Polar, two major manufacturers of household appliances, and the demise of consumer electronics manufacturers in the 1990s such as Diora, ZRK, and Elemis tell us something about the shifts in Polish consumer culture. The most important features required by consumers of household appliances are utilitarian values, ergonomics, and durability, and the Polish manufacturers of these products were able to convince consumers that they, with their resources and knowledge base, were capable of designing and producing products with these features. In contrast, the Polish manufacturers of consumer electronics could not compete with Western potentates, who have vast R&D budgets for commercializing technological innovation, who benefit from the economies of scale, and who could ascribe hedonistic values into their products with substantial marketing and advertising budgets.

The changing attitudes of intermediary actors toward domestic products were one of the most significant elements of the reconfiguration of the consumer mediation junction after the year 1989, but when a host of intermediary actors attempted to convince Polish consumers to buy Polish products, the meaning of this term became more elusive in the context of the emergence of hybrid products, particularly on the consumer electronics market. In the 1990s, Polish electronics manufacturers, whose representatives took part in public debates and argued for the support of "Polish electronics," were often only assembling products from imported components.

This was particularly visible in the advertising of Polish television sets. The adverts for both Elemis and Unimor from the early 1990s included claims that these products were made from high-quality imported components. For instance, Elemis advertised its products with the sales pitch, "Modern television set built with components from the best world's companies: Toshiba, Philips, Siemens."[77] This advert summarizes the demise of the category "made in Poland" consumer electronics, as they were replaced by hybrid products assembled in Poland.

"EXPORT REJECTS"

As Fehérváry notes in her quoted remark, in the opinion of state socialist consumers, domestically made goods produced solely for export had more in common with commodities imported from the West than local products made for the domestic market.[78] This was particularly the case for "wersja eksportowa," or export version electric appliances that constituted a special category of highly prized consumer goods. In this section, I will investigate how the expansion of trade across the Iron Curtain by Polish manufacturers and trade organizations influenced the local consumer culture. I will focus on a category of electric appliances that were made for export but were actually distributed by the domestic retail trade after being classed as an "odrzut eksportowy," or export reject.

An export version of an electric appliance became an "odrzut eksportowy," when it did not pass internal quality control due to some minor flaws. We may say that the cultural meaning of an "odrzut eksportowy" was drawn not from the country-of-origin stereotypes but rather from stereotypes about the "country of destination." An evaluation of the quality of "odrzut eksportowy," can be described as, to quote Apparadai, a form of knowledge that accompanies "relatively complex, long distance, intercultural flows of commodities."[79] Products for export were intended to undergo such an intercultural flow, but instead they made only a short journey to a domestic retail store.

The high evaluation of the quality of any product, which had the halo of an export version, came from the understanding that both central planners and manufacturers, who badly needed hard currency, would pay closer attention to the quality of products that were to be sent in the "intercultural flow" to the Second Currency Region (Drugi obszar płatniczy), which included both the West and the Third World. While business partners from these places paid with convertible currencies, partners from the First Currency Region (Pierwszy obszar płatniczy), that is the COMECON area, were obliged to make payments in transfer rubles, a virtual currency developed by Soviet economists more than fifty years before the introduction of Bitcoin. It is worth noting that even export goods that were supposed to go to the COMECON region were considered superior to domestic products. However, customers had the highest regard for products that were waiting for a real "intercultural flow" into the Second Currency Region but for some reason did not manage to arrive there.

Marketing science scholar Robert King in his study of Polish marketing practices notes that in the 1970s, when decision-makers introduced the policy of extensive license purchases and several Polish manufacturers became OEMs for Western companies, export sales became an important part of the total sales of the enterprise for some product lines such as automobiles and refrigerators.[80] This increase in the international marketing activity of Polish manufacturers created the need for additional marketing research. The requirements to market their products and to pay attention to the quality of products was a challenge for industrial managers. Porter-Szűcs notes problems that they had to face:

> Industrial managers in the PRL had not previously needed to worry much about pleasing customers, and almost no one in Poland had any experience in marketing or sales. Polish products that were sold abroad had a notorious reputation for shoddy workmanship, and an unsustainably high percentage were returned because of defects. This wasn't because Polish workers were incompetent, but because they lived within an economic order that systematically de-emphasized consumer satisfaction. This became a major problem when the "consumer" was a foreign firm buying industrial goods.[81]

The regular cooperation of Polish manufacturers as OEMs with several Western companies such as Grundig, Telefunken, Sanyo, Philips, and Thomson, however, suggests that they were satisfied with the quality of the products. During my research, I found a glossy trade catalog of Diora export products that was published in 1980 by the UNITRA Foreign Trade branch, the one responsible for foreign trade contacts, with texts in both English and French.[82] The high quality of the catalog seems comparable with its Western counterparts. While I don't have the technical expertise to comprehensively compare the nuances of design and technical parameters of stacking systems from the 1970s, my browsing of an extensive collection of similar trade catalogs of sound systems from the extensive HiFi Archiv online database clearly shows that UNITRA was capable of making a "world-class" trade catalog.[83] Unfortunately, the broader pattern of establishing trade contacts between Western and Eastern business partners and its impact on the work culture in state socialist industries is still overlooked in the scholarship.

As a part of the mediation junction, journalists regularly quoted official data about the rise of production output but also regularly noted that this increase was linked with a rise of "produkcja eksportowa." For instance, a report on recent developments in the Polish consumer electronics industry from 1988 noted that: "The Polish electronics industry [is going to] increase the production output for the domestic market and export. Despite difficulties in supplies in 1987 [the production output of consumer electronics], the domestic market has increased by 5 percent and export to the Second Currency Region by 19,6 percent."[84]

Media stories with claims about large shipments of electric goods for export were framed by a specific narrative of modernization to explain why products that were in high demand were being sent abroad instead of being sold by the domestic retail trade. According to this narrative, in order to be able to modernize their products by introducing new technologies of production, which required the purchasing of machinery, components, or materials in the West, the Polish manufactures required hard currency known as "wsad dewizowy," or hard currency investment.

A columnist for *Życie Gospodarcze*, while writing a report about the slow demise of Fonica, the main manufacturer of record players, and the feeling of idleness among the staff during the system transition, quoted an employee who remembered manufacturing export versions of record players as an instance of "special production," when the enterprise had many orders from abroad:

> We were making the Telefunkens [that is record players for Telefunken made as an OEM] for 12 hours on a 12-hour shift. The foreman was standing behind our backs and hastening us and the truck was already waiting outside for our products. The same story was with record players for Novosibirsk and the same with manufacturing for the military. The assembly line was moving on in 27-second intervals. One could not have any breaks.[85]

We may assume that the foreman not only hastened workers but also, as other sources about the production of "wersja eksportowa" suggest, paid much more attention to the quality of the "special production."

In media sources, which quoted representatives of manufacturers who admitted that part of their production was exported, one can hardly find any claims about differences between the products made for the domestic market and those made for export. In order to be able to distinguish between the domestic and export versions, specific information about the technical differences between both versions was shared between customers when they were choosing electric goods. To obtain an export product from the retail trade required both knowing when this product would be available in a retail store and more informal knowledge from an office clerk or someone working in transportation or the wholesale trade to be able to distinguish the export version from the ordinary domestic product. This knowledge might be the information that a shipment that was being delivered to a retail store on a specific day would include some "odrzut eksportowy." The second was information about particular design features since the export goods were mostly indistinguishable from ordinary versions at first sight.

Generally, this kind of information could not be found in the press. However, in a 1987 article in *Pan*, a Polish version of *Playboy*, a magazine columnist who regularly wrote about the consumer electronics market provided detailed information about specific meanings of alphanumeric codes on Tonsil products, which he obtained from Tonsil representatives. One of these codes provided by the author indicated that this particular shipment of loudspeakers was part of a batch that Tonsil had made for Sanyo as an OEM, which for an unspecified reason would be instead delivered to the domestic retail trade.[86] Thus, plausible knowledge about the availability of an export version of the loudspeakers came through a semiofficial channel, but this type of communications was rare.

In the 1980s, the other way that export goods appeared on the domestic market was through *giełdy,* an informal bazaar, where it was regularly claimed that the appliances that were being sold were the export versions. It was a popular sales pitch since the potential buyer was probably not knowledgeable enough to verify this claim. A commentator in *Veto* in the "Na giełdach" section noted the practice he observed while visiting a popular *giełda* in Rembertów, on the outskirts of Warsaw: "Everything which is offered here is sold like commodities of foreign origin, even domestic products (vacuum cleaners, food processors, and coffee grinders) are sold as an export reject (at least they are recommended as such) and they are offered for such prices as if they had arrived from a far distance."[87]

In the context of the practices of traders from *giełdy*, the informal nature of knowledge about distinguishing domestic and export versions was used as an element of bargaining in the bazaar economy. As the export version of an appliance could not be easily distinguished from a domestic product by a cursory examination, an asymmetry of knowledge resulted between the bazaar trader and the consumer.[88]

The end of state socialism resulted in the instant demise of the "odrzut eksportowy" category, as these products no longer had any place in the buyer's market. However, after 1989, Polish manufacturers frequently used the fact that they export their products in advertising as a suggestion that their products were in high demand among the picky consumers of highly developed countries. For instance, a promotional text about Zelmer vacuum cleaners in *Veto* from 1992 listed countries where Zelmer exported its products: Germany, France, the Netherlands, Sweden, Italy, and Belgium.[89] Such claims were situated within a broader narrative of a corporate history of a state enterprise that had undergone a successful reconfiguration after 1989 and that was now capable of making "world-class" products desired by demanding consumers in highly developed countries.

Information about the practice of producing separate export versions of a different quality after 1989 was the subject of a different narrative about those manufacturers who were not willing to change their attitude. In a lengthy report from 1991 about the marketing of kitchen appliances, a *Veto* commentator, who praised Zelmer as a manufacturer who makes products of the same high quality for both domestic and foreign markets, condemned the attitude of Polar: "Products [made by Polar] for export are still made much more carefully than products for the domestic market. The disrespect for the Polish consumer is a sin of several of our manufacturers. It is no surprise that they are losing out to foreign competitors. After all, we already know what good appliances should look like."[90] This critical article shows how differences in the quality of the products made for domestic consumption and foreign markets was identified as a practice that was simply not acceptable by the consumers in the context of the emerging buyer's market, and that it was one of the leftovers of the work culture from the state-socialist era.

"RADMOR 5102 RADMOR 5100 UNITRA #TOP 10 BEST #VINTAGE"

The last section of this chapter is dedicated to the contemporary practices of reproduction, strengthening, and negotiating the sociotechnical imagery of the qualities of Polish audio electronics made under late state socialism by UNITRA enterprises, particularly by Diora and Radmor. Here, I demonstrate how the notion of the modernity of the Polish electronics industry from the 1970s is embedded in the cultural memory of late state socialist Poland. Moreover, the imagery of the perceived high quality and modernity of products released by UNITRA enterprises has been used to construct a nostalgia-fueled imaginary alternative modernity in which the Polish high-tech industry played a central role.

I argue that this process of constructing cultural memory related to some technological artifacts from the past is a way of coping with the bitterness of the memory of the transition to the postsocialist system and the imposition of the market economy that resulted in the demise of virtually all Polish electronics manufacturers. While Polar, the main manufacturer of refrigerators and washing machines, was acquired by Whirlpool, a global potentate in the home appliances industry, Diora, ZRK, and Polkolor went into bankruptcy in the 1990s after unsuccessful attempts to compete with imported audio electronics.

This section is based on an analysis of several internet sources that share and reproduce the imagery of an alternative modernity performed through narratives of the past and present social lives of products from the UNITRA association. Moreover, UNITRA is used here as a cultural symbol of such imagery. The title of this section came from a contemporary YouTube video, in which a vintage audio collector, as the title suggests, demonstrates the qualities of Radmor amplifiers and praises these products as "Top 10 Best Vintage audios."[91] The hashtags included in the title "#Top 10 Best #Vintage" correspond with the language forms used in contemporary internet-based materials that commemorate the qualities of some practices and objects from the past by using the phrase "vintage."

I refer to the work by fashion studies scholar Heike Jenss on the practices of mediating cultural memory with the practice of using vintage clothing.[92] As she notes, her agenda is to understand "how clothing of the 1960s is used, refashioned and forms a material part of practices and processes of identification and social relationships in the context of youth culture."[93] While answering this question, she investigates "the performance of vintage style, and their framing through perspectives and theories on the dynamics, mediation and experience of cultural memory, modernity and the temporalities of fashion."[94] Due to the specificity of the technological culture related to consumer electronics here, I do not refer to the body of work on post-socialist nostalgia but rather introduce only literature that offers an extensive outline of other relevant work on this subject.[95] In papers about postcommunist nostalgia, there is a knowledge gap in the theoretically informed studies on the contemporary uses of state socialist era technologies.[96]

Thus, I focus on exploring the "performance of vintage style" in relation to Polish audio electronics from the 1970s and to a lesser extent from the 1980s. The use of vintage audio electronics and the construction of cultural memories from the past are some of the tendencies of the audiophile culture. This trend can be illustrated not only with the practices of documenting vintage products through databases but also by their popularity and the prices of selected products.[97] The popularity of alternative modernities in this culture can be illustrated by the shared assumption that some past technologies offer better fidelity than contemporary products, particularly vacuum tubes that were replaced by transistors and vinyl records that were replaced by compact discs.

The introduction to the exhibition catalog on the history of Radmor, which I discussed earlier in the section on industrial design, is an exemplar of the cultural logic of the nostalgia of the 1970s, which is identified in the discourse as a successful period of technological innovation, product quality, and industrial design. This can be seen in the short introduction to the exhibition catalog by Wojciech Szczurek, the mayor of Gdynia:

> One of the largest and most innovative Polish companies which set new standards in Europe was established here—on the seaside, in Gdynia. Radmor's devices—radiotelephones, echo sounders, maneuver stations, military radio stations or popular hi-fi equipment made Polish engineering ideas famous far beyond our country's borders. Radmor's products are renowned and competitive not only on today's consumer market but also on the demanding and unique military products' market I do hope you will accept the invitation to this sentimental journey and the exploration of Polish engineering solutions' heritage which Gdynia is very proud of. The exhibition will probably be especially popular with those who have their own musical memories connected with the then luxurious Radmor 5100 Stereo HiFi Quasi Quadro radio and its successors. And there are many of such people among us.[98]

This remark also mentions the possible visitors to the exhibition, the generation of people who had some personal experience with the OR 5100 in their youth. As Piotr Metz notes: "I dreamt of the ICF Sony series—6800 is still my pride. I could never afford the 320. But a Radmor 5100 extension—the AM tuner (which sounds way better than medium frequency) is still very impressive today."[99]

These quotes demonstrate some of the central themes of the cultural memory of UNITRA audio electronics, their relative modernity for the 1970s, their competitiveness in comparison even with the products of the Western electronics potentates, and the recognition of good industrial design. The central site for expressing and sharing such memories is the "UNITRA-Klub" website, which includes an extensive database of the products released by major state enterprises and a thriving online trade platform with UNITRA products that are offered at rather high prices, particularly Radmor products. It also has a forum for sharing opinions and know-how.[100]

My research about the forum shows that the most frequent discussion topic is the serious and sometimes everyday contemporary use of UNITRA electronics according to the original purpose. Forum members carefully preserve, repair, and overhaul their precious possessions to use them in their original function: to listen to radio broadcasts and listen to music. The latter practice is rather limited due to the lack of recorded music and the problems with the reliability of stored music on magnetic media.

On the other hand, some technologically skilled users managed to use UNITRA products as an element of contemporary home cinema systems. The milieu of UNITRA products fans and their practices closely resembles the milieu of TRS-80 computer users, as they are users of products of manufacturers which are long gone. These fans all play roles mentioned by Lindsay: designers, producers, marketers, distributors, and technical support.[101] The practice of using vintage radio receivers and record players in the contemporary media world closely corresponds with the practices of using vintage clothing to "recollect" a selected period around which the community builds some form of nostalgia. As Jenss notes, these intersections play out in everyday dress and consumption practices—focusing in on youth and young adults, who through clothing and style recollect "the sixties" in the early twenty-first century.[102]

An analysis of the UNITRA-Klub website and several other internet websites and Facebook groups also shows the centrality of the age issue. There are two age groups, an older generation, those who previously had these products, usually in their adolescence or early adulthood, but also a new generation of younger users whose experience of UNITRA products is as vintage for the first time, with no "original" experience. Jenss explains the construction of the reversal of "newness" as a significant form of shaping identity: "The use and valuing of second-hand clothing as vintage, a kind of reversal of the idea of 'newness' in fashion by dressing in outmoded clothes, has been particularly popular among youth, raising questions with regard to the intersections of fashion, time, age/generation and cultural memory."[103]

Another remark by Jenss demonstrates the cultural logic of using vintage material culture artifacts to celebrate a vision of a specific era bounded by the notion of modernity:

As part of a youth cultural scene that bridges past and present, contemporary sixties enthusiasts form a particularly interesting case study for an exploration of vintage style and cultural memory. They are remembering a decade intricately bound up with ideas of modernity and the expansion of fashion and consumer culture. By immersing themselves into the fashion and music of the 1960s, hunting for old clothes, and modeling themselves on past styles as closely as possible, "the sixties" are not a distant, even though they were not even born in the time they now recall with their bodies.[104]

A unique way to commemorate this vision of Polish modernity from the late state socialism was an attempt to revive UNITRA as a brand. In 2014, a group of entrepreneurs bought the rights to the UNITRA name and logo from another privately owned company that had acquired it in the 1990s, and they released a series of headphones under this old/new brand. Most of these headphones were stylized to look like original Polish products from the 1970s and 1980s. This attempt received large media coverage but as journalists pointed out, these were headphones made in China.[105]

It is necessary to explain that at the time, Tonsil, the original manufacturer of headphones and loudspeakers, was still active as one of the very few remaining Polish consumer electronics manufacturers from the state socialist era. One of the journalists noted that there was some tension between Tonsil managers and the new UNITRA since the latter company tried to make copies of the original Tonsil products, in China, while Tonsil still continued its production in Poland. As noted at the time, the core elements of the tension were "polskość," or the Polishness and the authenticity of the products.[106]

NOTES

1. Brey, "Theorizing Modernity," 35.

2. Jutta Scherrer, "'To catch up and overtake' the West: Soviet discourse on socialist competition," in *Competition in Socialist Society*, ed. Katalin Miklóssy and Melanie Ilic (London and New York: Routledge, 2014), 10–22 here 19.

3. Wasiak, "VCRs, Modernity"; Wasiak, "The production of High Fidelity"; Wasiak and Švelch, "Designing educational."

4. Hebdige, "Object as Image," 102.

5. Hebdige, "Object as Image," 102.

6. Hebdige, "Object as Image," 102.

7. Jackie Clarke, "Work, Consumption and Subjectivity in Postwar France: Moulinex and the Meanings of Domestic Appliances 1950s–70s," *Journal of Contemporary History* 47, no. 4 (October 2012): 838–59, here 840. Cf. also Jackie Clarke, "Closing Moulinex: thoughts on the visibility and invisibility of industrial labour in contemporary France," *Modern and Contemporary France* 19, no. 4. 2011: 443–58.

8. Clarke, "Work, Consumption," 844.

9. Małgorzata Mazurek, *Socjalistyczny zakład pracy. Porównanie fabrycznej codzienności w PRL i NRD u progu lat sześćdziesiątych* (Warszawa: Wydawnictwo Trio 2005); Malgorzata Fidelis, *Women, Communism, and Industrialization in Postwar Poland* (Cambridge: Cambridge University Press, 2010).

10. Elizabeth C. Dunn, *Privatizing Poland: Baby Food, Big Business, and the Remaking of Labour* (Ithaca and London: Cornell University Press, 2004).

11. Danuta Mąkowa, "Polar ze znakim Q," *Magazyn Rodzinny*, Issue 6, 1975, 47–50; Danuta Mąkowa, "Zelmer 03," 19–20; Danuta Mąkowa, "MK Magnetofony Kasprzaka," *Magazyn Rodzinny*, Issue 3, 1974, 19–21.

12. Cf. Clarke, "Closing Moulinex."

13. *30-lecie Zelos*; Władysław Połeć, Mieczysław Wierzbiński, and Henryk Pawelec, eds., *Zakłady Elektromaszynowe EDA w Poniatowej* (Poniatowa: Zakłady Elektro-Maszynowe Eda, 1969).

14. A similar narrative can be found in a unique source, an amateur documentary movie by the moviemaking club affiliated with the cultural centre in Poniatowa: *25 lat Edy (1949–1974). Poniatowa w XXX-lecie PRL*, dir. Bolesław Nowak, AKFF "Foka" w Poniatowej, 1974, https://www.youtube.com/watch?v=Of1TOYaacC4.

15. *30-lecie Zelos,* 6.

16. Clarke, "Work, Consumption," 848.

17. Becky Conekin, "'Here Is the Modern World Itself.' The Festival of Britain's Representations of the Future," in *The Design History Reader*, ed. Grace Lees-Maffel and Rebecca Houze (Oxford and New York: BERG, 2010): 143–51, here 145. Originally published as: Becky Conekin, "'Here Is the Modern World Itself,'" the Festival of Britain's Representations of the Future," in *Moments of Modernity: Reconstructing Britain 1945–1964*, ed. Becky Conekin, F. Mort, and C. Waters (London and New York: Rivers Oram Press, 1999): 228–46.

18. Conekin, "'Here Is The Modern," 146.

19. Susan E. Reid and David Crowley, eds., *Style and Socialism: Modernity and Material Culture in Post-War Eastern Europe* (Oxford: Berg, 2000); David Crowley, "People's Warsaw/Popular Warsaw," Journal of Design History 10, no. 2, 1997: 203–23; Victor Buchli, "Khrushchev, Modernism, and the Fight against *'Petit-bourgeois'* Consciousness in the Soviet Home," *Journal of Design History* 10, no. 2 (1997): 161–76; Susan Reid, "This is Tomorrow!" Becoming a Consumer in the Soviet Sixties," in *The Socialist Sixties: Crossing Borders in the Second World,* ed. Anne Gorsuch and Diane Koenker (Bloomington: Indiana University Press, 2013), 25–65.

20. Cf. the section on the history of design in Russia in Bernhard E. Bürdek, *Design. History, Theory and Practice of Product Design* (Basel, Boston, and Berlin: Birkhäuser, 2005), 172–75, here 172.

21. Eli Rubin, "The Trabant: Consumption, Eigen-Sinn, and Movement," History Workshop Journal 68, no. 1 (Autumn 2009): 27–44; Stokes, *Constructing.*

22. Regina Lee Blaszczyk, *The Color Revolution* (Cambridge and London: MIT Press, 2012).

23. Danuta Mąkowa, "Zelmer 03," 19–20.

24. Mąkowa, "Zelmer 03," 20.

25. Danuta Mąkowa, "Wielkie pranie w automacie," *Magazyn Rodzinny*, Issue 4, 1975, 47–49, here 48.

26. Ewa Miłoszewska, "Ocena jakości sprzętu zmechanizowanego," *Gospodarstwo Domowe*, Issue 4, 1978, 11–13, here 13.

27. Agnieszka Drączkowska, "Victorius and on a Roll," in *Legenda Radmoru/The Legend of Radmor*, ed. Agnieszka Drączkowska and Paweł Gełesz (Gdynia: Muzeum Miasta Gdyni, 2020): 24–27, here 25. This is a bilingual Polish/English catalogue. Here and later, I quote the English texts of the articles included in the catalog.

28. Zbigniew Faust, "Gramofon elektryczny WG 400 Mister Hit," *Radioamator*, Issue 6, 1972, 152.

29. Jerzy Waglewski, "Typ MOT-772 Lena," *Przegląd Techniczny*, June 1, 1980, 35.

30. Jerzy Auerbach, "Wzornictwo dyktatorem w elektronice powszechnego użytku," *Przegląd Techniczny*, November 20, 1977, 24–25.

31. Agnieszka Drączkowska and Paweł Gełesz, eds., *Legenda Radmoru/The Legend of Radmor* (Gdynia: Muzeum Miasta Gdyni, 2020).

32. For the description and detailed photograph of Radmor 5100, see: Drączkowska and Gełesz, *The Legend,* 152–53.

33. "Radmor 5102 Manual," 3–4.

34. Czesława Frejlich, "Radmor: Contribution to the Polish History of the Industrial Design," in Drączkowska and Gełesz, *The Legend*, 45–52, here 49.

35. Piotr Metz, "Radmor Forever," in Drączkowska and Gełesz, *The Legend*, 61–63, here 63.

36. Frejlich, "Radmor," 49–50. Quotation after: Agnieszka Wróblewska, "Osiem lat elektroniki," *Wiadomości Instytutu Wzornictwa Przemysłowego,* Issue 6, 1987, 15–16.

37. Law, *Aircraft Stories*, 8–9.

38. Jerzy Waglewski, "Potrzebny gromowładny Jowisz," *Przegląd Techniczny*, October 29, 1978, 8–10, here 8; Andrzej Kulik, "Początek drogi," *Przegląd Techniczny*, October 29, 1978, 11–13.

39. "Wojna w kolorze," *Przegląd Techniczny*, May 1, 1977, 38–39.

40. For a discussion on the role of television in the Eastern Bloc and its political and cultural significance, see: Paulina Bren, *The Greengrocer and His TV: The Culture of Communism after the 1968 Prague Spring* (Ithaca, NY: Cornell University Press, 2010); Ellen Mickiewicz, *Split Signals: Television and Politics in the Soviet Union* (New York and Oxford: Oxford University Press, 1988); Kristin Roth-Ey, "Finding a Home for Television in the USSR, 1950–1970," *Slavic Review* 66, no. 2 (Summer 2007): 278–306; Martin Štoll, *Television and Totalitarianism in Czechoslovakia: From the First Democratic Republic to the Fall of Communism* (New York et al.: Bloomsbury Academic, 2019).

41. Poznanski, *Poland's Protracted Transition,* 66–67.

42. *Radioamator*, Issue 12, 1971, 285.

43. Jerzy Auerbach, "Odbiornik telewizji kolorowej T5601," *Przegląd Techniczny*, September 10, 1978, 26–27.

44. *Radioamator*, Issue 7, 1974, 155.

45. Auerbach, "Odbiornik telewizji," 26.

46. Karol Mieczykowski, "TVC," 14–15.

47. Mieczykowski, "TVC," 14.

48. Mieczykowski, "TVC," 14.

49. Mieczykowski, "TVC," 14.

50. In *Przeglad Techniczny*, from 1983, we can find a story of a fire caused by Jowisz, seeking a warranty claim and covering the damages by the WZT: Donat Zatoński, "Niespodziewane skutki pożaru telewizora," *Przegląd Techniczny*, September 11, 1983, 20–21; Donat Zatoński, "Problemy pod wysokim napięciem," *Przegląd Techniczny*, December 11, 1983, 16–17.

51. Marek Hauszyld, "Potyczki z "JOWISZEM," *Veto*, January 16, 1983, 4.

52. Marek Hauszyld, "WZT podjęły rękawice," *Veto*, January 16, 1983, 4–5.

53. Michael J. Chattalas, Thomas Kramer, and Hirokazu Takada, "The impact of national stereotypes on the country-of-origin effect: A conceptual framework," *International Marketing Review* 25:1 (2008): 54–74, here 55. For a comprehensive discussion on using COO stereotypes in the scholarship of consumer research, see: Michael J. Chattalas, *The Effects of National Stereotypes on Country of Origin–Based Product Evaluations*, PhD dissertation, City University of New York, 2005. See also: Durairaj Maheswaran, "Country of Origin as a Stereotype: Effects of Consumer Expertise and

Attribute Strength on Product Evaluations," *Journal of Consumer Research* 21, no. 2 (1994): 354–65. For an instance of using this framework as market research tool in the postsocialist Europe, see: Richard Ettenson, "Brand name and country of origin effects in the emerging market economies of Russia, Poland and Hungary," *International Marketing Review* 10, no. 5 (1993): 14–36. An interesting investigation in the origin of COO image in the age of industrial production can be found in Rolf Sachsse, "Made in Germany as image in photography and design," *Journal of Popular Culture* 34, no. 3 (Winter 2000): 43–58.

54. Chatallas, *The Effects*, 1.

55. Celia Lury, *Brands: The Logos of the Global Economy* (London and New York: Routledge, 2004), 16.

56. Ingrid M. Martin and Sevgin Eroglu, "Measuring a multi-dimensional construct: country image," *Journal of Business Research* 28, no 3 (1993): 191–210.

57. Chatallas, *The Effects*, 23.

58. Chatallas, *The Effects*, 24.

59. Appadurai, "Introduction," 41.

60. Appadurai, "Introduction," 41.

61. David Crowley, "Warsaw's Shops, Stalinism and the Thaw," in *Style and Socialism: Modernity and Material Culture in Post-War Eastern Europe*, ed. Susan E. Reid and David Crowley (Oxford: Berg, 2000), 25–47, here 41. See also discussion on this matter in: Fehérváry, "Goods and States," 433.

62. Lury, *Brands*, 16.

63. Fehérváry, "Goods and States," 429. Yurchak extensively discusses the meanings of the West in the popular discourse in the Soviet Union in several places in his book: Alexei Yurchak, *Everything Was Forever*. Cf. also: György Péteri, ed., *Imagining the West in Eastern Europe and the Soviet Union* (Pittsburgh: University of Pittsburgh Press, 2010).

64. *Dyrektorzy*, dir. Zbigniew Chmielewski, 1975.

65. *Dyrektorzy*, Episode 4.

66. *Dyrektorzy*, Episode 5.

67. Mazurek and Hilton, "Consumerism."

68. Bożena Zapaśnik, "Kuchenne szaleństwa," *Veto*, August 25, 1991, 5.

69. Irena Krzyżanowska, "Kuszenie biedaków," *Veto*, March 31, 1991, 5.

70. "Konsumenckie gusty," *Gazeta Bankowa*, October 10, 1993, 4.

71. "Polska po zniknięciu blondynek. Rozmowa z Anną Gizą-Poleszczuk," *Kultura Popularna* 14, no. 4 (2005): 105–8, here 108.

72. Chattalas et al., "The impact of national stereotypes," 68.

73. "Teraz Polska," http://www.terazpolska.pl/pl/Historia-Fundacji.

74. *Życie Gospodarcze* published the results of a survey on consumer preferences by Demoskop pollster company: Halina Frańczak, "Wolę polskie," *Życie Gospodarcze*, August 6, 1995, 30–31, here 30. The OBOP survey from 1994 includes research on the perception of the "Teraz Polska" campaign: OBOP, "Opinie konsumentów o towarach z Polski i zagranicy," Warszawa 1994.

75. Krystyna Panek, "Promujmy polskie wyroby!" *Przegląd Techniczny*, September 13, 1992, 6–7, here 6.

76. For instance, see Unimor advertorial: "Kolorowy świat z Unimoru," *Przegląd Techniczny*, August 1, 1993, appendix "High Tech," 4–5. It is understandable that advertorials placed in *Przegląd Techniczny* used vocabulary addressed to technically savvy readers, but we can find similar vocabulary in advertorials in titles which were addressed to different audiences; for instance, see Elemis advertorial in *Przekrój*: "Daleko od "Wisły," *Przekrój*, April 17, 1994, 9.

77. *Przegląd techniczny*, November 22, 1992, 27.

78. Fehérváry, "Goods and States," 429.

79. Appadurai, "Introduction," 41.

80. Robert L. King, "Enterprise-level marketing research activity in Poland: The predom/polar experience," *Academy of Marketing Science Journal* 11, no. 3 (Summer 1983): 292–303, here 293.

81. Porter-Szűcs, *Poland*, 280.

82. Unitra Diora/Unitra Przedsiębiorstwo Handlu Zagranicznego "Radio 80," place unknown, 1980(?), author's collection.

83. "HiFi Archiv," http://wegavision.pytalhost.com/.

84. Tadeusz Piechniewicz, "Czy sięgnie?" *Audio Video* 1, 1988, 1.

85. Irena Dryll, "Patefony strajkują," *Życie Gospodarcze*, July 14, 1991, 1.

86. Adam Jamiołkowski, "Słyszeć coraz więcej," *Pan*, November, 1987, 46–47, here 46.

87. *Veto*, April 23, 1989, 3.

88. Frank S. Fanselow, "The Bazaar Economy or How Bizarre is the Bazaar Really?" *Man, New Series* 25, no. 2 (June 1990): 250–65, here 251.

89. "Compacty z Rzeszowa," *Veto*, April 26, 1992, 11.

90. Zapaśnik, "Kuchenne szaleństwa," 5.

91. "Radmor 5102 Radmor 5100 UNITRA #Top 10 Best #Vintage tuner amplifier receiver Verstärker," YouTube video, added on April 1, 2018, https://www.youtube.com/watch?v=a1RNhhHFukA.

92. Heike Jenss, *Fashioning Memory. Vintage Style and Youth Culture* (London et al.: Bloomsbury, 2015).

93. Jenss, *Fashioning*, x.

94. Jenss, *Fashioning*, xi.

95. See: Maria Todorova, Zsuzsa Gille, eds., *Post-communist nostalgia* (New York and Oxford: Berghahn Books, 2010); Olga Shevchenko, "'In Case of Fire Emergency': Consumption, security and the meaning of durables in a transforming society," *Journal of Consumer Culture* 2, no. 2 (2002): 147–70; Ina Merkel, "From Stigma to Cult. Changing Meanings in East German Consumer Culture," in *The Making of the Consumer: Knowledge, Power and Identity in the Modern World*, ed. Frank Trentmann (Oxford: Bloomsbury, 2005), 249–70.

96. Here I refer to the seminal work on the contemporary use of a vintage TRS-80 home computer originally released in 1977: Christina Lindsay, "From the Shadows: Users as Designers, Producers, Marketers, Distributors and Technical Support," in *How Users Matter: The Co-Construction of Users and Technology*, ed. Nelly Oudshoorn and Trevor Pinch (Cambridge: MIT Press, 2003), 29–50.

97. There are a substantial number of databases of vintage electronics, for instance: "Hi Fi Database," https://www.hifidatabase.com/. For a contemporary evaluation of the qualities of vintage audios, see: Gary Gottlieb, *How Does It Sound Now? Legendary Engineers and Vintage Gear* (Boston: Course Technology, 2010).

98. Drączkowska and Gełesz, *The Legend*, 9. See also the exhibition website, "Wystawa Legenda Radmoru," https://www.muzeumgdynia.pl/wystawa/legenda -radmoru/; "Historia," "Radmor," https://www.radmor.com.pl/historia.php.

99. Metz, "Radmor Forever," 63.

100. "Unitraklub.pl," https://unitraklub.pl/.

101. Lindsay, "From the Shadows," 29.

102. Jenss, *Fashioning*, 1.

103. Jenss, *Fashioning*, 1.

104. Jenss, *Fashioning*, 1.

105. Karol Żebruń, "Unitra: Born in Poland—reaktywacja legendarnej marki," May 25, 2014, "Benchmark.pl," https://www.benchmark.pl/aktualnosci/unitra-marka -powraca-nowe-produkty-replika-sn-50.html; Paweł Pilarczyk, "Unitra-reaktywacja," May 22, 2014, "AGDLab," https://agdlab.pl/aktualnosci/Unitra-reaktywacja,4142.

106. Michał Fal, "Unitra powraca—reaktywacja kultowej marki z czasów PRL. Coraz więcej firm gra na konsumenckiej nostalgii," May 23, 2014, "Natemat.pl," https://natemat.pl/103495,unitra-powraca-reaktywacja-kultowej-marki-z-czasow-prl -coraz-wiecej-firm-gra-na-konsumenckiej-nostalgii.

Conclusion

In this book, I have discussed how the notion of technological innovation was deeply embedded in the politics of the modernization project of late state socialist Poland. The possibility to introduce technologically innovative consumer products, or later the perceived lack thereof, was deeply embedded in the political, social, and economic currents of the socialist state of Poland. In my investigation, I have presented several issues relevant to a specific "sociotechnical order" in which technology was supposed to play a significant role in strengthening the existing social and political order and securing economic growth.

State socialism is a fascinating and still overlooked historical setting for studying how a host of social actors can attempt to establish this order through "projectness," and then later attempt to renegotiate it when drawbacks and failures of the project become apparent to all the parties involved. The most obvious case here is the Chernobyl nuclear reactor accident, in which the Soviet authorities unsuccessfully attempted to publicly "negotiate" the disaster as a minor accident, which had limited effects on people or the environment.[1] However, the history of the Eastern Bloc offers many other possible cases for studying not merely "successes" and "failures" in the introduction of technological innovation through "projectness." Studies of these socialist projects also offer an opportunity to study the epistemology relevant to the establishment and negotiations of the meanings of terms such as "quality," "reliability," "progress," and "obsolescence." Such terms are relevant not only to technologies but also to economic and social issues.

Surprisingly, there are virtually no works that discuss how social actors in the state apparatus "performed" state socialist projects through the production of publicly expressed narratives relevant to "sociotechnical imaginaries." There is, of course, an abundance of scholarly works on how state socialism "worked," that is, how a network of social actors embedded in the structure of the state apparatus carried out their actions. But there are very few scholarly works on how these actors publicly performed their identities and objectives.

One example of this is Yurchak's work on how the Soviet propaganda apparatus and Komsomol youth organization "performed" communist ideology in the late USSR.[2]

My book has shown how a host of social actors performed and negotiated key elements of such imagery. First, in the decade of the 1970s, the new ruling elite publicly performed a bold "technological promise" that the new party-government was capable of introducing a technology-based modernization project. The new elite used this ability as one of the key elements of its political legitimacy and offered generous subsidies to sponsor such a project. Only a few years later, the next ruling elite used Polkolor, one of the key symbols of this project, dubbed as the "pyramid near Piaseczno," in their strategy to publicly delegitimatize the Gierek-era ruling elite.

Secondly, for economists and the engineering community, the profitability of technological innovation, particularly following the opening of foreign markets, became a focal point in such an imaginary. Previously, historians of the Eastern Bloc covered technological projects, such as the military and space races and nuclear energy, where costs were of lesser importance. I have attempted to show that the mundane details of the production of technologically complex goods in an industry where the funding for investments and possible profit margins from the production was a top priority. While reading about the production of export versions of audiocassette recorders and automatic washing machines in the 1970s, my impression was that the slogan of "wysoka wartość dodana," or high added value, that comes with the production of such goods, was equally important as "social progress" and "socialist values."

Thirdly, the ability to constantly introduce new and more technologically advanced products became a widely discussed element of the currents in the politics of consumption. Several home technologies became ascribed with cultural meanings of the material symbols of the new, "modern," consumption regime of Poland of the 1970s. I moved away from discussing the shortage economy and instead have highlighted how manufacturers and intermediary actors performed the modernity of newly released products, particularly consumer electronics. As I have shown, studying the modes of representation of consumer goods can reveal how actors involved in the production, mediation, and consumption of these goods were embedded within the evolving power relations.

This process of articulating the problem of quality in public discourse about electric goods can be interpreted, according to Callon, as a "problematization" of a specific aspect of consumer technology. As he notes: "the problematization describes a system of alliances, or associations, between entities, thereby defining the identity and what they 'want.'"[3] Social actors, while expressing their opinions about the qualities of electric goods, defined what they wanted from other actors, attempted to execute their demands, and formed coalitions that were based on the common definition of these demands. Van Lente and Rip discuss the process of how social actors articulated their conviction that technology manufacturers did not fulfill their promises of paying attention to the product quality expressed previously through the public statements of state enterprise representatives.[4]

Cornelis Disco and Barend van der Meulen, in their introduction to the volume *Getting New Technologies Together* introduce the case of the Queen Elizabeth II, the Atlantic liner that in the 1980s underwent an extensive renovation, including a new propeller. During her first voyage, the new and carefully renovated propeller blade broke off, but after an extensive overhaul that took two years, a newly designed propeller was installed, and this time, it worked. As they note, this example shows how a failure of a single technological artifact, the propeller blade, indicated the failure of an entire network of human and nonhuman actors.

> Evidently, it was not only the blades of the Queen Elizabeth II that had been damaged on that first voyage, but also the standards, design rules, testing procedures, and the reputation of the manufacturer—and all had to be repaired. The "misbehavior" of a couple of propeller blades had not merely destroyed the propulsion system, but an entire, carefully planned, socio-technical order, and this forced the manufacturer to create a new one.[5]

This remark provides a suitable summary of the crisis in the quality of technical goods in the 1980s. To paraphrase the authors, the regular "misbehavior" of self-combusting television sets and failing washing machines significantly damaged the carefully planned, complex sociotechnical order that was based on a system of internal quality control in state enterprises, "quality police," quality certificates, and system of awards given during fairs.

My book does not offer any straightforward answers to whether the Polish technology-based modernization project was a success, that is, if those engaged in this project achieved their objectives. I sought instead to deconstruct the ideology of progress and the "projectness" of this specific historical setting. Moreover, I do not offer an investigation into how this project was experienced by consumers. There are already several insightful recent works on consumption in the Eastern Bloc that cover this experience. In contrast, I discuss how other relevant social actors discursively constructed consumers and consumption in their modes of representation of home technologies. This approach was part of my strategy to focus on how social actors performed innovation in consumer technologies, and how consumers were incorporated into such performances. I believe that this approach can provide a new framework for studying other aspects of social, economic, and cultural change in late state socialism, which does not necessarily involve any technological change.

State socialism is still fascinating, yet not fully explored: a universe of complex and opaque networks of interactions between social actors embedded in power relations. Similarly, state socialism was built from complex networks between the social and material worlds. Such interactions were dictated by ideological principles, economic structures, and the agenda of particular interest groups. What is particularly important is how the production and public communication of knowledge about other social actors embedded in such networks was an intrinsic element of these relationships. I believe that my book can offer some inspiration, particularly to young scholars who are interested in explorations of this system.

NOTES

1. Schmid, *Producing Power.*
2. Yurchak, *Everything.*
3. Michel Callon, "Some elements," 70.
4. van Lente and Rip, "Expectations."
5. Cornelis Disco and Barend van der Meulen, "Introduction," in *Getting New Technologies Together. Studies in Making Sociotechnical Order*, ed. Cornelis Disco and Barend van der Meulen (Berlin and New York: Walter de Gruyter, 1998): 1–13, here 1–2.

Bibliography

25 lat Edy (1949–1974). Poniatowa w XXX-lecie PRL. dir. Bolesław Nowak, AKFF "Foka" w Poniatowej, 1974. YouTube video, https://www.youtube.com/watch?v =Of1TOYaacC4.

"XXVI Targ Krajowe "Jesień 1970." *Życie Gospodarcze*, September 20, 1970.

30-lecie Zelos. Kronika wydarzeń. Piaseczno: Zakłady Kineskopów Monochromatycznych Zelos/Unitra Polkolor, 1986.

Andrykiewicz, Zofia. "Kształtowanie jakości towarów powszechnej konsumpcji w sferze przedprodukcyjnej i poprodukcyjnej (ze szczególnym uwzględnieniem psychospołecznych elementów wartości użytkowej towarów)." *Handel Wewnętrzny*, Issue 1, 1981.

Antoniszyn, Emil. "Unowocześnianie struktury organizacyjnej gospodarki." *Życie Gospodarcze*, September 22, 1974.

Appadurai, Arjun. "Introduction: Commodities and the Politics of Value." In *The Social Life of Things. Commodities in Cultural Perspective*, edited by Arjun Appadurai, 3–63. Cambridge: Cambridge University Press, 1986.

Auerbach, Jerzy. "Elektronika na cenzurowanym." *Przegląd Techniczny*, April 6, 1977.

Auerbach, Jerzy. "Odbiornik telewizji kolorowej T5601." *Przegląd Techniczny*, September 10, 1978.

Auerbach, Jerzy. "Wzornictwo dyktatorem w elektronice powszechnego użytku." *Przegląd Techniczny*, November 20, 1977.

Augustine, Dolores L. *Red Prometheus Engineering and Dictatorship in East Germany, 1945–1990.* Cambridge and London: MIT Press, 2007.

Autio-Sarasmo, Sari, and Katalin Miklóssy, eds. *Reassessing Cold War Europe.* London and New York: Routledge, 2011.

Baczyński, Jerzy. "Ciche granie." *Polityka*, April 28, 1984.

Barthes, Roland. "The New Citröen." In Roland Barthes, *Mythologies*. New York et al.: The Noonday Press, 1972, 88–90. First published 1957.

Bauman, Zygmunt. "Life-world and expertise: Social production of dependency." In *The culture and power of knowledge: Inquiries into contemporary societies*, edited by Nico Stehr, and Richard V. Ericson, 81–106. Berlin: Walter de Gruyter, 1992.

Beniger, James R. *The Control Revolution: Technological and Economic Origins of the Information Society*. Cambridge, MA: Harvard University Press, 1986.

Berner, Boel. "'Housewives films' and the modern housewife. Experts, users, and household modernization: Sweden in the 1950s and 1960s." *History and Technology* 18, no. 3 (January 2002): 155–79.

Białecki, Klemens, Zygmunt Kossut, and Andrzej Szanjder. "System socjalistycznej reklamy." *Życie Gospodarcze*, September 16, 1973.

Borowy, Michał. "Innowacje a jakość życia." *Życie Gospodarcze*, October 27, 1974.

Bren, Paulina. *The Greengrocer and His TV: The Culture of Communism after the 1968 Prague Spring*. Ithaca, NY: Cornell University Press, 2010.

Bren, Paulina, and Mary Neuburger, eds. *Communism Unwrapped: Consumption in Cold War Eastern Europe*. Oxford: Oxford University Press, 2012.

Brey, Philip. "Theorizing Modernity and Technology." In *Modernity and Technology*, edited by Thomas J. Misa, Philip Brey, and Andrew Feenberg, 33–71. Cambridge and London: 2003.

Brock, Gerald W. *The Second Information Revolution*. Cambridge and London: Harvard University Press, 2003.

Buchli, Victor. *An Archeology of Socialism*. Oxford and New York: BERG Publishers, 1999.

Buchli, Victor. "Khrushchev, Modernism, and the Fight against 'Petit-bourgeois' Consciousness in the Soviet Home." *Journal of Design History* 10, no. 2 (1997): 161–76.

Budziński, Michał. "Utworzenie Wielkich Organizacji Gospodarczych—założenia reformy przemysłu PRL lat 70." *Kwartalnik Kolegium Ekonomiczno-Społecznego. Studia i Prace*, no. 3 (2018): 163–77.

Bulgakov, Mikhail. *The Master and Margarita*. London: Penguin Books, 2001. First published 1967.

Bürdek, Bernhard E. *Design. History, Theory and Practice of Product Design*. Basel, Boston, and Berlin: Birkhäuser, 2005.

Busch, Lawrence. *Standards. Recipes for Reality*. Cambridge and London: MIT Press, 2011.

Callon, Michel. "Some elements of a sociology of translation: domestication of the scallops and the fishermen of St Brieuc Bay." In *The Science Studies Reader*, edited by Mario Biagioli, 67–83. London and New York: Routledge, 1999. First published in: John Law, ed., *Power, Action and Belief: A New Sociology of Knowledge?* London: Routledge, 1986, 196–223.

Callon, Michel, Cécile Méadel, and Vololona Rabeharisoa. "The economy of qualities." *Economy and Society* 31, no. 2 (2002): 194–217.

Chalmers, Johnson A. *MITI and the Japanese Miracle: The Growth of Industrial Policy, 1925–1975*. Stanford, CA: Stanford University Press, 1982.

Chandler, Alfred D. *Inventing the Electronic Century: The Epic Story of the Consumer Electronics and Computer Industries*. Cambridge et al.: Harvard University Press, 2005.

Chattalas, Michael J. *The Effects of National Stereotypes on Country of Origin-Based Product Evaluations*. PhD dissertation, City University of New York, 2005.

Chattalas, Michael J., Thomas Kramer, and Hirokazu Takada. "The impact of national stereotypes on the country of origin effect: A conceptual framework." *International Marketing Review* 25 no. 1 (2008): 54–74.

Chernyshova, Natalya. *Soviet Consumer Culture in the Brezhnev Era* London and New York: Routledge, 2013.

"Chłodziarki i zamrażarki z "Polaru." *Veto*, July 18, 1982.

Cholewicka-Goździk, Krystyna. "Ceny a jakość." *Polityka*, February 27, 1982.

Clarke, Adele. E., Carrie Friese, and Rachel Washburn. *Situational Analysis in Practice: Mapping Research with Grounded Theory.* Walnut Creek, CA: Left Coast Press, 2015.

Clarke, Jackie. "Closing Moulinex: thoughts on the visibility and invisibility of industrial labour in contemporary France." *Modern and Contemporary France* 19, no. 4 (2011): 443–58.

Clarke, Jackie. "Work, Consumption and Subjectivity in Postwar France: Moulinex and the Meanings of Domestic Appliances 1950s–70s." *Journal of Contemporary History* 47, no. 4 (October 2012): 838–59.

Cockburn, Cynthia. "Domestic Technologies: Cinderella and The Engineers." *Women's Studies International Forum* 20, no. 3 (May-June 1997): 361–71.

"Compacty z Rzeszowa." *Veto*, April 26, 1992.

Conekin, Becky. "'Here Is the Modern World Itself,' The Festival of Britain's Representations of the Future." In *The Design History Reader*, edited by Grace Lees-Maffel and Rebecca Houze, 143–51. Oxford and New York: BERG, 2010. Originally published as: Conekin, Becky. "'Here Is the Modern World Itself,' the Festival of Britain's Representations of the Future." In *Moments of Modernity: Reconstructing Britain 1945–1964*, ed. Becky Conekin, F. Mort, and C. Waters, 228–46. London and New York: Rivers Oram Press, 1999, 228–46.

Crowley, David. "People's Warsaw/Popular Warsaw." Journal of Design History 10, no. 2, (1997): 203–23.

Crowley, David. "Warsaw's Shops, Stalinism and the Thaw." In *Style and Socialism: Modernity and Material Culture in Post-War Eastern Europe*, edited by Susan E. Reid and David Crowley, 25–47. Oxford: Berg, 2000.

"Czy zapomnimy o Hi-Fi?" *Przegląd Techniczny*, August 15, 1982.

"Daleko nam do luksus." *Atut*, Issue 10–12, 1989.

"Daleko od Wisły." *Przekrój,* April 17, 1994.

Dąbrowski, Janusz. "Dlaczego nie kochamy elektroniki." *Życie Gospodarcze*, December 15, 1974.

Dąbrowski, Janusz. "Strategia 'oszczędnego dobrobytu.'" *Przegląd Techniczny*, January 9, 1983.

Disco, Cornelis, and Barend van der Meulen. "Introduction." In *Getting New Technologies Together Studies in Making Sociotechnical Order*, edited by Cornelis Disco and Barend van der Meulen, 1–13. Berlin and New York: Walter de Gruyter, 1998.

Drączkowska, Agnieszka, and Paweł Gełesz, eds. *Legenda Radmoru/The Legend of Radmor.* Gdynia: Muzeum Miasta Gdyni, 2020.

Drączkowska, Agnieszka. "Victorius and on a Roll." In *Legenda Radmoru/The Legend of Radmor*, edited by Agnieszka Drączkowska and Paweł Gełesz, 24–27. Gdynia: Muzeum Miasta Gdyni, 2020.

Dreilinger, Danielle. *The Secret History of Home Economics. How Trailblazing Women Harnessed the Power of Home and Changed the Way We Live.* New York: W.W. Norton & Company, 2021.

Dryll, Irena. "Patefony strajkują." *Życie Gospodarcze*, July 14, 1991.

Dudley, Leonard. *Information Revolutions in the History of the West.* Cheltenham: Edward Elgar, 2008.

Dudziński, Władysław. "Efektywność społeczna." *Życie Gospodarcze*, January 18, 1970.

du Gay, Paul, Stuart Hall, Linda Janes, Hugh Mackay, and Keith Negus. *Doing Cultural Studies: The Story of the Sony Walkman.* London, Thousand Oaks, and New Dehli: SAGE, 2003. First published 1997.

Dunn, Elizabeth C. *Privatizing Poland. Baby Food, Big Business, and the Remaking of Labour.* Ithaca and London: Cornell University Press, 2004.

Duraj, Jan. *Socjalistyczny model konsumpcji.* Warszawa: Książka i Wiedza, 1973.

Dyrektorzy, dir. Zbigniew Chmielewski, 1975.

"Dzień jutrzejszy krajowego rynku sprzetu elektronicznego." *Radioamator*, Issue 7/8, 1975.

Elias, Megan J. *Stir It Up: Home Economics in American Culture.* Philadelphia: University of Pennsylvania Press, 2010.

"Eliminacja targowych bubli." *Przegląd Techniczny*, January 20, 1985.

Ettenson, Richard. "Brand name and country of origin effects in the emerging market economies of Russia, Poland and Hungary." *International Marketing Review* 10, no. 5 (1993): 14–36.

Fal, Michał. "Unitra powraca—reaktywacja kultowej marki z czasów PRL. Coraz więcej firm gra na konsumenckiej nostalgii." May 23, 2014, "Natemat.pl." https://natemat.pl/103495,unitra-powraca-reaktywacja-kultowej-marki-z-czasow-prl-coraz-wiecej-firm-gra-na-konsumenckiej-nostalgii.

Fallan, Kjetil. "Culture by Design: Co-Constructing Material and Meaning." In *Assigning Cultural Values*, edited by Kjerstin Aukrust, 135–63. Frankfurt: Peter Lang Publishing, 2013.

Fanselow, Frank S. "The Bazaar Economy or How Bizarre is the Bazaar Really?" *Man, New Series* 25, no. 2 (June 1990): 250–65.

Faust, Zbigniew. "Gramofon elektryczny WG 400 Mister Hit." *Radioamator*, Issue 6, 1972.

Fehérváry, Krisztina. "Goods and States: The Political Logic of State-Socialist Material Culture." *Comparative Studies in Society and History* 51, no. 2 (April 2009): 426–59.

Fidelis, Malgorzata. *Women, Communism, and Industrialization in Postwar Poland.* Cambridge: Cambridge University Press, 2010.

Forester, Tom. *High-Tech Society: The Story of the Information Technology Revolution.* Cambridge, MA: MIT Press, 1987.

Frankowski, Stanisław. "Bubel?" *Przegląd Techniczny*, July 27, 1987.

Frańczak, Halina. "Wolę polskie." *Życie Gospodarcze*, August 6, 1995.

Frejlich, Czesława. "Radmor: Contribution to the Polish History of the Industrial Design." In *Legenda Radmoru/The Legend of Radmor*, edited by Agnieszka Drączkowska and Paweł Gełesz, 45–52. Gdynia: Muzeum Miasta Gdyni, 2020.

Froelich, Lech. "Znak znany już na świecie." *Życie Gospodarcze*, June 2, 1974.

George, Alexander L., and Andrew Bennett. *Case Studies and Theory Development in the Social Sciences.* Cambridge and London: MIT Press, 2005.

Gerovitch, Slava. *From Newspeak to Cyberspeak: A History of Soviet Cybernetics.* Cambridge and London: MIT Press, 2002.

Gille, Zsuzsa, Cristofer Scarboro, and Diana Mincytė. "The Pleasures of Backwardness." In *The Socialist Good Life. Desire, Development, and Standards of Living in Eastern Europe*, edited by Cristofer Scarboro, Diana Mincytė, and Zsuzsa Gille. Bloomington: Indiana University Press, 2020, epub.

Gooday, Graeme. "Re-writing the 'book of blots': Critical reflections on histories of technological 'failure.'" *History and Technology* 14, no. 4 (1998): 265–91.

Gorsuch, Anne E., and Diane P. Koenker, eds. *The Socialist Sixties, Crossing Borders in the Second World.* Bloomington: Indiana University Press, 2013.

Gottlieb, Gary. *How Does It Sound Now? Legendary Engineers and Vintage Gear.* Boston: Course Technology, 2010.

"Gra zwana kooperacją." *Przegląd Techniczny*, January 20, 1980.

Haffer, Mirosław, and Tomasz Skąpski. "Sprzęt trwałego użytku w gospodarstwach domowych." *Polityka Społeczna*, June 1980.

Hand, Martin, and Elizabeth Shove. "Orchestrating Concepts: Kitchen Dynamics and Regime Change in Good Housekeeping and Ideal Home, 1922–2002." *Home Cultures: The Journal of Architecture, Design and Domestic Space* 1, no. 3 (2004): 235–56.

Hauszyld, Marek. "250 telewizorów dla czytelników 'Veto.'" *Veto*, December 18, 1983.

Hauszyld, Marek. "Potyczki z 'JOWISZEM.'" *Veto*, January 16, 1983.

Hauszyld, Marek. "WZT podjęły rękawice." *Veto*, January 16, 1983.

Hebdige, Dick. "Object as Image: The Italian Scooter Cycle." In Dick Hebdige, *Hiding in the Light: On Images and Things.* London and New York: Routledge 2002, 77–115. First published 1988.

Hecht, Gabrielle, ed. *Entangled Geographies: Empire and Technopolitics in the Global Cold War.* Cambridge and London: MIT Press, 2011.

Henderson, Jeffrey. *The Globalisation of High Technology: Production, Society, Space and Semiconductors in the Restructuring of the Modern World.* London and New York: Routledge, 2003. First published 1989.

Herf, Jeffrey. *Reactionary modernism: Technology, culture, and politics in Weimar and the Third Reich.* Cambridge and New York: Cambridge University Press, 1984.

Hess, David J. "Technology- and Product-Oriented Movements: Approximating Social Movement Studies and Science and Technology Studies." *Science, Technology, & Human Values* 30, no. 4 (Autumn 2005): 515–35.

Houze, Rebbeca. "Introduction." In *The Design History Reader*, edited by Grace Lees-Maffel and Rebecca Houze, 175–77. Oxford and New York: Berg, 2010.

Hutnik, Mieczysław, and Tadeusz Pachniewicz. *Zarys historii polskiego przemysłu elektronicznego do 1985 r.* Warszawa: Stowarzyszenia Elektryków Polskich, 1994. *Zeszyt Historyczny SEP*, 1994, no. 2.

Iriye, Akira, and Rana Mitter. "Series Editors' Preface." In *The Making of European Consumption: Facing the American Challenge*, edited by Per Lundin and Thomas Kaiserfeld, x–xi. Houndmills: Palgrave Macmillan, 2015.

Isenstadt, Sandy. "Visions of Plenty: Refrigerators in America around 1950." *Journal of Design History* 11, no. 4 (1998): 311–21.

Jadczyk, Michał. "Zamiast ABC ocena jakości." *Życie Gospodarcze*, April 16, 1972.

"Jakość, wygoda i uroda życia." *Magazyn Rodzinny*, Issue 1, 1974.

Jameson, Fredric. *Postmodernism, or, The Cultural Logic of Late Capitalism.* Durham: Duke University Press, 1991.

Jamiołkowski, Adam. "Słyszeć coraz więcej." *Pan*, November, 1987.

Jasanoff, Sheila. "Ordering knowledge, ordering society." In *States of Knowledge: The Co-production of Science and Social Order*, edited by Sheila Jasanoff, 13–45. London and New York: Routledge, 2004.

Jasanoff, Sheila, and Sang-Hyun Kim. "Containing the Atom: Sociotechnical Imaginaries and Nuclear Power in the United States and South Korea." *Minerva* 47 (2009): 119–46.

Jasanoff, Sheila, and Sang-Hyun Kim, eds. *Dreamscapes of Modernity. Sociotechnical Imaginaries and the Fabrication of Power.* Chicago and London: University of Chicago Press, 2015.

Jasanoff, Sheila, Sang-Hyun Kim, and Stefan Sperling, "Sociotechnical Imaginaries and Science and Technology Policy: A Cross-National Comparison." Program on Science, Technology & Society, Harvard University. Accessed 1 June 2023. https://sts.hks.harvard.edu/research/platforms/imaginaries/iii.proj/nsf-summary -and-proposal/.

Jaskólski, Lucjan. "Jesteśmy krytykowani." *Przegląd Techniczny*, February 2, 1977.

Jaworski, Jerzy. "Reklamacje jakościowe temat nadal aktualny." *Życie Gospodarcze*, April 4, 1972.

Jędrzejczak, Mateusz. "Problemy dystrybucji nowości w branży elektroakustycznej." *Handel Wewnętrzny*, Issue 5, 1980.

Jenss, Heike. *Fashioning Memory. Vintage Style and Youth Culture.* London et al.: Bloomsbury, 2015.

Jones-Imhotep, Edward. "Disciplining technology: Electronic reliability, Cold-War military culture and the topside ionogram." *History and Technology* 17, no. 2 (2000): 125–75.

Jones-Imhotep, Edward. *The Unreliable Nation: Hostile Nature and Technological Failure in the Cold War.* Cambridge and London: MIT Press, 2017.

Josephson, Paul R. *Would Trotsky Wear a Bluetooth? Technological Utopianism under Socialism 1917–1989.* Baltimore: Johns Hopkins University Press, 2009.

Karns, Alexander Jennifer. *The Mantra of Efficiency: From Waterwheel to Social Control.* Baltimore: Johns Hopkins University Press, 2008.

Karpiński, Andrzej, ed. *Problemy nowoczesności w gospodarce.* Warszawa: Państwowe Wydawnictwo Ekonomiczne, 1974.

Khrushchev, Sergei N. *Nikita Khrushchev, and the Creation of a Superpower*. University Park: Pennsylvania State University Press: 2000.

King, Robert L. "Enterprise-level marketing research activity in Poland: The predom/ polar experience." *Academy of Marketing Science Journal* 11, no. 3 (Summer 1983): 292–303.

"Kolorowy świat z Unimoru." *Przegląd Techniczny*, August 1, 1993, appendix "High Tech."

"Konstytucja Polskiej Rzeczypospolitej Ludowej z dnia 16 lutego 1976 r." Accessed July 1, 2023. http://libr.sejm.gov.pl/tek01/txt/kpol/1976-01.html.

"Konsumenckie gusty." *Gazeta Bankowa*, October 10, 1993.

Kopeć, Aleksander. "Polski przemysł radioelektroniczny." *Życie Gospodarcze*, February 24, 1974.

Kopytoff, Igor. "The Cultural Biography of Things: Commoditization as a Process." In *The Social Life of Things: Commodities in Cultural Perspective*, edited by Arjun Appadurai, 64–91. Cambridge: Cambridge University Press, 1986.

Kornai, János. "The Soft Budget Constraint." *Kyklos* 39, no. 1 (February 1986): 3–30.

Kosicki, Stanisław. "Technika i Technologia Radmor S.A." In *Legenda Radmoru/The Legend of Radmor*, edited by Agnieszka Drączkowska and Paweł Gełesz, 65–77. Gdynia: Muzeum Miasta Gdyni, 2020.

Kostrzewa, Andrzej. *Ekonomiczne podstawy sterowania jakością produkcji*. Warszawa: Państwowe Wydawnictwo Naukowe, 1974.

Kotowicz-Jawor, Joanna. *Presja inwestycyjna w latach siedemdziesiątych*. Warszawa: Państwowe Wydawnicwo Naukowe, 1983.

Krzyżanowska, Irena. "Kuszenie biedaków." *Veto*, March 31, 1991.

Kulik, Andrzej. "Początek drogi." *Przegląd Techniczny*, October 29, 1978.

Kurzyk, Ryszard. "Edukacja konsumenta jako działalność informacyjna." *Gospodarstwo Domowe*, January–February, 1971.

Kuszko, Anna. "Francja zmienia oblicze." *Życie Gospodarcze*, July 30, 1972.

Law, John. *Aircraft Stories. Decentering the Object in Technoscience*. Durham and London: Duke University Press, 2002.

Lee Blaszczyk, Regina. *The Color Revolution*. Cambridge and London: MIT Press, 2012.

Lees-Maffei, Grace. "The Production-Consumption-Mediation Paradigm." *Journal of Design History* 22, no. 4 (December 2009): 351–76.

Lees-Maffei, Grace, and Rebecca Houze, eds. *The Design History Reader*. Oxford and New York: BERG, 2010.

Lenin, Vladimir Ilyich. "The role and functions of trade unions under the New Economic Policy." In *Lenin's Collected Works*, 2nd English Edition. Vol. 33, 188–96. Moscow: Progress Publishers 1965. First published 1922.

Lewis, Robert. "Hierarchy and Technological Innovation in Soviet Industry: The Science-Production Associations." *Minerva* 22, no. 2 (June 1984): 129–59.

Lindsay, Christina. "From the Shadows: Users as Designers, Producers, Marketers, Distributors and Technical Support." In *How Users Matter: The Co-Construction of Users and Technology*, edited by Nelly Oudshoorn and Trevor Pinch, 29–50. Cambridge: MIT Press, 2003.

Linenthal, Edward Tabor. Symbolic Defense: The Cultural Significance of the Strategic Defense Initiative. Urbana: University of Illinois Press, 1989.

Lundin, Per. "Introduction." In *The Making of European Consumption: Facing the American Challenge*, edited by Per Lundin and Thomas Kaiserfeld, 1–16. Houndmills: Palgrave Macmillan, 2015.

Lundin, Per. "Mediators of Modernity: Planning Experts and the Making of the 'Car-Friendly' City in Europe." In *Urban Machinery: Inside Modern European Cities*, edited by Mikael Hård and Thomas J. Misa, 257–79. Cambridge: MIT Press, 2008.

Lury, Celia. *Brands: The Logos of the Global Economy.* London and New York: Routledge, 2004.

MacKenzie, Donald. *Inventing Accuracy: A Historical Sociology of Nuclear Missile Guidance.* Cambridge and London: MIT Press, 1990.

Mackrakis, Kristie, and Dieter Hofman, eds. *Science under Socialism, East Germany in Comparative Perspective.* Cambridge, MA: Harvard University Press, 1999.

Maheswaran, Durairaj. "Country of Origin as a Stereotype: Effects of Consumer Expertise and Attribute Strength on Product Evaluations." *Journal of Consumer Research* 21, no. 2 (1994): 354–65.

Mąkowa, Danuta. "MK Magnetofony Kasprzaka." *Magazyn Rodzinny*, Issue 3, 1974.

Mąkowa, Danuta. "Polar ze znakiem Q." *Magazyn Rodzinny*, Issue 6, 1975.

Mąkowa, Danuta. "Wielkie pranie w automacie." *Magazyn Rodzinny*, Issue 4, 1975.

Mąkowa, Danuta. "Zelmer 03 na taśmie." *Magazyn Rodzinny*, Issue 1, 1974.

Marcinakówna, Anna. "Kto pomoże Nowoczesnej Gospodyni." *Miesięcznik ZMW*, March 1972.

Marres, Noortje, and David Stark. "Put to the Test: For a New Sociology of Testing." *The British Journal of Sociology* 71, no. 3 (2020): 1–34.

Martin, Ingrid M., and Sevgin Eroglu. "Measuring a multi-dimensional construct: country image." *Journal of Business Research* 28, no. 3 (1993): 191–210.

Matuszewski, Maciej. "Zasady kwantyfikacji jakości środków konsumpcji." *Zeszyty Prawnicze*, no. 63, 1974.

Mazurek, Małgorzata. *Socjalistyczny zakład pracy. Porównanie fabrycznej codzienności w PRL i NRD u progu lat sześćdziesiątych.* Warszawa: Wydawnictwo Trio, 2005.

Mazurek, Malgorzata, and Matthew Hilton. "Consumerism, Solidarity and Communism: Consumer Protection and the Consumer Movement in Poland." *Journal of Contemporary History* 42, no. 2 (April 2007): 315–43.

Merkel, Ina. "From Stigma to Cult. Changing Meanings in East German Consumer Culture." In *The Making of the Consumer: Knowledge, Power and Identity in the Modern World*, edited by Frank Trentmann, 249–70. Oxford: Bloomsbury, 2005.

Metz, Piotr. "Radmor Forever." In *Legenda Radmoru/The Legend of Radmor*, edited by Agnieszka Drączkowska and Paweł Gełesz, 61–63. Gdynia: Muzeum Miasta Gdyni, 2020.

Miastkowski, Lech. "Ceny a jakość wykonawcza wyrobów." *Życie Gospodarcze*, September 24, 1972.

Mickiewicz, Ellen. *Split Signals: Television and Politics in the Soviet Union.* New York and Oxford: Oxford University Press, 1988.

Mieczykowski, Karol. "TVC—opium dla mas?" *Przegląd Techniczny*, January 2, 1983.

Miedziński, Paweł. *Centralna Agencja Fotograficzna 1951–1991*. Szczecin and Warszawa: Instytut Pamięci Narodowej, 2021.

Miklóssy, Katalin, and Melanie Ilic, eds. *Competition in Socialist Society*. London and New York: Routledge, 2014.

Miłoszewska, Ewa. "Ocena jakości sprzętu zmechanizowanego." *Gospodarstwo Domowe*, Issue 4, 1978.

Misa, Thomas J. "The Compelling Tangle of Modernity and Technology." In *Modernity and Technology*, edited by Thomas J. Misa, Philip Brey, and Andrew Feenberg, 1–30. Cambridge and London: 2003.

"Modernity's Powerful Imaginations." Program on Science, Technology & Society, Harvard University. Accessed June 1, 2023. http://sts.hks.harvard.edu/research/platforms/imaginaries/i.ant/modernitys-powerful-imaginations/.

Mosco, Vincent. *The Digital Sublime: Myth, Power, and Cyberspace*. Cambridge and London: MIT Press, 2004.

Myśliński, Jerzy. *Kalendarium polskiej prasy, radia i telewizji*. Warszawa: Bel Studio, 2012.

Nałęcz Jawecki, Andrzej. "Nowości rynkowe na huśtawce." *Życie Gospodarcze*, September 23, 1973.

Neuburger, Mary C. *Balkan Smoke: Tobacco and Making of Modern Bulgaria*. Ithaca and London: Cornell University Press, 2013.

Nowastowski, Janusz. "Ocena jakości wyrobów przemysłu elektrotechnicznego w Polsce." January 24, 2014, "Elektroonline.pl." Accessed May 5, 2023, http://elektroonline.pl/a/6946,Ocena-jakosci-wyrobow-przemyslu-elektrotechnicznego-w-Polsce,,Elektrotechnika.

OBOP. "Opinie konsumentów o towarach z Polski i zagranicy." Warszawa, 1994.

Oiva, Mila. "Creation of a Market Space: The Polish Clothing Industry, Soviet Union, and the Rise of Marketing, 1949–1961." PhD thesis, University of Turku, 2017.

Oiva, Mila. "Selling fashion to Soviets. Competitive practices in Polish clothes export in the early 1960s." In *Competition in Socialist Society*, edited by Katalin Miklóssy and Melanie Illic, 71–88. London and New York: Routledge, 2015.

Oiva, Mila. "Something New in The Eastern Market: Polish Perceptions of the Developing Soviet Consumerism, 1961–1972." In *Fashion, Consumption and Everyday Culture in the Soviet Union between 1945 and 1985*, edited by Eva Hausbacher, Elena Huber, and Julia Hargaßner, 99–113. München, Berlin, and Washington/D.C.: Verlag Otto Sagner, 2014.

Oldenziel, Ruth, and Karin Zachmann, eds. *Cold War Kitchen. Americanization, Technology, and European Users*. Cambridge and London: MIT Press, 2010.

Oldenziel, Ruth, and Karin Zachmann. "Kitchens as Technology and Politics: An Introduction." In *Cold War Kitchen. Americanization, Technology, and European Users*, edited by Ruth Oldenziel and Karin Zachmann, 1–29. Cambridge and London: MIT Press, 2010.

Oldenziel, Ruth, Adri Albert de la Bruhèze, and Onno de Wit. "Europe's Mediation Junction: Technology and Consumer Society in the 20th Century." *History and Technology* 21, no. 1 (March 2005): 107–39.

"Opłacalność postępu technicznego." *Życie Gospodarcze*, January 18, 1970.

Ostrowska, Elżbieta. "Handel—zapora czy autostrada między produkcją i konsumpcją." In unpublished collection of conference papers from the IRWiK seminar "Konsumpcja-Rynek-Wzrost Gospodarczy," 1988, IRWiK, archive file 203, page 5, Archiwum Akt Nowych.

Oushakine, Serguei. "'Against the Cult of Things': On Soviet Productivism, Storage Economy, and Commodities with No Destination." *Russian Review* 73 (April 2014): 198–236.

Oudshoorn, Nelly, and Trevor Pinch. "Introduction: How users and non-users matter." In How users matter: The co-construction of users and technology, edited by Nelly Oudshoorn and Trevor Pinch, 1–25. Cambridge and London: MIT Press, 2003.

Paczkowski, Andrzej. *The Spring Will Be Ours. Poland and the Poles from Occupation to Freedom.* University Park: Pennsylvania State University Press, 2003. First published 1995.

Panek, Krystyna. "Promujmy polskie wyroby!" *Przegląd Techniczny*, September 13, 1992.

Partner, Simon. *Assembled in Japan: Electrical Goods and the Making of the Japanese Consumer.* Berkeley, Los Angeles, and London: University of California Press, 1999.

Patterson, Patrick Hyder. *Bought and Sold: Living and Losing the Good Life in Socialist Yugoslavia.* New York: Cornell University Press, 2011.

Patterson, Patrick Hyder. "Just Rewards: The Social Contract and Communism's Hard Bargain with the Citizen-Consumer." In *The Socialist Good Life: Desire, Development, and Standards of Living in Eastern Europe,* edited by Cristofer Scarboro, Diana Mincyte, and Zsuzsa Gille. Bloomington: Indiana University Press, 2020, epub.

Perez, Carlota. "Technological revolutions and techno-economic paradigms." Cambridge Journal of Economics 34, no. 1 (2010): 185–202.

Péteri, György, ed. *Imagining the West in Eastern Europe and the Soviet Union.* Pittsburgh: University of Pittsburgh Press, 2010.

Peters, Benjamin. *How Not to Network a Nation: The Uneasy History of the Soviet Internet.* Cambridge and London: MIT Press, 2016.

Piechniewicz, Tadeusz. "Czy sięgnie?" *Audio Video,* Issue 1, 1988.

Pilarczyk, Paweł. "Unitra—reaktywacja." May 22, 2014, "AGDLab." Accessed May 1, 2023. https://agdlab.pl/aktualnosci/Unitra-reaktywacja,4142.

Pinch, Trevor. "'Testing—One, Two, Three . . . Testing!': Toward a Sociology of Testing." *Science, Technology, & Human Values* 18, no. 1 (Winter 1993): 25–41.

Połeć, Władysław, Mieczysław Wierzbiński, and Henryk Pawelec, eds. *Zakłady Elektromaszynowe EDA w Poniatowej.* Poniatowa: Zakłady Elektro-Maszynowe Eda, 1969.

"Polska po zniknięciu blondynek. Rozmowa z Anną Gizą-Poleszczuk." *Kultura Popularna* 14:4 (2005): 105–8.

Poprzeczko, Jacek. "Bylejakość." *Polityka*, August 28, 1982.

Poprzeczko, Jacek. "Samodzielność z rozdzielnikiem." *Polityka*, February 27, 1982.

Porter-Szűcs, Brian. "Conceptualizing Consumption in the Polish People's Republic." In *The Socialist Good Life. Desire, Development, and Standards of Living in Eastern Europe*, edited by Cristofer Scarboro, Diana Mincytė, and Zsuzsa Gille. Bloomington: Indiana University Press, 2020, epub.

Porter-Szűcs, Brian. *Poland in the Modern World: Beyond Martyrdom*. Chichester: Wiley Blackwell, 2014.

Poznanski, Kazimierz Z. *Poland's Protracted Transition: Institutional Change and Economic Growth 1970–1994*. Cambridge: Cambridge University Press, 1996.

Radmor 5102 Manual. Gdynia: Zakłady Radiowe Radmor, 1977.

"Radmor 5102 Radmor 5100 UNITRA #Top 10 Best #Vintage tuner amplifier receiver Verstärker." YouTube video, added on April 1, 2018. https://www.youtube.com/watch?v=a1RNhhHFukA.

Reid, Susan E. "The Khrushchev Kitchen: Domesticating the Scientific-Technological Revolution." *Journal of Contemporary History* 40, no. 2 (April 2005): 289–316.

Reid, Susan E. "'This is Tomorrow!' Becoming a Consumer in the Soviet Sixties." In *The Socialist Sixties: Crossing Borders in the Second World*, edited by Anne Gorsuch and Diane Koenker, 25–65. Bloomington: Indiana University Press, 2013.

Reid, Susan E., and David Crowley, eds. *Style and Socialism: Modernity and Material Culture in Post-War Eastern Europe*. Oxford: Berg, 2000.

Rip, Arie, and Siebe Talma. "Antagonistic Patterns and New Technologies." In *Getting New Technologies Together: Studies in Making Sociotechnical Order*, edited by Cornelis Disco and Barend van der Meulen, 299–322. Berlin and New York: Walter de Gruyter, 1998.

Roth-Ey, Kristin. *Moscow Prime Time: How the Soviet Union Built the Media Empire that Lost the Cultural Cold War*. Ithaca and New York: Cornell University Press, 2014.

Roth-Ey, Kristin. "Finding a Home for Television in the USSR, 1950–1970." *Slavic Review* 66, no. 2 (Summer 2007): 278–306.

"Rozporządzenie Rady Ministrów z dnia 25 marca 1985 r. w sprawie szczegółowego zakresu działania Urzędu Postępu Naukowo-TechnicznIgo i Wdrożeń." *Dziennik Ustaw* 1985, nr 21 poz. 93.

Rubin, Eli. "The Trabant: Consumption, Eigen-Sinn, and Movement." History Workshop Journal 68, no. 1 (Autumn 2009): 27–44.

Sachsse, Rolf. "Made in Germany as image in photography and design." *Journal of Popular Culture* 34, no. 3 (Winter 2000): 43–58.

Samotyj, Marek. "Do czego służy jakość?" *Przegląd Techniczny*, September 15, 1976.

Sanchez-Sibony, Oscar. *Red Globalization: The Political Economy of the Soviet Cold War from Stalin to Khrushchev*. Cambridge and New York: Cambridge University Press, 2014.

Sarewitz, Daniel. *Frontiers Of Illusion. Science, Technology, and the Politics of Progress*. Philadelphia: Temple University Press, 1996.

Scarboro, Cristofer. "The Late Socialist Good Life and Its Discontents: *Bit*, *Kultura*, and the

Scarboro, Cristofer, Diana Mincyte, and Zsuzsa Gille, eds. *The Socialist Good Life. Desire, Development, and Standards of Living in Eastern Europe.* Bloomington: Indiana University Press, 2020.

Schein, Louisa. "Performing Modernity." *Cultural Anthropology* 14, no. 3 (August 1999): 361–95.

Scherrer, Jutta. "To catch up and overtake the West: Soviet discourse on socialist competition." In *Competition in Socialist Society,* edited by Katalin Miklóssy and Melanie Ilic, 10–22. London and New York: Routledge, 2014.

Schmid, Sonja D. *Producing Power: The Pre-Chernobyl History of the Soviet Nuclear Industry.* Cambridge and London: MIT Press, 2015.

Shevchenko, Olga. "'In Case of Fire Emergency': Consumption, security and the meaning of durables in a transforming society." *Journal of Consumer Culture* 2, no. 2, 2002: 147–70.

Sikora, Marian. "Za czyje grzechy cierpi konsument?" *Życie Gospodarcze,* September 13, 1970.

Sikorski, Andrzej. "Bariery dźwięku." *Życie Gospodarcze,* April 1, 1974.

Sikorski, Andrzej. "Rozwiązania częściowe czy systemowe?" *Życie Gospodarcze,* June 13, 1971.

Sitarski, Piotr, Maria B. Garda, and Krzysztof Jajko. *New Media Behind the Iron Curtain: Cultural History of Video, Microcomputers and Satellite Television in Communist Poland.* Kraków: Jagiellonian University Press, 2021.

Slade, Giles. *Made to Break: Technology and Obsolescence in America.* Cambridge and London: Harvard University Press, 2006.

Slater, Don. *Consumer Culture and Modernity.* Cambridge: Polity Press, 1997.

Slay, Ben. *The Polish Economy: Crisis, Reform, and Transformation.* Princeton, NJ: Princeton University Press, 1994.

Social Life of Goods." In *The Socialist Good Life. Desire, Development, and Standards of Living in Eastern Europe,* edited by Cristofer Scarboro, Diana Mincytė, and Zsuzsa Gille. Bloomington: Indiana University Press, 2020, epub.

Stage, Sarah, and Virginia B. Vincenti, eds. *Rethinking Home Economics: Women and the History of a Profession.* Ithaca, NY: Cornell University Press, 1997.

Stanek, Łukasz. *Architecture in Global Socialism: Eastern Europe, West Africa, and the Middle East in the Cold War.* Princeton and Oxford: Princeton University Press, 2020.

Starkowski, Mieczysław. "Jesień'88." *Veto,* October 23, 1988.

"Status Zjednoczenia Przemysłu Zmechanizowanego Sprzętu Domowego PREDOM." 1976. Ministerstwo Przemysłu i Handlu, Archiwum Akt Nowych.

Steiner, André. "The globalisation process and the Eastern Bloc countries in the 1970s and 1980s." *European Review of History* 21, no. 2 (June 2014): 165–81.

Stępień, Stanisław. "Imperatyw rozwoju—albo wizja upadku." *Przegląd Techniczny,* January 2, 1983.

Stępień, Stanisław. "Kiedy dogonimy?" *Przegląd Techniczny,* January 6, 1985.

Stępiński, Jerzy. "Normy i normalizacja a jakość produkcji." *Życie Gospodarcze,* May 24, 1970.

Stokes, Raymond G. "Autarky, Ideology, and Technological Lag: The Case of the East German Chemical Industry, 1945–1964." *Central European History* 28, no. 1 (1995): 29–45.

Stokes, Raymond G. *Constructing Socialism: Technology and Change in East Germany 1945–1990.* Baltimore et al.: Johns Hopkins University Press, 2000.

Štoll, Martin. *Television and Totalitarianism in Czechoslovakia: From the First Democratic Republic to the Fall of Communism.* New York et al.: Bloomsbury Academic, 2019.

Taylor, Charles. *Modern Social Imaginaries.* Durham and London: Duke University Press, 2004.

"Tensions of Europe Intellectual Agenda," 2005 Accessed on May 10, 2023. https://www.histech.nl/projects/SHT/www/nl/files/get/Intellectual_Agenda.pdf.

Tischleder, Babette B., and Sarah Wsserman. *Cultures of Obsolescence: History, Materiality, and the Digital Age.* New York: Palgrave Macmillan, 2015.

Todorova, Maria, and Zsuzsa Gille, eds. *Post-communist nostalgia.* New York and Oxford: Berghahn Books, 2010.

Trentmann, Frank. "Beyond Consumerism: New Historical Perspectives on Consumption." *Journal of Contemporary History* 39, no. 3 (July 2004): 373–401.

Trentmann, Frank. "Knowing consumers—histories, identities, practices: an introduction." In *The making of the consumer: knowledge, power and identity in the modern world,* edited by Frank Trentmann, 1–27. Oxford: Berg Publishers: 2005.

Tymowski, Andrzej. "Rozważania o jakości spożycia." *Polityka Społeczna,* Issue 4–5, 1980.

"Uchwała Nr 97/75, Rady Ministrów z dnia 30 maja 1975." Ministerstwo Przemysłu i Handlu, Archiwum Akt Nowych.

"U 'Kasprzaka' i w elektronice." *Przegląd Techniczny,* September 19, 1982.

Unitra Diora/Unitra Przedsiębiorstwo Handlu Zagranicznego. "Radio 80." Place unknown, 1980(?), author's collection.

"Ustawa z dnia 3 grudnia 1984 r. o utworzeniu Komitetu do Spraw Nauki i Postępu Technicznego przy Radzie Ministrów oraz Urzędu Postępu Naukowo-Technicznego i Wdrożeń." *Dziennik Ustaw* 1984 nr 55, poz. 280.

"Uzasadnienie do Uchwały Nr 97/75, Rady Ministrów z dnia 30 maja 1975." Ministerstwo Przemysłu i Handlu, Archiwum Akt Nowych.

van Lente, Harro, and Arie Rip. "Expectations in Technological Developments: An Example of Prospective Structures to be Filled in by Agency." In *Getting New Technologies Together: Studies in Making Sociotechnical Order,* edited by Cornelis Disco and Barend van der Meulen, 203–29. Berlin: Waiter de Gruyter, 1998.

Waglewski, Jerzy. "Potrzebny gromowładny Jowisz." *Przegląd Techniczny,* October 29, 1978.

Waglewski, Jerzy. "Typ MOT-772 Lena." *Przegląd Techniczny,* June 1, 1980.

Waglewski, Jerzy. "Zaczęło się od Melodii." *Przegląd Techniczny,* June 8, 1980.

Waliszewski, Jan. "Gdzie sprawdzać jakość wyrobów." *Życie Gospodarcze,* August 15, 1971.

Wasiak, Patryk. "Debating consumer durables, luxury and social inequality in Poland during the system transition." *Zeitschrift Für Ostmitteleuropa-Forschung*, no. 4 (2015): 544–65.

Wasiak Patryk. "The production of high fidelity audio electronics, and the politics of technological and social modernization in late state socialist Poland." *Journal of Sonic Studies*, forthcoming.

Wasiak, Patryk. "VCRs, Modernity, and Consumer Culture in Late State Socialist Poland." In *The Socialist Good Life: Desire, Development, and Standards of Living in Eastern Europe*, edited by Cristofer Scarboro, Diana Mincyte, and Zsuzsa Gille. Bloomington: Indiana University Press, 2020.

Wasiak, Patryk, and Katarzyna Stańczak Wiślicz. "Deconstructing 'nowoczesna gospodyni': The home efficiency movement, gender roles, and material culture in late state socialist Poland." *Slavic Review*, forthcoming.

Wasiak, Patryk, and Jaroslav Švelch. "Designing educational and home computers in state socialism: Polish and Czechoslovak experience." *Journal of Design History*, forthcoming.

Werblan, Andrzej, and Zbigniew Sufin. "Technika a cele społeczne." *Przegląd Techniczny*, February 3, 1980.

Wiktorowska, Bożena. "Super bubel." *Razem*, December 14, 1986.

Williams Rutherford, Janice. *Selling Mrs. Consumer: Christine Frederick and the Rise of Household Efficiency*. Athens and London: University of Georgia Press, 2003.

Wiszniewski, Edward. *Polityka konsumpcji w Polsce*. Warszawa: Państwowe Wydawnictwo Ekonomiczne, 1979.

"Wojna w kolorze." *Przegląd Techniczny*, May 1, 1977.

Woodall, Jean. *The Socialist Corporation and Technocratic Power: The Polish United Workers' Party, Industrial Organisation and Workforce Control 1958–80*. Cambridge et al.: Cambridge University Press, 1982.

Woźniczko, Grażyna, Andrzej Wolin, and Paweł Wyrzykowski. "Jego wysokość bubel." *Razem*, November 30, 1984.

Wróblewska, Agnieszka. "Osiem lat elektroniki." *Wiadomości Instytutu Wzornictwa Przemysłowego*, Issue 6, 1987.

Wróblewski, Andrzej. "Pod presją." *Polityka*, February 21, 1981.

Yurchak, Alexei. *Everything Was Forever, Until It Was No More: The Last Soviet Generation*. Princeton and Oxford: Princeton University Press, 2005.

Zachmann, Karin. "Managing Choice: Constructing the Socialist Consumption Junction in the German Democratic Republic." In *Cold War Kitchen. Americanization, Technology, and European Users,* edited by Ruth Oldenziel and Karin Zachmann, 259–84. Cambridge and London: MIT Press, 2010.

Zalewska, Joanna. "Consumer revolution in People's Poland: Technologies in everyday life and the negotiation between custom and fashion (1945–1980)." *Journal of Consumer Culture* 17, no. 2 (2017): 321–39.

Zapaśnik, Bożena. "Kuchenne szaleństwa." *Veto*, August 25, 1991.

Zatoński, Donat. "Niespodziewane skutki pożaru telewizora." *Przegląd Techniczny*, September 11, 1983.

Zatoński, Donat. "Problemy pod wysokim napięciem." *Przegląd Techniczny*, December 11, 1983.

"Z działalności edukacyjnej Instytutu Handlu Wewnętrznego i Usług." *Handel Wewnętrzny*, Issue 4, 1980.

Żebruń, Karol. "Unitra: Born in Poland—reaktywacja legendarnej marki." May 25, 2014, "Benchmark.pl." https://www.benchmark.pl/aktualnosci/unitra-marka -powraca-nowe-produkty-replika-sn-50.html.

Zielinski, Janusz G. "New Polish reform proposals." *Soviet Studies* 32, no. 1 (1980): 5–27.

Zimmer, Ben. "The 'Bubble' That Keeps on Bubbling." August 27, 2013, "Vocabulary. com." Accessed on January 10, 2023, https://www.vocabulary.com/articles/ wordroutes/the-bubble-that-keeps-on-bubbling/.

Żmuda, Andrzej. "Nasz start—nadzieje i obawy." *Atut*, Issue 1, 1988.

Index

181

About the Author

Dr. Patryk Wasiak (1978) holds MA degrees in sociology and art history (Warsaw University) and a PhD in cultural studies (Warsaw School of Social Sciences and Humanities). He is a recipient of grants and fellowships from the Volkswagen Foundation, the Center for Contemporary History Potsdam, the Netherlands Institute of Advanced Study, and the Andrew W. Mellon Foundation.

His research interests include the cultural history of the Cold War and the history of computing. He has published articles in *IEEE Annals of the History of Computing, International Journal of Communication,* and *History and Technology.*